# TESTED

## ADVENTURES OF
## AN AMERICAN SCIENTIST
## IN PANDEMIC CHINA

## MATTHEW J. KOHN

TWO-TRACK
PRESS
BOISE, IDAHO

# TESTED

## ADVENTURES OF AN AMERICAN SCIENTIST IN PANDEMIC CHINA



Published by Two-Track Press, Boise, Idaho



Library of Congress Control Number: 2022922316

Publisher's Cataloging-in-Publication
(Provided by Cassidy Cataloguing Services, Inc.)

| | |
|---|---|
| Names: | Kohn, Matthew J., author. |
| Title: | Tested : adventures of an American scientist in pandemic China / Matthew J. Kohn. |
| Description: | Boise, Idaho : Two-Track Press, [2023] \| Includes bibliographical references and index. |
| Identifiers: | ISBN: 979-8-9874088-0-3 (paperback – black and white edition) \| 979-8-9874088-3-4 (paperback – color edition) \| 979-8-9874088-1-0 (Kindle) \| 979-8-9874088-2-7 (ePub) \| LCCN: 2022922316 |
| Subjects: | LCSH: Kohn, Matthew J.--Travel--China. \| Scientists--United States--Biography. \| COVID-19 Pandemic, 2020---China. \| Science--China. \| China--Description and travel. \| Food--China. \| LCGFT: Autobiographies. \| Travel writing. \| Humor. \| BISAC: TRAVEL / Asia / East / China. \| HUMOR / Topic / Travel. \| BIOGRAPHY & AUTOBIOGRAPHY / Personal Memoirs. |
| Classification: | LCC: Q143.K556 A3 2023 \| DDC: 509.2--dc23 |

# DEDICATION

For Xiaochi and Huixia, who gave so much,
and for Heather, who gave up so much.

# CONTENTS

# THE BEFORE TIMES

Back in 2018, before the COVID-19 pandemic, two Chinese scholars came to work with me at Boise State University. It was quite unusual for two scientists from the same country to contact me at the same time. But they did, and everything worked out beautifully! Dr. Xiaochi Liu arrived in Boise on November 1, 2018, and returned to China in October 2019. Dr. Huixia Ding arrived December 1, 2018, and returned in November 2019.

You'll notice that they returned to China just before the COVID shit hit the fan. They were lucky. Little did we know.

Xiaochi is a professor at the Chinese Academy of Sciences in Beijing. He works on the origins of a special type of granite (called a leucogranite) that is common in the Himalayas. Huixia is a professor at the China University of Geosciences, Beijing. She works on metamorphic rocks in the Himalayas that have started to melt because they have reached such high temperatures. Both Huixia and Xiaochi wanted to come to Boise because I also work in the Himalayas. We could (and did) all learn a lot from each other.

Geographically, the part of the Himalayas that is inside China is on the southern edge of Tibet. So, both Xiaochi and Huixia also work in southern Tibet. I've always wanted to go to Tibet . . .

All visiting scholars to the US are required to have their English language skills evaluated, normally via recorded interview. Even before they came to Boise, during their interviews, both Huixia and Xiaochi asked me whether I had ever visited China, and whether I might want to do field work in Tibet. I could travel on some kind of academic exchange visa or tourist visa. And my wife, Heather, could come on a tourist visa. Of course, I'd jump at the chance to go to Tibet, especially if Heather could come with me. But Heather and I don't have travel money like that because salaries in Idaho are . . . conservative.

It turns out the Chinese Academy of Sciences in Beijing (where Xiaochi works) has a visiting scholars program, called the President's International Fellowship Initiative (PIFI). It pays for foreign scholars to come to the Academy for periods ranging from as little as a single week (for wizened old geezers) to multiple years (for sparkly young students) to engage in collaboration with Academy personnel. I'm considered a wizened old geezer now, and the fellowship that I could receive would pay a weekly honorarium to give a set of lectures on a topic in my specialty. Although the honorarium was for a maximum of two weeks, the amount it would pay could cover a much longer stay.

There's an unfortunate side to PIFI, which I'll explain another time, but all PIFI literature refers to those foreign scientists who warrant support from the Academy as foreign talent. That phrase—"foreign talent"—comes back to haunt another part of this story.

In August 2019 (still before the pandemic), Xiaochi and his boss, Fuyuan Wu, helped me apply for a two-week PIFI Distinguished Scientist fellowship. This is the highest level fellowship, and at the time it paid roughly $7,500 per week, or $15,000 total. Not chump change for an academic. The Chinese Academy approved my fellowship in early January 2020, when there were only a few cases of COVID-19. The plan was for me to travel to Beijing at the end of the 2020 spring semester, and we would do field work during summer 2020. This aligned nicely with the academic year. I would be in Beijing for a couple weeks after my spring semester ended, give a couple lectures, Heather would join us, and we'd go to Tibet.

Then, with the mounting pandemic, China and the US closed their borders. So, no travel to China, no fellowship, no Tibet for Matt and Heather. Of course, the pandemic changed everything else, too, and we all had other things on our minds. Stay-at-home orders. The election. Black Lives Matter. A lot happened in 2020. Personally, I doom-scrolled pandemic statistics and watched the old *Star Trek* television episodes. Seriously. We all coped in different ways.

But then, the Chinese Academy of Sciences told me that I could defer my fellowship. So Xiaochi and I cooked up another plan. I would teach during the 2020–2021 academic year in Boise, then request sabbatical for 2021–2022. I would go to China, not in summer 2020 as originally planned, but in summer 2021. If I were on sabbatical, I could go to Tibet anytime during 2021, even in the fall (because I wouldn't be teaching). Surely, after a year, travel would be allowed, right?

Everything worked! Well, sort of.

The pandemic didn't really diminish that much, at least not in the US (at the time of this writing in summer 2021, cases are increasing again for what, the third time?). But as some kind of equilibrium developed, China started approving travel visas, the Chinese Academy sent me a letter of invitation, and Boise State approved my sabbatical, including travel to China. I was on my way!

There were only two problems. Well, there were many more than two, but at the time it seemed like two.

First, China now required quarantine for all incoming travelers: two weeks in the city of arrival, and, because it's the capital, an additional week of quarantine upon arrival in Beijing. There was also a week of post-quarantine observation afterward, but after official quarantine you could start wandering around and getting into mischief. So, visiting in Beijing actually meant three weeks of solid quarantine (because you could no longer fly directly to Beijing from the US). And that meant that visiting China was not for the casual traveler. If you wanted to spend any significant time there (say a couple weeks), especially in Beijing, you were committing to over a month of travel. That was fine for a professor on a year's sabbatical, but it was way too much time for Heather to take off of her job teaching music. Hmm . . .

The second, and bigger, problem was that China still wasn't allowing tourist visas. Although in principle I could get a different kind of visa (well, maybe),

Heather was going to be stuck in the US, regardless. So, we had to think about how long I would stay in China. Given the quarantine time sink, it made sense for me to stay as long as possible. But that meant a longer time apart from Heather. Hmm . . .

Well, Biden got elected, Trump's rhetoric sparked a revolt, COVID started abating in the US, and I decided not to worry too much about how long I might stay. After all, I still didn't have a visa. But I would apply for one, and see how far down the road I could go. After all, the stars were aligning, right?

Right?

**XIAOCHI LIU**

**HUIXIA DING**

**THE AUTHOR AND FUYUAN WU**

# MAY

# GETTING AN F-ING VISA

In the United States, you can't apply for a Chinese visa yourself. Well, that's not true—you can, but you're taking a big risk. My sister-in-law, Heidi, who has traveled to China often, told me all the paperwork has to be filled out perfectly, and (this is important) it has to be hand-delivered to the consulate. Someone else can deliver it, but it can't be mailed.

Now, I don't get to choose which consulate I submit my application to, either: each block of states has its own. For example, Washington, Oregon, Northern California, and Nevada all deal with the consulate in San Francisco. Southern California, Arizona, and New Mexico deal with the consulate in Los Angeles. There are other consulates in New York City, Houston, and Chicago.

Any guesses about where an Idaho resident like me applies for a Chinese visa? Why, naturally, at the Chinese Embassy in *Washington, DC!* I kid you not. If I wanted to apply for a Chinese visa myself, I would have to fly to Washington, DC, and hand-deliver the application, my passport, and the application fee to the visa office of the Chinese Embassy. Which is open only during certain hours. And doesn't answer their phone. Ever. Believe me, I tried calling. *Many* times.

To accommodate people like me, there are visa application companies that help with visa applications. They're not cheap, close to $1,000 total, but that's a hell of a lot cheaper than roundtrip airfare across a continent plus a hotel for two weeks while waiting to see if the visa application is approved. Which it might not be, if the form wasn't filled out perfectly. If it's denied for any reason, you have to pay that application fee and start all over again. And wait two weeks. Or more.

So, I hired a company. And here's how that went.[1]

———

### MAY 4

*Brrrriiiiinnnngggg!* (sound of a telephone ringing)

> **TC:** Hello, how can I help you?
>
> **Me:** Hi, my name is Matt Kohn, and I'm a professor at Boise State University. I'm a US citizen, and the Chinese Academy of Sciences has invited me to come give a series of lectures in Beijing this summer. [Gosh, I'm so proud of myself.] I'd like to apply for a travel visa. I see there are lots of different kinds of visas, but I'm not positive which one I need. Can you help me?
>
> **TC:** Sure, but China isn't issuing tourist visas.
>
> **Me:** OK. Do I need a tourist visa? I'm not sure I need a tourist visa.
>
> **TC:** And they're issuing business visas only for extreme cases. You're unlikely to get a business visa.
>
> **Me:** OK. I'm not sure I need a business visa either.
>
> **TC:** Well, what kind of visa do you need?
>
> **Me:** That's what I'm asking you to help me figure out.

---

1. All the following conversations are from memory, and are strongly colored by the emotions I felt at the time. The company I worked with (let's just call it "TC") records all their calls, so somewhere there's verifiable documentation that what I've written is not 100 percent accurate. It's close, but mostly I'm trying to give you a sense of what it felt like for me at the time. Also, keep in mind that the visa is *the* most important step in getting to China. If this falls through, our plans for the last two years are scuttled. And, if the process drags on too long, my documents from the Chinese Academy of Sciences will expire, and/or I'll arrive too late in China for travel to Tibet. There's a lot of time pressure.

TC:     I see. Well, do you have a PU letter?

Me:     What's a PU letter?

TC:     It's a letter that you need to apply for a visa.

Me:     OK, but what's in the letter?

TC:     The information the consulate needs to issue you a visa. It's important to know if you have a PU letter already, or if you want us to request one for you. But China isn't issuing PU letters either.

Me:     OK, let's do this: I'll get in touch with the Chinese Academy of Sciences and ask about a PU letter, and I'll see what kind of visa they think I need. Then I'll call you back and we can go from there.

TC:     OK, sounds good.

I texted Xiaochi.

Me:     Xiaochi, the visa application company I'm working with says I need a PU letter. Do you know what a PU letter is? Oh, it's an invitation letter? I should look at the letter that the Academy sent me? Oh! Yes, there's a stamp right at the top that says PU letter. [Geez, why didn't TC tell me it was a friggin' invitation letter?] OK, well at least that's one mystery solved. Do you know what kind of visa I should ask for? OK, thanks for checking . . .

Oh, your administrative office just calls it a visitor's visa? [That doesn't sound like an official visa. But surely TC will know, right?]. OK, I'll talk to the visa company again.

MAY 6

*Brrrriiiiinnnngggg!*

TC:    Hello, how can I help you?

Me:    Hi, this is Matt Kohn. I'm a US citizen, and I called a couple days ago about getting a visa to travel to China. I was asked to determine what kind of visa I would need, and also whether I had a PU letter. Well, it turns out I have the PU letter [Gosh, I'm so proud of myself.].

TC:    OK, great! What kind of visa do you need?

Me:    Well, the Chinese Academy says it's just a visitor's visa.

TC:    Hmm . . . there is no visitor's visa. You're sure they didn't say something else, like a business visa or student visa?

Me:    Well, it's not a student visa because I'm not a student. Here, let's do this: why don't I start the application process, and when it comes time to figure out what visa I need, we can fill that in.

TC:    OK.

Me:    Can you help me get started?

TC:    Glad to. First go to www . . .

Five minutes later:

Me:    Great, so I'll get an email from someone who will help guide me through the application process?

TC:    Yes, your personal visa assistant will contact you within twenty-four hours. Anything else I can help you with?

Me:    Nope, I'm good. Thanks!

TC:    You're very welcome.

Wow, that guy in Chicago was good. Clear, on point, helpful. What a relief!

MAY 7

I receive an email from Mark, my personal visa assistant in Washington, DC. Actually, I'm only guessing he's in Washington, DC, because that's where my visa application will be submitted. He has a UK accent and keeps slightly odd hours. He could live in Uzbekistan for all I know. We arrange a phone call.

Me:     Hi, Mark. Thanks for handling this.

Mark:   Glad to help. Now, what type of visa do you need?

Me:     Well, it's unclear. The Chinese Academy of Sciences says it's called a visitor's visa. But there's no such visa. I think it's likely an academic exchange visa, but I'm not positive.

Mark:   Not a student visa.

Me:     Not a student visa.

Mark:   OK, an academic visa is an F visa, but I don't think China is issuing F visas.

Me:     OK, I'm still not positive I need an F visa.

Mark:   Well, if you need an M visa [business visa], they're very hard to get. Most are denied, and some take months. When are you leaving?

Me:     I haven't made any reservations yet, but I'd like to leave around June 30.

Mark:   Oh, so seven or eight weeks. I have to be honest with you: there's no guarantee you'll get a visa, and it might take months.

Me:     Sure, but I think we should try. Even if it fails, I'll be kicking myself if we don't try. I know it's expensive, but I'm willing to take the risk.

[We talk more. blah, blah blah. Mark emphasizes the business visa—several times. I emphasize how the trip is not business-related. blah, blah, blah.]

Mark: OK, I'll send you some materials via email, and we can go from there.

Me:    Sounds good. Thanks again.

Mark: You're welcome.

MAY 8

I emailed Xiaochi.

*Dear Xiaochi, I've been in touch with a company that helps apply for Chinese visas. The guy I talked to there was discouraging. He thinks there have been no F visas issued in over a year. There are a few M visas (essential business) that have been approved. However, part of the application process will include two letters—one from the Chinese Academy of Sciences and one from Boise State University—and the consulate is not likely to think that two academic institutions are engaged in business. With two academic institutions, it's going to look like academic exchange, which is an F visa.*

*No visas are being issued for teachers or students either. The consulate's opinion is that instruction can all be done remotely.*

*At this point, my contact is checking to see if there have been any F visas issued (or attempted) recently. I'll talk with him again on Monday.*

*Best,*
*Matt*

So, here's the way this works:

## MAY 11

Mark sends me a link to the application form, which contains a long list of questions about who I am, where I'm going, what I'm doing, where my mother lives (seriously, where my mother lives? I'm fifty-seven years old), passport info, driver's license, credit card, etc. I also have to send various other stuff like a visa photo, the PU letter, a letter from my employer asking for a visa, and a bunch of other stuff I don't remember offhand. It's a long list. Mark will use this information to fill out a draft application form and send it to me for proofing. This forms the basis of the application, so I need to be careful that all the information is exactly correct.

## MAY 14

After spending a lot of time going back and forth with Xiaochi (poor guy has to relay all the questions to his administrative offices, and with a fourteen-hour time difference between Boise and Beijing, it's hard to coordinate) we get it all straightened out. The Academy says I need a plain vanilla, academic-exchange, F visa. I relay all the information to Mark, including the PU letter, and that I should apply for an F visa.

## MAY 18

I get the draft application form from Mark. It's a pdf. Well, no worries, I deal with editing pdfs all the time. For every correction, I highlight the problem area in bright green and leave a prominent electronic sticky note next to it with the correction. This is standard practice in pdf editing, albeit a little overkill. I'm not usually quite so in-your-face with edits, but I don't want there to be any slipups. When I send it back to him, I also include some explanations in the email. Keep in mind that *every* detail matters or the application could be rejected.

Here's the mental blow-by-blow as I look over the pdf for the first time on the eighteenth:

Geez, what kind of goofy form is this? "Equivilent"? Doesn't TC know how to spell, or is that from the Chinese application?

OK, fix Heather's birthdate.

OK, fix these phone numbers.

Wait a second. What's with the M visa? How many times did we talk about this? The academy said an F visa. Change that to F.

OK, fix that phone number too.

Weird, he sends me emails, but doesn't know my email address? Easy to add.

Wait, this itinerary doesn't make any sense. It's a ninety-day visa, I can't stay four months. And I can't depart and arrive Beijing on the same dates as Shanghai. Let's see . . . OK, fixed that.

Wait, the countries I've visited in the last *five* years? Mark asked me for only the last *three* years. They're gonna see that in my passport. OK, let's see, if it's five years, I need to add Argentina, Austria, and Finland.

OK . . . attach to email . . . and . . . good!

---

MAY 19

*Brrrriiiiinnnngggg!*

Hi, Mark, what's up? OK, glad you got that. No, I don't really know how I can apply for an M visa between two academic institutions. The Chinese Academy said I should apply for an F visa. Well, sure, but if no one's applied for an F visa in over a year, then of course none have been issued, right? So, how do you know I can't get an F visa? Sure, I understand that we *know*

M visas are at least possible for some situations. I'll ask again, but I still think we should stick with an F visa. OK, good.

Come again? The itinerary doesn't matter? The visa office isn't even going to look at it? [Dude, do your words even make sense to you?] I guess, sure, the itinerary could change after I get there. OK, whatever you say.

Sorry, what? Yeah, your questionnaire asked me about the last three years of foreign travel, but your form says five years. Well, it's right there on the sticky note I left on the form [Don't you read my sticky notes?]. Yeah, like I said in my email, there are sticky notes all through the document with my edits [Don't you read my emails?]. Uh, OK, sure, it's Argentina, Austria, and Finland. OK, sounds good. And I'll talk to my contact at the Academy again about the visa type. OK. Bye.

I email back and forth with Xiaochi about M versus F visas. Finally, because Mark seems so insistent on requesting an M visa, we give up and I write to Xiaochi:

*Dear Xiaochi, Thanks for talking with your administrative offices again. I'll ask whether TC thinks it's advisable to switch to an M visa. I just don't know anymore.*

Then, I write to Mark:

*Hi Mark,*

*Well, the Chinese Academy of Sciences now asks what TC's recommendation is regarding requesting an F versus an M visa. They seem to think that I could apply for either. Would you mind contacting your supervisor and getting a final recommendation?*

*Thanks for your thoughts (and those of your supervisor),*
*Matt*

From Mark:

> *Hi Matt,*
>
> *As mentioned, and confirmed with PU, application needs to show F visa, as per supervisor.*
>
> *Call me, should you have any queries,*
> *Mark*

What am I thinking now, you ask? Now I'm recalling each of the first letters of the last three days of the five-day workweek strung together (you can work it out).

Or, more specifically:

OK, Mark, so let me get this straight: The PU letter, which is the most important document of all and that you've had all this time, clearly indicates that I apply for an F visa. Not an M visa. And we've spent how much time dicking around with whether I should apply for an M visa or an F visa or some other kind of F-ing visa? Xiaochi has contacted his administrative offices how many times? This has taken how many days? And I'm spending how much money for your so-called expertise? What kind of dolt are you? Ugh.

---

## MAY 20

Here's what I actually wrote:

> *Hi Mark,*
>
> *OK, I just wanted to clear that up with the Chinese Academy of Sciences.*
>
> *You should get my materials today.*
>
> *Thanks for your help,*
> *Matt*

No email from Mark . . . ever again. Everything was due in the embassy the next day, May 21. Does it ever get there? No email from Mark.

So, what happened???!!!

Well, normally visas take up to ten business days (two weeks) to process, although, of course, these aren't normal times. OK, I really should have requested information from Mark immediately after sending the materials. But I was tired of dealing with the guy, and TC did reliably contact me whenever they needed anything. So, it was only after two weeks of hearing nothing but crickets (and four weeks after starting the whole deal), that I sent Mark an email:

> *Hi Mark,*
>
> *I'm just curious whether you can provide any updates on the visa request.*
>
> *You received my materials and submitted the request, correct?*
>
> *Best,*
> *Matt*

Auto-response from Mark: he's on vacation! Great, my "personal visa assistant" just took off without letting me know. So much for personal service.

So, I send another email to the contact in his auto-response:

> *Hello,*
>
> *I sent the [previous] message to Mark, but received an auto-response suggesting I get in touch with you. Please forward as necessary.*
>
> *Thanks,*
> *Matt*

Response:

> *Hello Matt*
>
> *Your order is complete and the passport was returned to you via UPS overnight delivery on May 28 to following address on file:*
>
> *MATTHEW KOHN: [my phone number]*
> *[my street address]*
> *BOISE ID [zip]*
> *Best regards,*

Huh? Order "complete" five days ago? Well, was the visa approved or not?

I look through all my email, including my spam folder—nope, nothing there. China made a decision on my visa, and my "personal visa assistant" didn't let me know? Is my passport sitting somewhere at home? Why hasn't anyone said anything?

I rush home. Yep, there's a little package (who picked that up? And why didn't I see that before?), and, yes, it's got my passport, and, yes, there's a visa!

*An f-ing F visa!*

Hurrah! I'm on my way now, right?

Right?

[My "personal visa assistant"—geez, Louise . . .]

**Application details**
**Validity of visa (months)**:   3
**Maximum duration of longest stay (days)**:   90
**Entries**:   Single
**Types of visa and major purpose of your visit to China**
**Types of visa and major purpose of your visit to China**:   ( M ) Commercial trade activities - Trade

This should be F-visa, not M.

Add a reply...

**EXAMPLE OF EDITS**

JUNE

# MAYBE I SHOULD RETIRE

I love the people in my university's research office. Sure, they're a little anal when it comes to regulations, etc. But it's their job to try to protect us academic researchers, they have innumerable rules to follow, and they work hard to be fair.

So, I didn't hesitate to contact them in March when they sent a message that all researchers at the university were now supposed to disclose:

- Travel expenses directly paid or reimbursed by an outside entity;

- Living expenses directly paid or reimbursed by an outside entity; and

- Other funding (for example, salary, stipend, honoraria, etc.) paid to a University researcher by an outside entity.

At that time, the support that I hoped to receive from the Chinese Academy of Sciences wasn't exactly spelled out. Maybe they would pay me two weeks' honorarium, and that would be it—I would pay for everything else. That's what I was thinking. Or maybe they would pay round trip airfare and two weeks of living expenses in addition to the honorarium. But it didn't really matter. They would be paying at least one of the three categories. And Huixia had talked about possibly providing support from the China University of Geosciences.

So, I emailed my research office:

*Hi, I am not currently receiving support from a foreign entity. However, during my sabbatical in China (currently planned for July through December of this year), the Chinese Academy of Sciences and possibly the China University of Geosciences, Beijing, have offered me support for travel and living expenses.*

*Can you help me figure out how to disclose this? I have received no money yet and probably won't until I arrive in China.*

Hard to believe that such a simple little message could set off such a shit storm of complications that they still haven't been sorted out. But here's the reason why the research office sent out that message (well, one of the reasons), and what it all boiled down to:

1. Congress was in the process of writing legislation that would ban federal funding to US researchers who receive support from a foreign government or institution.

2. My research and graduate student training program relies on federal funding, mainly the National Science Foundation (NSF). I was also in the process of submitting a research proposal to the U. S. Department of Energy (DOE), another federal agency.

3. The Chinese Academy of Sciences and the China University of Geosciences, Beijing are (surprise!) foreign institutions.

4. If the Chinese Academy of Sciences or China University of Geosciences paid for any of my travel, or provided an honorarium, I might not be permitted to receive research funding from NSF or DOE.

Ever again. End of career.

| Matt: | Are you serious? That doesn't make any sense. How can they punish me retroactively? |
|---|---|
| Research office: | I know, we agree, but that's the risk. |
| Matt: | OK, what do you think I should do? |

Research office: Honestly, we think you shouldn't accept any support at all from China. From the university's perspective, you should turn down the fellowship.

Maybe I should retire now. Then I can do whatever the hell I damn well please. But I can't afford to do that. Salaries in Idaho are . . . conservative.

The research office is right. From the university's perspective, it's crazy for me to risk the next ten years of support for student researchers for a couple weeks in Tibet. If I can even get permission to go to Tibet. Which is a whole other question.

But, it's not fair! And there's nothing that pisses me off more than an injustice. I decide to look up the legislation. OK, Senate bill 1260. What exactly does it say:

Oh, I might not be able to receive funding if I participate in a "foreign talent recruitment program." What's "foreign talent recruitment"? Oh, it's defined in one of Trump's last presidential memos: any foreign government or institution that directly or indirectly offers "cash, research funding, complimentary foreign travel, honorific titles, career advancement opportunities, promised future compensation, or other types of remuneration or consideration, including in-kind compensation."

Well, that's stupid. That could be anything! A Nobel Prize derives from a foreign institution that provides cash, other types of remuneration (a medal), and an honorific title. Maybe also foreign travel. Does that mean getting a Nobel Prize deep-sixes my research career in the US? That seems kind of hypocritical when the US provides a special pathway to a green card for Nobel Prize recipients. And what happens if I'm invited to give a talk in Canada, with a promise to cover my airfare and hotel ("complimentary foreign travel")? Compensation for foreign travel happens often in academia. Academic exchange (intellectual transparency) advances science.

What's especially disturbing for me is that the legislation specifically calls out China as a bad actor. It's one thing if I accept travel money from, say, Canada, to give a talk in Calgary (I have to disclose it, or I might lose funding). It's another thing if I accept travel money from China (goodbye, research program). And, there's no wiggle room. Even if I pay my entire travel expenses out of pocket, but the Chinese Academy of Sciences provides me with an office for an afternoon (in-kind compensation), my research career is over.

| Matt: | OK, I looked up the legislation, and what the Chinese Academy of Sciences is offering me is academic exchange. The legislation says that's OK. They're not trying to hire me or steal secrets. |
| --- | --- |
| Research office: | Sure, but they don't have to be trying to hire you. We contacted the FBI about your fellowship, and they say it's foreign talent recruitment. |
| Matt: | But the way the legislation is written, everything can be classified as foreign talent recruitment. |
| Research office: | Sure, but we can't change that. The FBI says you're risking your career if you go to China. |

Oh, and it gets better: *when* did this conversation take place? *When* did I learn that the FBI could (would?) tank my career if I went to China? Why, the day after I found out that China had approved my F visa! You know, the F visa that took a month of delightful banter with my "personal visa assistant," Mark? The first F visa issued in the US in over a year? The f-ing F visa?

One step forward, *two* steps back?

Next, I email and call NSF and ask their advice. We have a couple hour-long discussions. They're super-supportive, and generally encourage me to travel to China. Ultimately, I write a lengthy email to my research office, per NSF's recommendations. Their perspective differs rather markedly from the research office. But, then again, it's not NSF's butt on the line, is it? If I get cut off from research, my career is over, but it's only a few less proposals for them to handle. I love and respect my NSF program officers—they're all dedicated people, and they all have invested substantial time and resources in me, and helped me repeatedly. You will not find better people on the face of the Earth. But Boise State would be taking the risk.

Hmm . . . what to do?

Next, I email and call DOE, asking them about the implications of receiving travel money from China:

> DOE: Hi Matt. Yes, we received your email with all your questions. I want to let you know that you're not going to find anyone in DOE who is going to answer them.
>
> Me: Really? Uh, well, thank you for telling me [I guess]—I'd rather know that I'm not going to get answers, than to just not hear. [Don't you hate it when you ask a question and no one ever answers? I'd much rather hear "No" than nothing. Plus, DOE is super restrictive about collaborations in China.]
>
> DOE: Yeah, China's too sensitive. You're better off steering clear.
>
> Me: OK. Thanks.

End of conversation.

What else can I do? Sure, I could give up and stay home. But, like I said, nothing pisses me off more than an injustice, and people shouldn't risk their careers over inept legislation. I've also spent two years developing this collaboration, so I want to make this work. And, I feel like, if I can fix this, other people will benefit, especially younger scientists who can't stick their necks out with the same security as an old fart like me. So, I figure there's only one thing left: I call both my senators and my congressional representative, and see if I can get the legislation changed. Why not?

Now, you probably know that you rarely get to talk directly with your legislators, you normally talk to an expert on their staff. And that's usually better, because legislators can't be experts on everything (some would say "on anything"), and they don't have time to learn it all from you from scratch. It's more effective to have you explain it at length with people on their staff who are particularly knowledgeable (expert-to-expert), and then have them explain it to your legislator.

The staffs of all my legislators agree pretty quickly to my request to speak with them, and they all voice support for academic exchanges. But, as I expected, only up to a (politically-defined) point. I kind of have the same conversation three times. First, I send them all an email explaining the situation. Then I talk to them either over Zoom or by phone.

[Note: the following conversation is not verbatim. The staff members were all fantastic, and helpful, but a little more circumspect than what I wrote. I'm giving you my bottom line interpretation of what they meant. Also, this is distilled from three different conversations.]

Me: Hi, thanks for taking time out to talk with me. I realize there may not be much you can do, given the political winds, but I thought I would at least explain my concerns.

Staff: Yes, I'm happy to talk with you. We're always looking for feedback, especially if legislation can have unintended consequences.

Me: Right, that's exactly the situation here.

Staff: OK, can you explain what's going on, again?

Me: Sure. I'm on sabbatical this year, and the Chinese Academy of Sciences has offered me a fellowship to visit in Beijing. The fellowship would cover airfare and living expenses, maybe with a little left over. This is similar to fellowships that other universities around the world offer to visiting scholars, especially for sabbaticals. But in this case, with the current legislation, if I accept it from China, I may be giving up all hope of receiving federal funding for my research. I want to emphasize that my research is not sensitive in any way. This is purely an academic exchange. In fact, the visa I received is specifically for academic exchanges. And the Chinese Academy of Sciences has agreed to forego any intellectual property that might be developed while I'm there. [I had the Academy write me a letter saying that, just in case.]

Staff: OK, can you explain that in a little more detail? Exactly how does the wording of the legislation say that?

[we talk for a while]

Staff:  OK, I get it. Uh, I think there are a few things you should know.

Me:  Great, that's why I called.

Staff:  First, sometimes when legislation gets written, it's not always obvious what the implications will be. Basically, we can make mistakes.[2]

Me:  OK, sure, I understand that.

Staff:  So, we rely on our constituents, like you, to help us understand what the problems are and how to fix them. So, thank you for contacting us.

Me:  Glad to.

Staff:  Second, one of the few things [some would say "the only thing"] that Democrats and Republicans agree on in Washington right now is that we all want to be tough on China.

Me:  Yeah, I kind of got that. I think the Senate bill passed committee by a vote of twenty to four. It can't get much more bipartisan than that.

Staff:  Right. So that means it's unlikely we're going to be able to change the wording in the Senate bill at this point. I'll ask, but no one is going to want to look like they're soft on China.

Me:  OK, I wish that weren't true, but I understand that. I'm not surprised.

Staff:  Last, I'll get in touch with the committee that's drafting the House legislation. It's possible their wording will be different.

Me:  OK, thanks for doing that.

Staff:  Sure thing. Is there anything else in the bill that you want to talk about?

---

2. No one actually ever said "mistake," but this is pretty clearly what they meant.

> Me:    Honestly, I've been so focused on this one part, I haven't paid much attention to the rest. Increasing funding for NSF is always a good thing, though. They've been underfunded for a long time.
>
> Staff:  OK. Thanks for taking time to talk with us.
>
> Me:    Oh, thank you! I appreciate all the work you do.

OK, I admit it, I'm a bit of a suck-up to legislative staff. But do you know how hard these folks work? And have you seen their salaries (which are publicly available)? I don't know how they live in DC on that pittance. Also, just think, they have to be nice to people like me all day long!

So, the Senate bill passes anyway (surprise!), and it's still badly written (surprise!). Now it's the House's turn. Surely this would be better, right?

Right?

Actually, it *is* better!

I'll spare the details—here's the bottom line:

Yes, my federal funding could still be in jeopardy if I receive any money or other support from China (hey, that just wasn't gonna change), but:

1.  Only if I am participat*ing* in a program. That's big. I can be in China this summer, and still receive US research funding next year. Whew! That's a relief!

2.  Implementation could take as long as a year. So, there's time to work out the kinks.

3.  An office will be set up to identify problem programs. So, if I'm offered something next year, I'll know who to contact to see if it's OK.

4.  It's OK to receive foreign travel and in-kind support, for example, to give a talk in Canada.

I guess I won't retire just yet.

# JULY

# TESTING, TESTING . . .

Even with a visa, it's surprisingly difficult to get to China. Here's how:



04:45   Get up.

06:00   Drive to airport and catch flight to Dallas.[3]

11:45   Arrive Dallas, pick up checked bag and catch Lyft to one of only two testing sites in Texas. It's not exactly close. This would be like flying into San José and taking a cab to San Francisco. At least I don't have to go to the testing center in Houston.

12:15   What? Guy at testing center tells me payment is only in cash, and it will cost $450? I have an appointment, you know. What? Appointments don't matter? OK I'll just get some cash from a local bank and mass with everyone else. But what am I going to do with these two suitcases? Thankfully, guy from testing

---

3. Why Dallas? Because China requires a negative COVID test from one of three or four testing labs in the country. Dallas has one of them and has the cheapest flights. Flying out of San Francisco would cost me $13,000.

center offers to let me store them in an air-conditioned building (or the chocolate would melt).

Wait, where the hell is my backpack with my computer?! Really?! I left it in the Lyft vehicle? Oh geez, probably because I had only four hours of sleep last night. Call driver, get backpack, and take Lyft to local bank.

12:30   Bank: Can I help you?

Me: Please let me take out a cash advance for hundreds of dollars on a debit card for an account with a completely different bank, even though I don't have a PIN yet because my account is too new.

Bank: No problem!

1:00    I walk back to testing center. It's 93°F (34°C) and high humidity, so I'm totally soaked in sweat now. First test—nasal swab. Stand in line listening to cicadas for about half an hour before they even take my paperwork. Woman in front of me in line tells me that Dallas issues travel permits only for F-1 student visas. I have an F visa, but it's not F-1 because I'm not a student. Is this a waste of time?

2:00    Nasal swab done. Now I get to pay that $450 cash for a blood draw. Did I mention I have to get it taken by 3:00 p.m. or I won't have the test results in time to get my health approval? While waiting in line, I find out that China won't issue me travel clearance unless I have a picture of myself in front of the testing center, showing my passport, receipt, and bandage from the blood draw. And I was supposed to know that . . . how? Now it's 95° (35°C). Very slow line . . .

2:50    Blood draw. What was I worried about? I got up at 4:45 a . m . and had a full ten-minute buffer. But why did they give me Caucasian skin-color tape? That won't show up in the picture. Why couldn't it be blue, like everyone else's? Is it because I'm the only white guy in a one kilometer radius?

3:00 Selfie in front of testing center, trying to make an inconspicuous bandage show.

3:10 Pick up suitcases and call Lyft.

4:00 Ride to the Airbnb rental. This would be like driving from San Francisco back to San José, then on to Santa Cruz. Driver asks why I would be doing all this, if I don't actually know it will work. I've been asking myself the same question for the last three months.

5:00 On pins and needles wondering if I'll get my test results in time. Walk to the grocery store and get some takeout from a Nepali restaurant. Now it's 97°F (36°C).

6:00 Still on pins and needles. Watch Chinatown on Amazon Prime account. One of the tests could be positive because I've been vaccinated. In that case, I'll have to upload a third test (that's why it cost me $450, not $350).

9:00 Get test results, and they're both negative (Whew! Step one done!). Now start application process. Where the hell is that again? Supposedly I can use WeChat (ubiquitous China app on my phone), but how do I find an application on a chat app? Finally settle for an online link from the Chinese embassy.

9:30 Fill out innumerable bits of information (why do they need my mother's maiden name and my father's middle name?) and upload numerous documents (copy of my passport, copy of my visa, results of nasal swab and blood test, date of last COVID vaccination, copy of vaccination card, photo of me in front of the testing clinic). Good thing I have all that stuff! In fact, they have most of it, too, because it was in my visa application from last month.

10:00 Finished uploading. Now just waiting. It's morning in China, so I'm in constant contact with Huixia and Xiaochi. They say it takes about one to one-and-a-half hours to get approval, so I should know by midnight.

Midnight Still no word. Try to find alternate means of uploading same data using WeChat. It turns out I can't do it through the app. Why? Because I don't have a Chinese phone number. Hmmm . . . this won't be a problem when I get to China, right?

---

## SUNDAY, JULY 18

01:00 Give up waiting for response from China and go to sleep.

03:00 Wake up with food poisoning and faint in hallway. Another guest revives me and helps me up. I make it to the bathroom.

04:00 Better now (good thing food poisoning passes fast). Clean as a whistle, inside and out! Still no response from China. Go back to sleep.

09:00 Walk to grocery store for food. Only 85°F (29.5°C), but still soaked in sweat by the time I get back to the Airbnb rental.

10:00 Eat breakfast. Cleaning staff arrives. Why haven't I heard anything from China? Xiaochi suggests maybe I need to upload my invitation letter, even though there wasn't any obvious option for it. But, if I revise the application, it withdraws the old one and I start all over again. Xiaochi, Huixia, and I decide to leave it alone. Xiaochi and Huixia go to sleep.

2:00 Eat lunch. Why does that melon on the counter have rodent tooth marks in it? They weren't there this morning. And why are they the size of a squirrel or rat? Notify the Airbnb rental owner and throw it away. He says he'll talk to his staff.

We had rats in South Carolina. They'd come up from the river every once in a while. It turns out they like to eat cockroaches. Oops! I meant to say they like to eat "palmetto bugs." I don't think this house has rats. It's way too clean. Probably a squirrel got in.

3:00   Get my approval from China (woohoo! Step two done!). What a relief! Now I just have to get to the airport for my flight.

3:00   Write out report for National Science Foundation (due in two weeks) so that Boise State doesn't cut off my grants and start paying everything through my development account. Oh, NSF has a new rule? I have to upload "archivable" pdfs of all publications? Hmmm . . . despite having worked with pdf creation and editing for literally twenty years, archivable pdfs are new to me, and I can find no method on my Mac to create an acceptable file. Maybe my software is too old. Too bad NSF's instructions are for a PC only . . .

6:30   Submit report anyway, without required pdfs. Whatever. Too excited to sleep. I'm finally going!

12:00  Eventually get to sleep.

## MONDAY, JULY 19

04:00 Guy in room next to me wakes me up, talking loudly on the phone. I was going to get up soon anyway, right?

04:45 Really? There's no Lyft anywhere close by? Try Uber.

05:15 Uber arrives. My flight is at 8:15, but I can't check in online, and who knows how full the flight will be? At least I have my health code. With my passport and visa, that's all I need, right?

05:40 Long line at check-in, but it's not horrible. Plenty of time—what was I worried about?

05:45 What? I have to fill out the customs form before I can check in? What kind of country requires that? Oh, right. China. OK, how do I do that? Helper guy from airlines tells me I have to scan a QR code and fill out a form on WeChat app. I know how to do that.

06:00  The form has to send a confirmation code to a phone, but it won't accept my US phone number. Hmmm . . . that's not going to be a problem when I get to China, right? It's afternoon in China, so I contact Huixia and Xiaochi. They help me get the code.

06:15  Form completed. (Whew!) Submit . . . failed? What the hell—I did too check that box!

06:16  Really? All the information I just entered is gone? Start customs form again from scratch. Get code from Huixia . . .

06:45  Form completed. Submit . . . success! OK, now I have a second confirmation code for check-in. Start checking in. Oh, a screenshot of the health code isn't sufficient, I have to find it online? By some miracle, I do. What? I need a third code? The helper guy didn't say anything about a third code. Just the two. Leave line and talk to him again.

06:50  Helper guy: No, I just need two codes. The gate agent doesn't know what she's talking about. Back to gate agent.

06:55  Where did that second code go? You mean I can't access both my health code and customs code online? Leave check-in line again to talk to helper guy. Oh, I'm supposed to show an online version of the health code and a screen shot of the customs code. And I was supposed to know this, how?

07:00  By some miracle, the customs code hasn't disappeared, and I get my screen shot. Back to gate agent. Get checked in. Now I just have to get through security.

07:10  Through security (quick because I have TSA PreCheck).

07:30  I have to check in again? OK, fine, whatever.

07:45  Board flight.

08:15  Really? The flight is delayed? Someone left a camera case in the jetway and won't claim it, plus there are thunderstorms?

I'm tempted to claim the camera, just to get a new camera. But, beside the fact that it's dishonest, I don't want to have to lug something else around. Ah, who cares? I'm on the flight. China's stuck with me now.

08:45  Take off for China.

## TUESDAY, JULY 20

Noon  Arrive in Seoul. Have to stay on plane. Captain says we have to stay out of the aisles because . . .? Well, just because.

2:30  Arrive in Shanghai. Now they really are stuck with me.

**TESTING VERIFICATION!**

# WHEN IN CHINA . . .

To continue the saga.

2:30  Arrive Shanghai airport.

2:45  Arrive at gate. But everyone's staying on the plane. What's going on?

3:00  Captain announces the immigration and customs halls are overflowing, so no one is allowed off the plane. We have to wait until there's room for us.

3:01  Power goes out. Climate in plane immediately equilibrates with human body temperature and water content: approximately 95°F (35°C) and 100 percent humidity. Remember those scenes of southern churches in the summertime, with everyone fanning themselves? I always knew those flight instruction cards were good for something.

3:15  Emergency power and air conditioning start. Temperature starts to drop. Slowly.

3:30  Entertainment is restarted. Start watching movies: Feeling Through, The Neighbors' Window, and Hair Love, which all received Oscars. I thought The Neighbors' Window was a little predictable, but they were all good, and I'd recommend them.

4:45　We're off the plane and in a corridor (thankfully sort of air conditioned). No indication what we're doing here. This isn't immigration, but it's good to be standing again.

5:00　Entering a long hallway. No idea where we're going. The line moves quickly for a minute (hurry! Hurry!), then stops for five. Hurry for a minute, stop for five.

5:15　Pick up free Wi-Fi. This is good, otherwise my China data plan would run out with all the texting I'm doing with Xiaochi and Huixia.

5:20　Xiaochi and Huixia start sending me images of what they plan to eat for dinner. It reminds me that I haven't eaten in about eight hours.

5:30　Oh, I get it, we're waiting to have our customs code scanned again (glad I have that screenshot), but . . . this isn't where I get tested? No, a guy in a hazmat suit hands me a fifteen-milliliter centrifuge tube and a small plastic ziplock labeled "hazardous waste," and points down a flight of stairs. Hmmm . . .

5:45　Exit the building to a relatively short line outside [90°F (32°C), high humidity—did we just circle back to Dallas?], then enter a testing building, about the size of a diner, with multiple stations. Recalling that people in Dallas don't generally wear hazmat suits at airports, just because of COVID, I cleverly deduce this must be China, and where I get tested.

First is a nasal swab. No worries, I've done that before.

Holy cow! I didn't think my nasal passages went that far back! Is my nose running or am I bleeding? Oh, OK, at least it's not blood. Maybe it's cerebrospinal fluid?

What now? A throat swab? OK, that doesn't sound so bad.

Holy cow! This woman is ruthless! She better hope I don't barf all over her. Other people are retching, too, so I guess I'm not being singled out. Whew, that's done.

What do I do with the baggy? Oh, I give it to the heartless woman. No idea what she does with it. She doesn't seem to know what to do with it either. Why do I have it?

Back outside, I go up an escalator and on to immigration.

6:00    Immigration. OK, here's my customs code, and here's my health code, and here's my intake form. What? Letter of invitation? Uh, sure, it's on my computer somewhere. Here it is—whew, disaster averted.

What? My phone number is right there on the form. Oh, you need a Chinese phone number? Damn, where did I put Xiaochi's phone number? I send a panicked text to Xiaochi and Huixia. OK, got that. Whew, disaster averted. I bet the people waiting behind me are getting impatient. Just their luck to get stuck behind an American who doesn't have a Chinese phone number . . .

What's my schedule, you say? I'm in Shanghai for two weeks in quarantine, then Beijing for a week in quarantine, then staying with a colleague. Oh, you need a final home address in Beijing. OK, got that.

Oh, I see, you will confiscate my passport until I arrive at the hotel. Then I'll get it back. Sure, no problem. Why would an American traveling alone in China worry about being separated from his passport? What could go wrong?

6:30    Through immigration and on to a new line. What's this? I need to fill out another form for the hotel? Oh, I scan another QR code and fill out the corresponding online form? OK, no problem. Wow, this time I already have all the information at my fingertips. Why? Because I've already provided it before.

Yes, I'm happy to provide you with my customs code for the fourth time. Or, is it the fifth?

6:45    OK, now I'm in a group of people standing around waiting for . . . what? Maybe we get on a bus that takes us to the hotel? No, that would make too much sense.

7:00    Oh, we're getting on a bus that's taking us to the hotel! Altogether, I was in the Shanghai airport for a little over four hours. One of Huixia's students was in the airport for seven hours. I guess I'm lucky.

Wow, Shanghai is really flat, and really wet. And even from a bus you can't see any distance. Where the heck are we going? This looks like South Carolina with Chinese graffiti. And lots of institutional housing that looks like it's from the 1950s or 1960s. Fascinating but a little depressing, all at the same time.

7:45    Too dull, I fall asleep.

8:00    Arrive at the hotel. More people in Tyvek hazmat suits. What's this? More paperwork? Sure thing—love it! Good thing I have a pen with me. I suppose it's like registering for a hotel/motel in the US, except it's a three-page document in a language I don't read. I don't know what I'm signing away, maybe the rights to my firstborn child? Sorry, Tavi.

8:15    Exit bus and have my bags spray-washed in disinfectant. I'm looking forward to having a disinfectant-soaked backpack against my skin.

Now I'm at hotel check-in. Say what? I have to scan this QR code and fill out another online form? Sure thing!

Wait, this isn't working for me. No, I don't know why the form isn't responding. When I tap on the area to type in my name, nothing happens. No, none of the other areas respond either. I'm directed to talk to a woman who is also trying to check in, and who speaks English. She's polite, although obviously a little annoyed to have to deal with me. Why is it her turn to deal with the American whose app doesn't work and who doesn't have a Chinese phone number? No, she doesn't know why the app isn't accepting text from me. Suddenly— yes! It starts to work. We have no idea why, but, OK, should be easy now.

Oh, I have to list a local Chinese contact phone number? Let's see, could I have that paper form back that I just handed you? It has the phone number on it that you need.

Yes, of course the emergency contact also has to have a Chinese phone. Why would I think of listing Heather's? Glad I have Huixia's phone, also.

8:45    Finally cleared. Where am I, anyway? Oh, Ruitai Hotel, Changning District, Room 324. I take an elevator ominously labeled "sterilized" to the third floor. Wait a second. How do I get in the room? Is there a scanner? I have a QR code on my passport now (surprise!). How does this work? I leave my two suitcases (damned if I'm going to drag them back downstairs) and go back to the hazmat folks at check-in. Oh, I have to wait. For what? No idea.

Two guys from Jamaica are also having problems checking in. Their apps don't work, and they really don't work. As in, they can't even get an app to come up on their phones. Why do we need smart phones to travel to China, anyway? We're the last ones to check in.

9:00    Oh, I have to be escorted to the room. I probably broke a half dozen rules by taking an elevator by myself and by touching an elevator button with a plague-ridden fingertip. At least we take the same sterilized elevator, so that must not have been a mistake. My hazmat guide lets me in the room, and says I can't leave for two weeks. Without a key, I wouldn't leave if I could.

9:15   Let's see, what's for dinner? A bowl of instant noodle soup (I have a hot pot in my room), a giant Vienna sausage, and a spherical brown proteinaceous blob. I check with Xiaochi and Huixia. The brown blob is a cooked, shelled egg. Probably.

Let's see, what other supplies did they give me? Four rolls of toilet paper, a case of bottled water, five toothbrushes, two combs, three packages of tissues, four pairs of flip-flop slippers (what is it with giving guests flip-flops in Asia, anyway? I heard it was to protect against foot parasites, but surely no longer), four bars of soap, three shower caps, ten chlorine disinfectant tablets, a half-dozen trash bags, and a half dozen yellow hazmat bags. The room has a spray bottle that's supposed to be prepared each day with a disinfectant tablet so I can disinfect every scrap of material that goes into the hazmat bags. I can also disinfect all the surfaces, although COVID dies within a couple of days, so why would I do that until around day twelve? Each time I poop, I'm supposed to drop six tablets in the toilet, and let it all sit for at least thirty minutes before flushing. Of course, even concentrated chlorine solutions won't penetrate a turd. This isn't going to sterilize my poop. Also, my toilet runs, so there's water slowly circulating through the bowl anyway. I doubt the hotel staff is likely to listen to me, so I choose not to inform them.

Other rules: I can't leave the room. If the door is open more than a few seconds, an alarm starts to sound. I'm not supposed to order food from outside the hotel: no alcohol, fast food, fresh food, or prepared food. The hotel does provide meals that include cooked vegetables and fresh fruit. I just can't order anything from outside.

10:00  I take a shower and go to sleep. Except for a couple of brief naps, I've been up for twenty-nine hours. At least I have a bed. And no bedbugs either—I started checking in the cheap motels in the US, and now it's a habit.

Other interesting features: Google doesn't work. Great, so I created a whole new Google account for travel/security, and am directing all communications through it, and now it doesn't work. That won't be a problem, right?

I get my temperature checked twice per day.

The room has air conditioning, but is pretty warm (80–85°F, 27–29°C). I consider stripping down and not bothering to put on clothes when I answer the door. No one talks to me, and maybe the hazmat folks will find their job a little more interesting if I show up naked. If they even notice. They're pretty single-minded. There's a young woman in the room across from mine who gets her meals and is tested at the same time. She never looks at me and deliberately ignores my greetings. I decide I should stay clothed.

If I had tape and wire, I'd try to figure out how to jimmy the door open without triggering the alarm. Why didn't anyone tell me to pack tape and wire ahead of time? Huixia recalls the movie *Shawshank Redemption*, and I suggest I slowly take apart my door, flushing bits down the toilet, until I can roam the halls. Sadly, I don't have a poster to mount over a hole in the door. Another packing oversight.

How do I pay for the hotel? It's about $60 per day, which includes food (cheap by US standards, all things considered). Was that one of the forms I signed early on? I guess that means my son Tavi's worth about $850. They have no credit card information that I know of, although I do have bank account info in WeChat. I check my bank account, and they haven't been taking money out. Hmm. Thank goodness Xiaochi will be meeting me in Shanghai to extract me from the hotel. He can help sort all that out when I check out. What could go wrong?

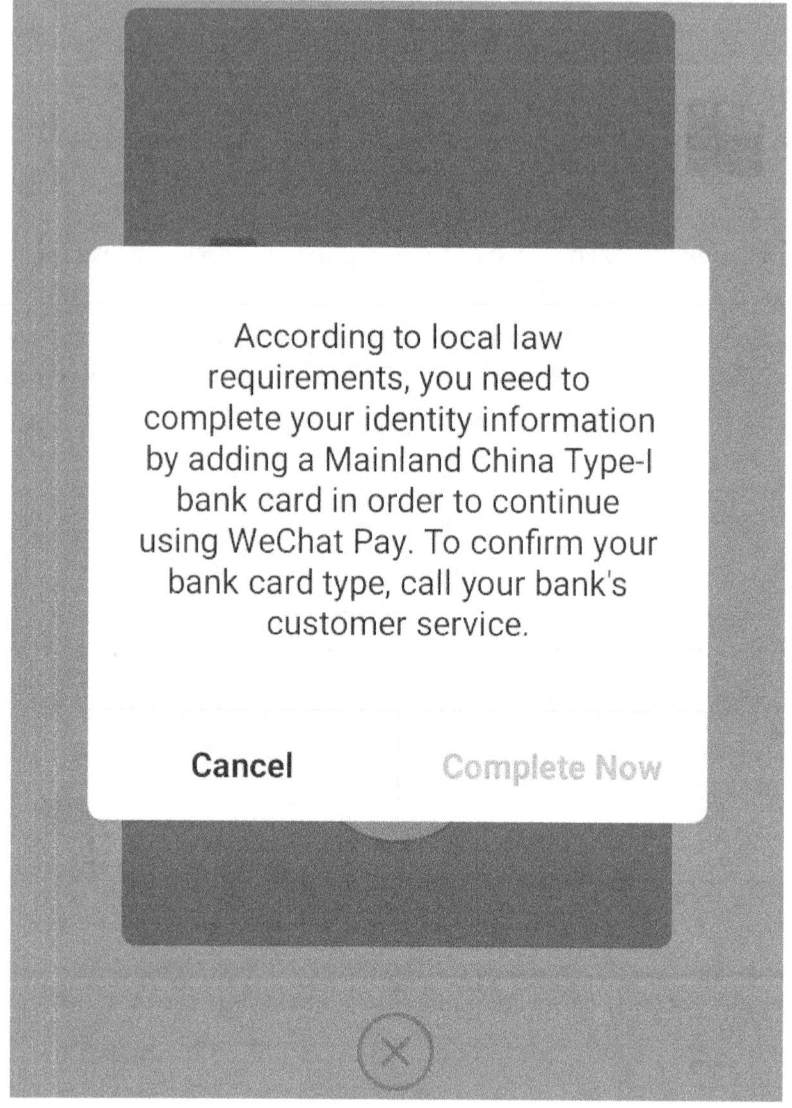

According to local law
requirements, you need to
complete your identity information
by adding a Mainland China Type-I
bank card in order to continue
using WeChat Pay. To confirm your
bank card type, call your bank's
customer service.

Cancel          Complete Now

**TYPICAL . . .**

# FISH HEADS



Bing! Wide awake (gotta love that jet lag)! It occurs to me it's lunch time in Boise, but I'm not hungry at all.

I remember last night's dinner, though. For each lunch and dinner, I get a prepackaged meal, sort of like a TV dinner. It's an approximately 8" x 9" clear plastic tray with five compartments and a tight-fitting lid. The center compartment contains soup of some kind: so far, it's been plain egg drop, tomato egg drop, or seaweed. If I rotate the big compartment of steamed rice to the upper left, the lower right always has steamed vegetables (cabbage stuff, bok choy, spinach-ey stuff, broccoli). Maybe I have a vitamin deficiency, because I'm digging the greens, even though they're just steamed and salted. The upper right is a mix of vegetables and meat. And the lower left is a meat-intensive dish.

Yesterday evening, the tray reeked of fish when I opened it. My mom is very sensitive to fish, and she probably smelled it in Ohio. The soup was tomato and egg drop. I don't remember what was in the upper right. Bok choy with tofu strips occupied the lower right, and in the lower left . . . fried fish.

Now when I say fried fish, I mean just that, two fried fish. Gutted (thankfully), floured, and pan fried, with the heads, tails, fins, and scales. Two fried eyeballs stare balefully up at me. I contact Xiaochi and Huixia via WeChat:

Matt:  Hey, I got whole fried fish for dinner!

Xiaochi: Yes, in China we eat the whole fish.

Matt:  Even the bones and head?

Xiaochi: Yes, the head is good.

Matt:  Really?

Well, I'm in China so that I can learn about China. I'd better try the fish head. Also, what goes around, comes around. I didn't eat that fish head with the sucker mouth in India when I had the chance. I have to do it now. I bite off the head. It's crunchy and salty, pretty good, actually, and—ow! How can such a small fish have such a big bone! I hope I don't crack a tooth over here.

Huixia:  I don't eat fish heads.

Matt:  What? Now you tell me?!

Xiaochi: No, it's good.

Huixia:  Oh, actually, I do eat this kind of whole fish.

She sends an image of fish poached in some kind of tomato sauce. A little like the fish in India, except it's much bigger and not a sucker. I'm glad I'm sticking with the fried fish. I could use the calcium and phosphorus anyway.

Matt:  If I get a stomachache tonight, you know who I'll blame.

Do fish brains carry prions? Aah, I'll probably die of something else before prions kick in, twenty years from now . . .

The memory of whole fried fish last night reminds me of the Lighthouse, a local fast-food restaurant in Spartanburg, South Carolina. I used to stop there for dinner while taking students to Great Smoky Mountains National Park for a geology field trip. As I lie in bed, I'm remembering my first visit:

I walk up to the counter. An enormous guy is waiting to take my order. Not super tall, but broad. If he had an order pad, it would look like a postage stamp in his hand. He says something thoroughly unintelligible, with an inflection at the end. I can tell he's asking me something. I take a guess that it's what I want to order.

"I'll have the fried catfish." He turns and yells something thoroughly unintelligible back over his left shoulder. Did he just order catfish for me, or did he hear "cat" and suddenly remember to tell his buddy that the cat litter box needs to be emptied? He turns back to me with an expectant look.

Now I'm less sure. "And a small order of fries?" He looks off to his left and yells something else unintelligible. Wait, did he say "Parivrrta Virabhadrasana," yoga's "revolved warrior pose?"

He turns back to me again.

"Uh, and a glass of water, and that's it." He turns his attention to the next person in line and says something thoroughly unintelligible, but with an inflection at the end. I guess I'm done ordering. What exactly am I going to get? Maybe cat litter soup.

I slide my plastic tray down the counter and eye the various slabs of pie. I love pecan pie, but this stuff looks so sugar laden, my teeth start to ache. I pass up the pie. I pass up the sweet tea, too. I like sweet tea well enough, but I don't need the extra 500 calories per cup.

I arrive at the register. My food arrives at the same time. It's breaded-and-fried catfish fillets in a little paper boat, and another little boat of fries—exactly what I ordered! It looks and smells awesome, at least if you're hungry for fried food. Which I am.

The clerk asks, "Something to drink, hon?"

Oh, I guess I wasn't supposed to tell the big guy about the water.

"Just a glass of water."

"OK-here's-a-glass-the-water-pitcher's-over-there-ice-is-at-the-coke-machine-that'll-be-six-seventy-five"

I pay. Good food.

Why does last night's dinner remind me of The Lighthouse? That's because my third time there I ordered a fried fish sandwich, and that's exactly what I got. A gutted, floured, pan-fried whole fish—head, tail, fins, and scales (just like I ate last night)—inserted into a Wonderbread hamburger bun. Well, a sandwich is two pieces of bread with something else in between. A fried whole fish in a hamburger bun is a "fried fish sandwich." If I had had a bun last night, I could have made my own Chinese fried fish sandwich.

Now it's 3:00 a.m. Rain starts beating against the window. It's summer in Idaho, and I haven't heard rain like this in at least three months. I get up and push back the curtains. Heat from the window pushes back at me. The heat and rain remind me again of South Carolina. The last time I drove through Clemson was in 2007 during a tropical storm. Warm bands of rain occasionally swept across the highway, blinding me, but there were no other cars, so it's not like I was going to hit anyone. Unlike me, everyone else was smart enough not to hold their geology field trips during a tropical storm. Southeast Asia is a little like the southeastern United States. Warm. Wet. And green so bright it embeds itself into the inside of your skull. I remember now that it's hurricane season. Well, typhoon season. Am I going to experience a typhoon while in quarantine? That would be interesting. Where would they evacuate all us plague people?

I consider getting up and making some coffee. Xiaochi bought me some genuine American Peet's coffee. It comes in these ingenious little pouches that perch over your cup so you can make drip coffee. I don't know who thought of it, but I'm thankful.

Or, maybe I'll check Bilibili (www.bilibili.com—one of China's surrogate YouTube channels, because YouTube is banned). I uploaded one of my mineralogy videos there last night. It took fifteen minutes and I have 230 more to upload. That's roughly 60 hours.

Or, what was that, revolved warrior pose? I'll give that a try.

**EXAMPLE OF FRIED FISH
(AFTER ARRIVAL AT THE CHINESE ACADEMY OF SCIENCES)**

**SINGLE-SERVE, FRESH DRIP PEET'S**

# TERIYAKI VERTEBRATE

I'm a little worried that I should be working on manuscripts, but my thoughts focus on food, instead. Some people on my email list are thinking about food, too, because they've started writing back about my last story. I know they mean well, but really, eat the eyeball first? My growing daily obsession returns—what will dinner be?

Eventually, dinner arrives. Whoa, now that's different! When I place the rice in the upper left corner, the soggy steamed vegetables aren't in the lower right corner any more, they're in the *upper* right corner. There's some kind of dish in the lower left with potatoes and . . . is that vertebrate or invertebrate?

Other than aquatic organisms, I've never knowingly eaten invertebrates. Shellfish, sure—oysters, clams, lobster, crab, and crawdads (they're shellfish, right?). Mussels. Sea urchin eggs (are they shellfish?). Also octopus (I regret that now—they're really smart) and squid (not so regrettable). Maybe even sea cucumber. But I mean I haven't deliberately eaten terrestrial vertebrates, like insects, worms, and scorpions. Of course, we all do eat them. I've heard that, in a normal lifespan, a human will eat a half dozen or so spiders. Tiny ones occasionally venture into your open mouth while you sleep, and then you roll over, close your mouth, and . . . one down, five to go.

I've heard crickets taste pretty good. My brother Fred tells me they taste terrible, but I don't believe him. We conducted a geochemical analysis of grasshoppers in my lab once. We extracted water by heating them (they were already dead) in glass tubes for an hour at the boiling point and condensing the water vapor in a cold trap. We then analyzed the water. But, when we opened the grasshopper tubes afterwards, they smelled delicious. Intensely umami. I was too chicken to eat them, though.

Ironic, saying that I was too "chicken," because chickens do eat grasshoppers. How is it "chicken" not to eat them? Chickens eat everything, the little dinosaurs.

And the lower right dish—teriyaki . . . vertebrate? Yes, it's definitely a vertebrate because that's a chunk of spinal column. From my ventures into vertebrate paleontology, I know that spinal columns are not super diagnostic of species. The technical term is "plesiomorphic" and it refers to characteristics that are conserved during evolution. I happen to know that one spinal column looks pretty much like another. Well, OK, it's definitely not snake or turtle because their vertebrae actually are distinctive—they're not plesiomorphic. Well, not to mammals, anyway. And it's not fish. Could it be iguana? Ooh, I've never had teriyaki iguana before! It's probably chicken, at least the individual vertebrae are about the right diameter. I bet iguana's too expensive to waste on plague-riddled foreigners, anyway, especially the ones who lack Chinese phone numbers. Unless . . . is this my last meal? I was tested with nasal and throat swabs yesterday (thankfully, less aggressively than at the airport—I'm still picking splinters out of my uvula). Is there something they're not telling me? I don't remember listing teriyaki iguana on any of the forms I filled out, but I was pretty tired, and I didn't translate *all* the text. Could that have been one of those checkboxes on the customs form?

Thinking more about food, my mind drifts back to my food poisoning in Dallas. Did I mention that I collapsed at the top of a long flight of stairs? A little farther to the right, and I'd still be recuperating in a Texas hospital. Disaster averted.

In truth I should have revealed to the Chinese authorities that I had diarrhea within the previous forty-eight hours of arrival. But I know they were worried about COVID, not tandoori chicken, and it was forty-seven hours previous. In retrospect, the food poisoning wasn't such a bad thing, because it totally cleared out my GI tract. It's always a little awkward to poop on a plane. Should I start taking laxatives before long flights? Seems like it might backfire.

I make myself some more coffee. This will help me sleep tonight, right?

And . . . yes! My personal Wi-Fi has definitely stopped working. I'll wait to see if it recovers, otherwise, I guess I'll have to start emailing everyone at 5:00 a.m. again. Maybe the coffee was a good idea after all. Jet lag isn't always such a bad thing when you're competing with four hundred tech-savvy kids in a fifty-meter radius for the same Wi-Fi.

A TYPICAL LUNCH/DINNER AT THE RUITAI. IN THE LOWER LEFT, YOU CAN SEE PART OF A (FISH) SPINAL COLUMN. THE FOOD IN THE UPPER RIGHT IS . . .?

# PINBALL BRAIN

Bing! Wide awake again. My brain starts bouncing around like a pinball.

It's still dark. Let me guess. 2:30 a.m., right? Jet lag sure doesn't give up easily.

I roll over and push the button on my phone and the screen lights up. No, it's 4:12 a.m. That's normal. Normal for me anyway. Normal for middle age.

Bing! My mind asks: Which of the following answers is most correct?

Middle age is when you:

    a.   Start worrying about your parents

    b.   Have to pee in the middle of the night. More than once. Every night.

    c.   Get insomnia

Bing! Now my mind switches to the travel nurse at Lawrence Livermore National Laboratory when I was a postdoc.

Nurse:    Hey, have you heard about the three rules of male middle age?

Me:    No, what are they?

Nurse:    First: Never pass by a urinal without using it.

Me:    OK.

Nurse:    Second: Never trust a fart.

> Me:       Ha! OK.
>
> Nurse:    Third: Never let an erection go untended, even if you're alone.

Really? A fifty-something year-old woman is giving a thirty-something year-old guy masturbation advice? I mean, she's a nurse, but still. I chuckle. A little uncomfortably. We go back to talking about my knee problems. Still, I remember the joke twenty-five years later, and I follow the first two rules religiously, especially in airports. The momentary awkwardness was worth it.

Bing! My mind abruptly jumps to the topic I've been thinking about most for the last twenty-four hours: cookies.

Actually, sugar cookies and shortbread, because, yesterday, I got a care package. A *big* one. I still don't know whether the hotel relaxed its rule about outside orders, or if the ban applied only to orders from foreigners who lack a Chinese phone number and bank account. Anyway, in it were:

- Two tubes of potato chips (like Pringles)
- One package of chocolate sugar cookies
- One tub of beautifully-sculpted shortbread cookie rosettes
- Two large packages of biscotti
- One large package of soda crackers
- One large tub of cashew nuts
- One small box of . . . what's a "strawberry pretzel"?

Hey, there's a receipt! Let's see, how much did this all cost? OK, converting to dollars that's . . . forty dollars of unadulterated starch, fat, and salt. I'm not positive how food costs translate between China and the US, but I think a dollar in China may be roughly equivalent to two to four dollars in the US. In other words, this is like one hundred dollars of snacks.

Now there's a reason I don't buy snackie stuff, especially sugar cookies. Actually, there are several reasons. One of them is sleep.

Bing! My mind bounces back to Boise State, several years previous. My student, Robin, is introducing me to a new game.

[Oops! Hold on a sec—backstory: every Monday afternoon, our department hosts a speakers' seminar. A scientist from outside the department, usually from outside the state, comes to give a talk. This introduces our students to different ways of thinking about science, and helps the department keep up to speed on the latest research. Science advances through academic transparency, and this is one way we ensure that. We have a reception ahead of time, with tea, coffee, and . . . cookies. Usually sugar cookies. OK, back to Robin.]

Robin:     I call this "Seminar Bingo."

Me:     OK.

Robin:     Yeah, so every time one of these events happens during seminar, you get to fill in a square.

Me:     OK, just like regular bingo, except instead of calling out columns and numbers, like "B5," it's different events.

Robin:     Right. And if you get five in a row, you win!

Me:     OK, got it.

Robin:     So, for example, here's "speaker reads slide verbatim."

Me:     Yeah, good one.

Robin:     And here's another: "Professor comes to reception, but skips talk."

Me:     OK, sure, that happens sometimes.

Robin:     And here's yours: "Matt falls asleep."

Me:     Yeah—you should make that the center free square.

I always fall asleep at seminar. Partly, it's because I run around like a chicken with its head cut off all day long, and seminar is the one time I sit down . . . and . . . just . . . stop. I try to sit in the back, so speakers don't think their talks are boring. For a long time, I fell asleep because of sugar cookies. If I eat sugar cookies or bread, I get very sleepy in about ten minutes. Perfect if you want to fall asleep during seminar. Which I don't. So, I stopped eating them before seminar. Actually, it's one reason why I hardly ever eat them.

A second reason I don't eat sugar cookies is that, once I start eating them, I can't stop. Something about sugar and fat.

Bing! My mind jumps to field work in Bhutan. My colleague swears me out for eating our entire package of Oreo cookies for breakfast.

And reasons three and four are that they don't stick with me (I get really hungry soon after), and I'd rather invest in food that's more substantial—has more mouth feel, if you know what I mean.

Bing! my mind bounces to field work in western Turkey. Now I'm eating sugar cookies in the back of our field vehicle in a futile attempt to stave off late afternoon hunger.

I'm a little distressed about the care package from Huixia's husband, because my family wasn't exactly wealthy when we were growing up, and we never, ever, threw away food unless it was dangerously moldy, rotten, or infested. Sometimes, only if it was all three. And hardly anything lasted long enough to get that way. So, I'm morally opposed to throwing away edible food of any kind. And I can't give it away either. Well, not here, anyway. Sure, I'll give the potato chips to Xiaochi, because I know he likes potato chips. I filled half a suitcase with bags of assorted potato chips for him as a present (shhhh! don't tell him). But who else can I give food to? My co-quarantiners studiously avoid interacting with me. If I try tossing a package of unopened cookies to the young woman across the hall, she'll probably slam the door and report me for bioterrorism. In China, they'd probably take her seriously. Then I'd really be in prison.

Bing! Now I'm back to yesterday afternoon again. I might as well try the shortbread cookies. Those look good. I open the round box and eat one. Wow! That's *really* good! Sweet and buttery. I eat another. And another. Ten minutes later, the box is empty. Yes, Matt just downed seventeen thousand calories (seventy-one thousand kilojoules) of cookies in a tiny room with virtually no options for serious exercise. Stupid cookies. I'll be asleep in ten minutes, I just know it.

Still, my curiosity takes over. What, exactly, are "strawberry pretzels?" Salty . . . what's? I open the box. In it are two long, skinny foil packages. I pull one open. Well, those sure do look like pretzels. I take one out and tentatively nibble it. Wow! That's really good! It's basically a strawberry-flavored sugar cookie stick.

Bing! Now I'm ten years old, and my mom is making strawberry jam in our kitchen in Ohio. She carefully skims white foam off the top of a pot of slowly convecting, red, slimy goop and slides it into a shallow glass bowl.

| | |
|---|---|
| Me: | Mom, what are you doing? |
| Mom: | I'm making strawberry jam. |
| Me: | Yeah, but what are you doing with that white stuff? |
| Mom: | I'm skimming off the foam. |
| Me: | Why? |
| Mom: | The recipe says to do that. |
| Me: | Oh. What does it taste like? Can I eat it? |
| Mom: | Sure, but not too much. It's really sweet, and it will make you sick if you eat too much. Eat just a little. |

I eat just a little. She's not looking, so I eat a little more. And then a little more. Ten minutes later, it's gone, and I'm trying not to throw up in the sink. For the next ten years, I have trouble bearing the taste of strawberries. Nearly fifty years later, I like them well enough, but not *that* much. That's fortunate because I can eat a single strawberry pretzel now, and not feel compelled to eat the whole box. For once, caloric disaster has been averted. Good thing it wasn't *raspberry* pretzels.

Bing! Back in bed. What am I going to do with all these cookies? I'll eat some, for sure. They're probably good with coffee. Maybe when I get to Beijing I can put them out in my office for visitors to eat. Will they eat soda crackers?

It's starting to get light now. It's still raining—three days straight. I'm definitely not in Idaho any more.

Oh, well, it's time for my morning yoga routine. Maybe I can work off a few shortbread calories.

# GOTCHA!
# . . . MAYBE

---

## 4:06 A.M.:

Toodley-oodley-oodley-oodley-oo!

Toodley-oodley-oodley-oodley-oo!

What the—what time is it?

I roll over and look at my phone. 712-397-XXXX. Iowa? Geez Louise, someone's calling me from Iowa at 4:06 a.m.?

Toodley-oodley-oodley-oodley-oo!

OK, I'm tired of this.

I punch the green answer button:

| | |
|---|---|
| Matt [cheerily]: | Hello, is Matt there? |
| Telemarketer: | Uh . . . |
| Matt: | May I please speak with Matt? |
| Telemarketer: | Hi . . . uh . . . I'm Tammy, and . . . |

| | |
|---|---|
| Matt: | Hi, Tammy. Could you give Matt a message for me? Could you tell him to please stop calling me while I'm in China? It's 4:07 a.m. here, and I really don't like being woken up for anything less than an emergency. |
| Telemarketer: | Uh . . . |
| Matt: | Thanks! Bye! |

I punch the red hang-up button.

[Heh, heh, heh. Gotcha!]

I go back to sleep.

---

## 5:43 A.M.:

Toodley-oodley-oodley-oodley-oo!

Toodley-oodley-oodley-oodley-oo!

734-897-XXXX. Michigan?

I click the button that stops my phone ringing. And turn off my phone.

# UM SUM

I've been working on making captions for my mineralogy instructional videos, for uploading to Bilibili. Fortunately, Huixia found the perfect conversion site: you upload an audio file, and the site converts it simultaneously into both Chinese and English subtitles. It takes a while, but the Chinese is listed first in each caption, then the English. Huixia and I fix the text using simple text editing software, switch them so English is on top (harder to see) and Chinese on the bottom (easier to see), then upload it to Bilibili, and—voilà!—English and Chinese subtitles!

Unfortunately, as I go through these videos, especially the earlier ones, I'm shocked at how stupid I sound.

Audio: "OK, so . . . uh . . . this is quartz. And it . . . uh . . . has these relatively simple . . . uh . . . optical properties. Uh . . ."

How many times do I say "uh" or "um" when I'm speaking? Now I know—*lots!* How embarrassing is that?

And that reminds me:

I'm a graduate student at a meeting of the American Geophysical Union, and I'm sitting with two of my mentors. They're really good friends and they joke around a lot. I'll label them "M1" and "M2" (for mentor one and mentor two). One of my co-graduate students is about to give a talk. I'll call him "S" (for speaker).

> **M1:** Have you noticed how often S says uh or um when he speaks?

> M2:     No, I can't say I have.

> M1:     Oh, yeah, it's remarkable. I bet he says uh or um in this talk at least one hundred times.

> M2:     Seriously? That's almost ten times per minute.

[Talks are supposed to be twelve minutes long, although the total speaking slot is fifteen minutes.]

> M1:     Oh, I bet he could do it.

> M2:     I'll take that bet.

> M1:     OK.

> S:     Hi . . . uh . . . good morning . . . uh . . .

> M1 (grinning):   One, two . . .

[No, they don't verbalize them all, only the first couple, for fun, but not after that. It would be incredibly rude to have a conversation during someone's talk. Still, I know they're counting.]

[I should comment, too, that my mentors probably already knew everything about S's research, and didn't really have to listen to his talk to understand the science (unlike me, for whom it was all new). They may have even heard a practice talk. Plus, it's possible for seriously smart people like them to count and listen critically at the same time, if it's a topic they're familiar with. I think they attended the talk more to show support for S and to hear any questions than to learn what S was doing. And if they could have a little fun, well, so be it.]

Fourteen minutes later:

> S:     Thanks for listening.

> M2:     I got 98.

> M1:     I got 97.

> M2:     I guess you lose.

Session moderator: We have time for one quick question. Yes. Go ahead?

Audience member: Could you explain [something I don't remember].

S: Sure . . . uh . . .

One minute later:

M1: Four more!

M2: Guess you win after all.

M1: A new um sum record!

Surely, I couldn't rate as high an um sum, right? Or, could I? Well, it's not quite ten per minute, but some of my videos are truly Olympic.

So, because scientists pay attention to detail, and I don't want to appear stupider than I have to, I feel compelled to go into the audio portion of each video, and carefully clip out all (or most) of the ums. It's tedious work. But, actually, the audio flows better, and at least I'm spared a little embarrassment, in China, anyway. There are still all those unedited videos on YouTube.

Actually, I should count the ums there sometime. I wonder, did I beat S?

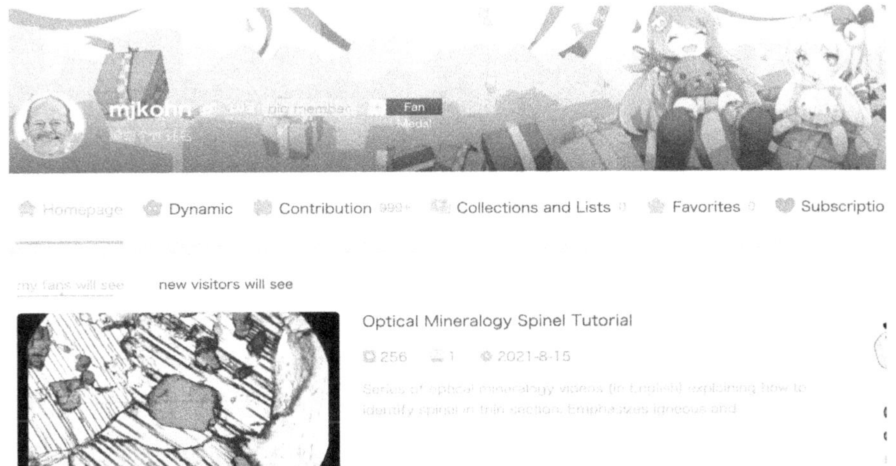


**MY WEBSITE IN CHINA**

AUGUST

# GETTING STONED IN ASIA

One of the curious things about construction in Asia is the amount of stone they use. India exports decorative stone—marble, granite, etc.—so maybe it's not so surprising there. I've always been impressed at how beautiful their hotels and public buildings are with respect to different facing stone. Everything else can be rundown, but the stone is spectacular.

OK, I'm a geologist, so I notice things like that. But I think even normal people would see it too.

Now, the hotel I'm staying at is not the highest quality. The carpets are permanently stained, there are black hairs sparsely scattered everywhere (did they vacuum before I arrived?), the floors are uneven, the chair I'm sitting in sags, the air conditioning is wimpy, the toilet runs . . .

But, the countertops in the bathroom are made of beautiful yellow fossiliferous limestone. I can easily make out turritellids and olivids (types of snails).

The turritellids make these skinny, spiral, dunce-cap types of shells. These are truly spectacular—the largest I've ever seen. At least five inches (twelve centimeters) long.

I don't think I've seen fossil olivids before, but these look just like the ones we collected as kids on the beaches of the southeastern US.

I can tell it's real stone, too, because it feels cold to the touch. Technically, that would mean it has relatively high heat conductivity and heat capacity, at least in comparison with petroleum products. Linoleum wouldn't feel this way.

In America, this would be like Motel 6 with granite countertops.

I guess it's a good thing I didn't pack a rock hammer. I'd be sorely tempted to—oops!—"accidentally" knock off a chunk.

**SNAIL FOSSILS AT MY SINK**

# FREE AT LAST! FREE AT LAST!

I've left my quarantine hotel! The transition was easier than I thought.

## SATURDAY, JULY 31

(Three days prior to transfer)

In the morning, at 9:00 a.m., I had my temperature checked (normal procedure, and my temperature was normal). And since nothing ever happens for several hours after that, I used that time to throw six bleach tablets in the toilet and sit in the cool of the bathroom for a couple minutes (the main room has large windows, so it's always about 5-10°F (3-5°C) hotter than the bathroom). And, of course, that's when . . .

Wham, wham, wham! (my door). *Brrrriiiiinnnnnggg! Brrrriiiiinnnnnggg!* (my doorbell). Somebody shouts something outside in the hall. In Chinese, of course. But I don't think language makes much difference—can you really understand what someone is shouting through a cloth mask, a plastic face mask, and a couple doors?

They don't sound alarmed enough for this to be a fire or typhoon evacuation (plus, for once, it's not raining). It would be too cruel a joke to hold fire drills during quarantines. What's going on?

It takes me a couple minutes to arrange myself (I give a couple yells, so whoever's in the hall knows I heard them). And, naturally enough, when I answer the door, there's no one there. Rather, I see the hazmat folk interrogating the woman across the hall. They turn and say something to me—I don't know what they say, because it's in Chinese. But the woman informs me I need to close the door. Curious: they insist I open the door, then leave, and then insist I close it?

Well, I expect they'll let me know eventually, so I close the door. A minute later the doorbell rings again. Good, now I'll find out.

Hi, what's going on? Oh, really? What a surprise! I have to scan another QR code . . .

I'll spare you the blow-by-blow, which is a little tedious because the app doesn't work right away (surprise!). But basically, the code takes me to a check-out form that I complete in the serenity of my hotel room. And hope that giving a hotel address as "across from Shuilu Park" isn't going to be a problem.

## SUNDAY, AUGUST 1

(Two days prior to transfer)

Wham, wham, wham! Brrrriiiiinnnnnggg! Brrrriiiiinnnnnggg!

Again, I'll spare you the blow-by-blow. The hazmat folks are waving a paper form and saying something. When they realize I don't understand them, they pull out their phones that have all their communications translated into English—great! I learn that they want me to check over the information (which is all correct, even "across from Shuilu Park"). They keep saying something about my name, so I sign the form, and that seems to satisfy them. At least, they leave after that and start banging on the door of the woman across the hall.

## TUESDAY, AUGUST 3

(Day of transfer and my last day of quarantine!)

Everything goes normally during the day: wake up at 5:00 a.m., breakfast at 7:30, temperature check at 9:00, lunch at noon, second temperature check at two, dinner at 5:30. But I don't know how I will leave the hotel, or get to the next one. All I really know is that I'm supposed to leave at 8:00 p.m.

I think I'm supposed to pick up an "all-clear" form from the front desk, verifying that I haven't contributed to a super-spreader event. Yet.

I'll need this form to leave the city. There isn't really a "front desk" though. More of a "back stairwell with service elevator."

A service elevator that is completely covered in plastic.

Otherwise, I'll have to wing it. Do I just walk out the door and the two and a half blocks down the street to the Quanji Hotel? Do I need an escort to get there? Do I need to douse myself in bleach and suit up in hazmat? I'll find out soon enough.

I communicate with Xiaochi, and he tells me I should just leave my room at 8:00, pick up a form, and walk out the door. He's arranged for someone from the next hotel (the Quanji) to come pick me up.

So, at 8:00, I leave the room and check out, easy peasy. There's a super-nice guy in line who volunteers to translate for me. He tells me I will have to get tested twice more: in two days and in seven days. Then I can leave Shanghai. There's a list of testing centers (except he doesn't show me the key list—more on that later). I don't have to make an appointment ahead of time.

I walk outside.

Maybe hanging around with people from other cultures makes you more comfortable with them, but the same can't be said of climates. Every time I come back to a tropical or subtropical locale, I feel like I'm being smothered in hot, wet cotton. My shirt is soaked in a minute. Fortunately, it's thin cotton, and I know it will dry quickly.

I hang out there about twenty minutes, texting with Xiaochi. Finally, I realize that no one's going to drive in, and that I should walk out to the street.

Immediately, I'm accosted by a couple guys who try to take my suitcases.

Who are you?

They don't speak English. They try to explain. I don't speak Mandarin.

Aha! I fire up my translation app. Glory be—it works perfectly! The two guys are from the Quanji Hotel, and have come to pick me up. But, there's no car. Rather, they start walking in the direction of the hotel. Slowly.

Well, if I'd known that, I would have just walked. Quickly. But hey, Matt, don't forget, it's not such a bad idea to walk slowly when you're wading through hot, wet cotton.

Xiaochi's map app told us it would take seven minutes to walk from the Ruitai to the Quanji. Fifteen minutes after we start our leisurely stroll, we arrive.

Of course, the guy at the front desk doesn't speak any English. But, aha! My translation app to the rescue! I get a room key (actually a card), and am escorted to my room. This time, though, I get to keep the card. So now I know that, in this hotel, I can run naked up and down the halls if I want to. Well, I might set off some alarms, but different alarms than in the Ruitai.

The room is stiflingly hot. It takes me a little while to find the controls for the air conditioner. And to fix the window so it closes. But, eventually the room becomes livable. All things considered, this worked out pretty painlessly.

I still don't know whether I can leave the hotel (other than to get tested). Xiaochi tells me the hotel told him I can't leave. How is this different from quarantine?

Huixia ordered me some antihistamines, and when they arrive, I take one. I almost immediately conk out for the next fourteen hours.

Freedom gives you the right to sleep late.

# WELL, NOT SO FAST

It's easy to get food when you're in hotel quarantine prison—they bring it to you regularly. And it's fairly well-balanced nutritionally, even if the cuisine is a little bland and soggy. And bony.

But, it's much harder to feed yourself when you're on hotel parole ("community observation"). According to the hotel, I'm not supposed to leave. Ever. Of course, it's not clear how I'll obtain my required tests tomorrow and in six days. But no doubt something will work out. Right?

Xiaochi managed to order me breakfast from the hotel (starch-o-rama!) and lunch from Taco Bell. Otherwise, we spent more or less all day trying to get apps to work on my phone. Just trying to find, install, and operate a simple map app took us an hour. And never worked.

The problems are:

1.  Nothing Google works well in China. Now, if you own an android phone and your main access to apps is through Google Play Store, this turns into a serious problem. I end up using an alternate app source, which doesn't even list apps that I know are available.

2.  Yes, there are apps that bypass some of the restrictions on Google, and we first tried to install them so I could use Google Play Store

and Google maps. However, none of the bypass apps work on my phone.

3. Whether an app runs also depends on what Wi-Fi I use. Not all the apps work on my portable Wi-Fi (why?). And the hotel Wi-Fi requires login information (which is a separate app that doesn't work particularly well).

4. Of course, *everything* is in Chinese. So, while I'm working on an app on my phone (downloading, opening, trying to register with my US phone number, cursing because that doesn't work, trying to register with Xiaochi's phone number, cursing again because *that* doesn't work, etc.), I'm using the translation app on my old phone to figure out what buttons I'm pushing and what information is needed. It's slow.

I'll have to ask my sister-in-law Heidi whether the Chinese voice translation of my cursing is accurate.

I now have multiple examples. In multiple languages.

So, we run through this sequence three or four times, then give up. The next day, Xiaochi helps me find the map function in WeChat, so I can at least see where I am (even if I can't read or search for anything). At minimum, I recognize the map patterns near the hotel, so I can get back. I guess that means I can still get lost (no navigation), but I can also get unlost.

Then, Xiaochi and I take on the food apps. Ugh.

Ultimately nothing works. The main problems appear to be that I lack a Chinese phone number and a Chinese bank account. This is all complicated and slowed with the two-phone translation process, but after four hours of work, we give up. Eventually, Xiaochi just orders me food. It's so much less effort.

Now, when you think about it, the whole situation is absolutely absurd. I mean, I'm OK because I have two seriously dedicated colleagues who are bending over backwards to help me. For example, they:

Check on testing sites to see which are closest (I have no workable map app or a Chinese character keyboard . . .).

Call the hotel to make sure I get breakfast (although this is something I could do myself).

Order me lunch (no workable food app, and the hotel doesn't serve lunch).

Order me dinner (again, no workable food app, and the hotel doesn't serve dinner either).

Order me anything else I might need (like toothpaste and antihistamines).

But what kind of system crashes for a foreign traveler just because he doesn't have a Chinese phone number or bank account? What foreign travelers *do* have them? To get them, you have to come to China. But to come to China (and navigate entry, quarantine/prison, testing, "observation"/parole), you have to have them already. And, technically, I'm not supposed to leave the hotel to either (a) get a Chinese SIM card, or (b) open a Chinese bank account. This seems like an unsolvable Catch-22.

I'm so thankful every day for Xiaochi and Huixia. And, I'm *so* looking forward to getting tested tomorrow.

# TESTING, TESTING ... AM I IN DALLAS AGAIN?

**7:30**  clatter, clatter, clatter! What the ...?

My room is on a sort of cul-de-sac hall spur, so any noise outside my door can't be associated with any other guests.

I look at my door. An eerie blue light illuminates the edges. Oh, I know what this is.

I open the door, and (sure enough) there s/he is: the little R2 robot unit that delivers meals. There's a button on the top that says "Open." I push it. Immediately the R2 unit starts chattering at me in Chinese, too fast for my translation app. A door slides open, and there's a bag of breakfast, which I remove.

The button on the top of the unit now says "Close," so I push it. The door slides shut, and I shut my door too. I know it's a little rude of me, because the unit is still chattering away. Is s/he asking for a tip? But I don't hear any alarms, and soon enough the clattering fades toward the elevator.

I eat the stir-fried rice with egg, the boiled egg, the glass of milk, and the fruit. But not the soupy porridge (congee) or the starchy, not-sweet, sweet corn. Corn in Asia always disappoints me—all the appealing texture of wilted lettuce, but less flavor. True, it exercises your jaws.

8:30   Xiaochi and I start texting to work out travel logistics to the testing site. For example, which site do I go to (there are five)? How will I avoid getting lost? I want to start early because afternoons are hot, just like Dallas. It sure ain't gonna be me standing in line at 3:00 p.m. this time!

We settle on a site that's second-closest, and passes by some universities and parks. It's only 3.6 kilometers (two-and-a-quarter miles), although the app says it will take me fifty-five minutes to get there. Maybe that's Shanghai walking speed? Normally it would take me forty minutes. Assuming I don't get lost . . .

Then we spend an hour trying to find a map app that works on my phone. The WeChat map app keeps defaulting to Google Maps, and Google doesn't work in China. Ugh. Finally, one map app starts working. It's in Chinese, but at least I can see where I am, and I have a route plotted on it.

9:50   Full of confidence and exuberance, I leave the hotel—I'm on my way!

9:51   I'm absolutely weaving around on the sidewalk. What's the matter with me? Could it be that I haven't walked anywhere in two weeks? (other than a casual saunter from the Ruitai to the Quanji). My muscles have forgotten how to walk! Fortunately, they're fast learners, and I steady as I go.

10:12   My map app stops working. Actually, it probably stopped working soon after I left the range of the hotel's Wi-Fi. But I didn't notice it until now, when Xiaochi asked me if I had a phone number for the testing center. And, not only has it stopped working, it has absolutely disappeared from my phone. I can't even bring it back up. I never manage to relocate it.

I contact Xiaochi and pull up the route images that he sent me this morning. How hard can this be? I'm a geologist, right? I don't need GPS to find my way. I keep walking.

10:30  OK, I'm getting pretty sweaty by now. It's hot, and it's humid . . . hmmm . . . am I in Dallas again? There are cicadas here, too, but unlike Texas, they're really loud. Not up to Brood X in the eastern US (which are active right now). Maybe only Brood V. I'm glad I'm getting this over with early.

10:50  After wandering briefly around a maze of tiny streets that don't interconnect, I stumble on the testing center. OK, no one understands English, but that's not surprising—it's just a neighborhood clinic. I get out my translation app, and with the help of another guy who comes up and speaks quite a bit of English, I get the story and call Xiaochi:

Matt:  Hi, Xiaochi. Yes, I got to the testing center just fine [OK, I wandered around a bit, but not that much]. No, they tell me that there's no testing until 1:30. Yes, I said that as long as I'm here now, they should just test me. But they said the company that does the testing won't even show up until 1:30. And they test only until 3:30.

No, there's no indication of hours of operation on any of the forms I received [Actually, that's not quite true, but I didn't know it at the time]. Sure, I could find some place for lunch, but two-and-a-half hours? That seems like a long time to wait. I suppose I could shop or look for a park, but with all this time, I think I'll just walk back to the hotel. No, thanks, I don't think I want a taxi. I didn't pay much attention to any of the shops when I walked past them, so this will give me some time to check them out.

12:00  Arrive back at the hotel. I have large blisters on both heels now (I haven't walked anywhere in 2 weeks), but no other shoe options. My shirt is absolutely soaked through, so I change to a new one. And take a nap - I'm exhausted.

12:45  Leave for the testing center. Again.

1:30  Arrive at the testing center. Again.

Same kind of deal as this morning: these folks also speak a little English, but with the help of the translation app and a kindly fellow, I find out that, no, I can't get tested. At least, not in a clean, air-conditioned clinic full of quiet corridors and calm- and efficient-looking medical staff who thankfully speak some English. No, instead, I have to stand outside in that line of people on the other side of the street, who are all desperately seeking the little shreds of shadow cast by the sycamores in among a rack of bikes. It's Dallas all over again.

I go to the end of the line.

Now, this line isn't TSA- or immigration-length or anything like that. There are maybe fifty people in front of me. But it's moving incredibly slowly. Why? The test itself takes less than a minute. How long can registration take? It can't be so bad, right?

2:00  Xiaochi checks in with me. Huixia has also joined the conversation. I've traversed one fourth to one third of the line in half an hour. At that rate, I'll be here until 3:00, at least. Hmm . . . just like Dallas.

Fortunately, I brought a bandana to wipe the sweat off my face. At least, I thought it would be for my face. Actually, it's for my face, top of my head, arms, neck, essentially any exposed skin. And I need it too. I notice little drops of wetness on the pavement, and realize, no, it's not rain, it's sweat dripping off the tips of my fingers. Yuck.

Every once in a while, a street cop comes by and demands we step out of the street and move forward, move forward! Now, let's be serious—do you really think anyone wants to stand close to anyone else when they're in a line to be tested for a highly contagious disease? Let's see, where's the bubonic plague line? Let's all squeeze together over there! I'm sure folks are delighted to press up against a potentially highly-contagious guy who is also super sweaty.

Why do people who live in the desert (like me) even visit subtropical climates?

2:30  Xiaochi asks me if I'm in the wrong line. Oh crap, is this the vaccination line? I send him a photo of a banner with all the information. He checks and—thank goodness!—I'm in the right line! The COVID-19 testing line is just very slow.

But, as we start texting, I notice the line is starting to move a little faster.

2:35  Now, I'm close enough to see inside the registration window. Why does everyone else have a QR code? Where was I supposed to get that? Xiaochi suggests I scan an emblem on the banner. It's supposed to bring up an app (surprise!) that lets me register for the test. But it doesn't work (surprise!) [In fact, we try this again the next day for about half an hour, and never get it to work, perhaps because I don't have a Chinese phone number.]

I'll just have to wing it. Again.

2:40  OK, it's my turn. Here's my passport. Yes, that's my last name, and that's my first name, and that's my date of birth.

Sorry, I speak only English. [At this point, a woman behind me in line comes forward and basically becomes my translator.

I do have my translation app, but this simplifies things considerably. People like her should be canonized.]

No, I didn't know I was supposed to pay. [Actually, I wasn't supposed to pay, but that's a whole other complication that we didn't figure out until the next day.]

No, I don't have Alipay. [Alipay is another ubiquitous Chinese app. It works similarly to WeChat Pay, but its primary use is for payments, not for texting.]

No, I don't have cash. Well, I have US cash, but not Chinese currency. I have WeChat—can I use that? Oh, just Alipay. No dice.

At this point—and this is pretty incredible, when you think about it—the woman behind me suggests I pay her using WeChat Pay, and she will pay my fee using Alipay. We pull up everything on our phones, and . . . it doesn't work. By this time, there's another guy from the clinic who speaks English pretty well, who is involved in the whole discussion. I make a last-ditch phone call to . . . well . . . you can guess:

Xiaochi, WeChat Pay isn't working for me. Is it OK if I give you the phone number of one of the clinic personnel here? You two can talk and maybe sort something out. OK, thanks.

Xiaochi and the clinic guy talk together, and make some arrangement with the woman behind me in line. [I find out later that Xiaochi pays her the testing fee using WeChat, she then pays my testing fee using Alipay]. After a minute, the clinic guy directs me to follow the woman, as she's headed for the testing center too. I start following.

The next thing I know, some guard is shouting at us. *Loudly!* Of course, I don't understand him, so I ignore him. Hey, it's easier to get forgiveness than permission, right? Plus, it's not like he's carrying a weapon (OK, clear indication that this is definitely not Dallas!). But he's insistent. It turns out, we were supposed to walk through the street, on the right side of the hedges, not on the sidewalk on the left side of the hedges. And the reason for this is . . .?

Whatever.

2:50    I'm now standing in the testing line. We're waiting to approach two different windows in a trailer the size of a mobile home. It's a little like takeout at a drive-through. At the first window, you place your order (Could I please have a Q-tip stuck up my nose? And another one down my throat?). At the second window, you actually get what you ordered.

2:58    Now I'm third or fourth in line. Why does everyone else have a QR code? Damn the QR codes, full speed ahead!

3:00    I'm at the first window. I hand the woman my passport. No, she doesn't speak any English (not surprising, of course), but she also doesn't want to speak into my translation app. I'm insistent, and we go through a couple rounds of exchanges where she keeps asking for my name, but it's not clear if she's asking for my last name or first name. Some kids behind me in line try to explain that she's asking for my name, but that's not really the problem. The problem, of course, is that it's customary in China to give your family name first, then your given name—the exact opposite of in the US. So, in China, Huixia would normally say her name is "Ding Huixia" (last name, first name), but in the US she would be "Huixia Ding" (first name, last name). I know that's the problem. And the woman at the window knows that's the problem. But we can't get past the language problem. Eventually, everything gets sorted out. Or maybe she gives up. She stops interrogating me, anyway, and I move to the second window for my tests.

3:08    OK, first it's down my throat, then it's up my nose.

3:10    I'm free!

I don't know what happens with the tests after this, or how I find out or receive my results. I'm just strangely pleased to have become briefly intimate with Q-tips again.

I now walk back to the hotel. Again.

I think I need some salt.

**R2 DELIVERY UNIT**

**WAITING TO GET TESTED**

# POCKY STICKS AND AFRICAN BUFFALO

Because I don't read Chinese characters, shopping in grocery stores in Shanghai for me is a lovely adventure. Many of the foods are the same, of course, but the style of packaging is different, so even the same foods look different. And there are some ingredients that are a little unusual, at least by American standards:

OK, that's potato chips, and that's milk, but what the heck is that? Oh, no worries, I'll just fire up my translation app. And it is . . . dried duck tongues? I'm definitely not in Kansas anymore. Or Idaho.

My first time shopping was on the long day after I got tested, and it was basically a trial run: Pocky Sticks.

If you're unfamiliar with Pocky Sticks, they're skinny cookies, shaped a bit like pretzel sticks, coated halfway with something sweet. My sister-in-law Heidi and her kid, Gaelan, introduced me to Pocky Sticks. I'm not sure whether to thank them or curse them.

Fortunately, my first purchase of Pocky Sticks was only slightly complicated.

I take my box of Pocky Sticks to the cash register, and I explain to the woman there (using my translation app) that I speak only English and that this is the first time I've tried to purchase anything in a store in China. Feeling a little nervous (does a Chinese app ever work correctly for me?), I fire up WeChat.

First, I have to enter a numerical password to get into WeChat Pay, just like the password you need to get into your phone. OK, I think I remember that password, and—it works! I cross the first hurdle.

Second, I have to enter a numerical password to activate WeChat Pay. This is where I got hung up at the testing center, so I have a little trepidation. I'm pretty sure I know what it is. Well, probably . . . Maybe?

I enter the password [please, please, please]. And I wait . . .

and wait . . . and wait . . .

The woman at the cash register is looking at me quizzically, but patiently. Fortunately, there's no one else in line. Unwittingly (as always) I picked a good store for that.

Finally, I realize—no, it's not going to work. All I'm getting is that all-too familiar "spinning wheel of death." Geez Louise, not again. I mean, it's only a box of Pocky Sticks, but what is going on?

I show the spinning wheel to the woman, and she gestures to the door. Strange, it doesn't look like she's telling me to shoo. I walk outside. Bingo! A QR code comes up. Was it a connection problem? Anyway, now I have a QR code. A QR code is a good sign, right?

I go back into the store, and she scans it. There's a beep. She prints out a receipt, and hands it to me. I look at her. She looks at me.

Then it hits me: Oh! I just bought some Pocky Sticks! Now I'm excited— it works!!!

I stash the Pocky Sticks in my pack, and walk a little farther in search of another store. This time, I'm looking for something substantial. Well, recognizable and proteinaceous, anyway.

I enter a second, larger grocery store. It turns out this store doesn't stock recognizable and proteinaceous food. It's either recognizable *or* proteinaceous, but not both. Still, I pick up some fruit and bottled water (Huixia is insistent that I don't drink the tap water from the hotel). At the counter, the woman at the register looks at my stuff, and calls over another woman.

Uh oh, did I do something wrong? Or, do they recognize me as the sweaty, potentially highly-infectious American from the clinic? I start edging toward the door.

Oh, I didn't weigh the fruit. Was I supposed to do that? Or was I supposed to ask someone to do that for me? Anyway, the second woman weighs out my produce, and prints out some stickers with—you guessed it—QR codes. I assume this is the price.

Back at the register, the first woman rings up everything, and I pull up WeChat pay on my phone. But this time, the QR code is already right there, I don't even have to enter my second password.

She scans the QR code. There's a beep, a receipt is printed out, and I'm good to go!

This looks simple, at least as long as I don't have to communicate with anyone.

I return to the hotel, and celebrate. How? By eating all my Pocky Sticks, of course. Damn you, Heidi and Gaelan! Good thing I bought only one box.

My second day of shopping, I first had to visit the clinic to pick up my test results. I confess, I succumbed to laziness (and a desire not to have to wash my clothes *too* often in a hotel sink), and had Huixia call me a taxi. What luxury! But I didn't see very much from the car.

Generally, I find it much more rewarding to walk places. How else would I have learned that some moped drivers put little cats' ears on their helmets? One woman mounted a propeller on hers, and another guy wore rabbit ears. I also would have missed the pink quilted blankets that some drivers install up front to protect themselves from road splash.

I admit, I'm not positive I would want to don a quilt in the summertime in Shanghai, but I can certainly see the value in the wintertime. I'd probably choose a different color than pink, though. Maybe mud-colored.

Another thing I noticed while walking is that, while Anurag Mathur's character Gopal in *The Inscrutable Americans* may comment that the "Most surprising thing about America is it is full of Americans," the same cannot be said of Shanghai. No, I can report with confidence that Shanghai is not full of Americans, at least not now anyway (remember—no tourist visas). Roughly speaking, my "whitey sighting" on the street comes in at only about one per hour. And most are probably not American—they're too thin (according to CDC statistics, about 75 percent of Americans are overweight, and over 40 percent are obese.)

Anyway, I planned ahead for my second trip. I knew the walk back from the testing center would be hot. So, I pulled the old African buffalo trick. And what is that, you ask?

Well, it's a way to keep cool in the heat. Sort of.

When I was researching water balance in East African animals, I learned that (not surprisingly) different animals do different things to conserve water and keep cool. Body temperature is a big deal. If you get too hot, your brain fries and you die. To keep cool, some animals are solely nocturnal, live in holes in the ground, or wallow in water or mud. Others keep cool, not only by hanging out in the shade (like we were doing, standing in line waiting for COVID-19 tests), but also by sweating (also what I was doing) or panting (not physiologically viable for primates). Unfortunately, sweating and panting use up a lot of water, and it's pretty easy to get dehydrated. So, temperature regulation is crucial, not just to keep your brain from frying, but also so you don't turn into topi jerky (topi is a type of East African antelope).

African buffalo are weird. They're black, and they belong to a group of animals that doesn't conserve water very well (subfamily Bovinae or bovines: cattle, bison, yaks, etc.), so they can get dehydrated easily. Seems like a bad combination if you live in a hot, dry place like East Africa, right? So, why are African buffalo often seen standing out in the sun, when all the other animals are keeping a low profile? How does this make any sense? Why don't they sweat themselves to death?

Well, it turns out that buffalo let their body temperatures decrease during the night, so they're actually rather chilly during the daytime. They don't really care if they stand out in the sun, because their bodies haven't gotten hot enough for their brains to fry, or for sweating to kick in. So, the "African buffalo trick" is to get as cold as possible before venturing out in the heat. That way it takes a while for your body to hit sweat-level temperatures.

In preparation for my second outing, I turned the air conditioning down as low as it could go and sat under it for half an hour until my toes started to go numb. I didn't start seriously sweating until at least a half hour after leaving the clinic. That's pretty good by Shanghai standards. At least it gave me one more day before I had to wash my shirts.

Anyway, the next store I visited had a wider variety of interesting foods. Ultimately, I bought a steamed bun (baozi) filled with greens (I wasn't quite sure what I was getting, but it was good), some jerky, yogurt, and . . . more Pocky Sticks! And more water, to keep Huixia happy.

Yes, it's a pain to get apps working on your phone in China, especially if you don't have a Chinese phone number or bank account. Xiaochi had to set me up with a WeChat account first. But, ultimately, it's a pretty sweet system. The clerks just scan your QR code, and you're done. I like it!

Now to get those duck tongues . . .

**QUILT ON MOTORBIKE**

**MORE QUILTS ON MOTORBIKES**

**POCKY STICKS**

# A SUNDAY STROLL IN SHANGHAI

It's 8:00 a.m. on Sunday morning, and I've just finished breakfast and deleting all the emails that I'd rather not deal with and can safely pretend I never received. With the whole day ahead of me, I decide to ignore the warnings from the hotel that I should absolutely, positively *never* leave my room, and I go for a walk.

I pack up everything I might need—passport (required for all foreigners at all times), cell phone, portable Wi-Fi, water bottle—and head out the door. Sure enough, the staff at the front desk barely looks up from their conversation as I boldly walk past. "Hide in plain sight"—that's my motto! So is "It's easier to receive forgiveness than permission." I hope that one applies in China too.

Stepping out the door, yes, another fine summer morning in Shanghai: super-humid and in the eighties. Of course, it's always super-humid and, as for temperature, you have only two choices: either in the eighties or nineties. Unlike the desert scrubland that I call home, daily temperature shifts in Shanghai are only approximately 10°F (typical of humid climates). So, low- to mid-nineties during the day, and low- to mid-eighties during the night. Not like Boise, where daily temperature shifts of 35°F are common. Usually, you can open your windows at night in Boise to cool off. Here in Shanghai? Not so much. That's why one of the first things I did when I walked into my hotel room was shut the window.

Anyway, I cross the street and head to a little park down the block. Now, the hotel staff has told me expressly (via Xiaochi) that I'm not allowed in the parks. But, how is anyone going to know, especially if I act like I know what I'm doing? Motto number one: hide in plain sight, right? Also, if I get stopped, I'll feign ignorance and apply motto number two: ask for forgiveness.

It's an interesting little park. It's long, skinny, and elongate parallel to the road, with a waterway running lengthwise down the middle. On the side of the waterway nearest the road are a series of plazas, with older people hanging out, mainly doing exercises, but also just chatting. One couple is practicing swing dance. This is clearly what some older people do on Sunday morning, head to the park and enjoy a little space and (relatively) fresh air. There are virtually no kids.

The waterway in the middle is mostly filled with water lilies. But they're restricted to rectangular enclosures. It's more of a hydroponics experiment than a "let's allow the water lilies to roam free" kind of park.

There's a little bridge that crosses the waterway, so (ever the intrepid explorer!) I cross it. That turns out to be a mistake. First, there's no way out from that side of the waterway. There are some meandering dirt paths among the trees, but otherwise that part of the park is walled off from surrounding streets and buildings. And the walls are unscalable (I checked). Second, there's trash everywhere. I'm surprised because Shanghai streets are super clean. I regularly see people sweeping up that one little piece of paper in that entire block. Third, there are a couple shifty-looking guys eying me suspiciously. Maybe they're homeless and I stepped into their living room. Or maybe they live in the apartment complexes next door and don't like trespassers. On the other hand, I'm also a sweaty white guy, wearing a tie-dyed shirt and ball cap. It's probably not every day that they see people who are essentially emblazoned with a sign saying "Hey, American here!"

Hmmm . . . one looks like he may be setting up a little drug processing kitchen. I cross back. Hastily.

Walking farther along the street in search of a second expressly forbidden park on my list, I pass a series of shops. Short lines of people wait at each. The shops here are fascinating. Each is tiny, fronts the street with an open counter, and is about the size of a food truck. You can walk into some (they're pretty deep), but most have a full-width display case with whatever the shop is selling, for example:

pastries, bread, steamed buns, fruit, prepared lunch, meat, etc. It's like a farmer's market, except with permanent structures.

One darkened doorway emits a steady stream of conversation that sounds a little like haggling. I peer into the gloom. Sacks and sacks of eggs. Not every seller has a counter.

I notice that every meat shop invariably contains lots of duck. I can tell it's duck, not only because the birds seem unnaturally skinny, but also because they have very long necks.

Now, what is it with duck and China? Or, to be more accurate, what is it with lack-of-duck and America? An entire supermarket in America might sport a couple measly frozen ducks around Christmastime, but always has row after row of chicken, both fresh and frozen. Does duck provide too little meat per pound to be economical? All I can say is that I'm glad the Chinese like to eat duck because it's delicious—much more tasty than chicken or turkey.

Actually, that's not quite fair, duck here is much more tasty than *American* chicken or turkey. That's not saying much. The chicken I've had here in China also has far more flavor. This, of course, reminds me of Thanhha Lai's book, *Inside Out and Back Again,* which won a Newbery Honor in 2012. As immigrants to Alabama, after the fall of Saigon in 1975, a Vietnamese family tries American fried chicken (possibly KFC, although the girl in the story, named Ha, doesn't say). Ha drools over the crunchy coating, but she describes the chicken as tasting like "bread soaked in water." I really didn't understand quite what she meant until I came to Shanghai. Chicken in America really is dreadfully soft and flavorless.

And that thought sends me back to Dehra Dun, India, and my good friend, Sudip Paul. I'm visiting him with my postdoc, Stacey Corrie, on an expedition to collect rocks in the Himalayas:

> **Sudip:**  Before we go to dinner, I want to take you to our new McDonald's. It's the first McDonald's in the entire Dehra Dun valley.
>
> **Matt:**  OK, sounds good. I'm surprised, though, because McDonald's serves hamburgers, and Indians generally don't eat beef.

Sudip:    Yes, they mainly serve chicken sandwiches. They say the chicken sandwich is identical to what you get in America. I wish you to try the chicken sandwich, and tell us if this is true.

Matt:    Sure, we'll give it a try.

We arrive at the McDonald's, and Sudip hands me and Stacey each a chicken sandwich.

I bite into it. In many ways, it's exactly like chicken sandwiches in America. Same squishy white bun, same processed chicken patty. But the flavor?

Matt:    Well, the texture is just like American chicken sandwiches, but the flavor is a little different.

Sudip:    Oh? How is that?

Matt:    In America, we use a lot less flavoring. It's basically just salt and pepper. Here, there's a mild curry flavor.

Stacey:    Yeah, it's good, but it's a little different.

Sudip:    Oh.

Matt:    Yeah, I like it, it's just a little different.

Sudip:    I see.

I'm not sure if he's disappointed or not. But the point is the same, "normal" American fast food is typically pretty bland.

Back to my Sunday stroll. I walk past a dance institute, find the second forbidden park, and walk around a bit. The style reminds me a little of the hydroponics park, but without the water—everything is carefully manicured. An entire bed of one species of shrub is trimmed to a specific height, like a flat-top haircut. Another bed with a different species of shrub is cut to a different height. Together, they give a two-tiered effect. It's pleasant, but doesn't exactly invite running around and playing. That's probably why there are relatively few people here, and virtually no kids.

Walking back toward the hotel, I realize the one shop I can't quite fathom is the combination vegetable and seafood. There are several of these in the area. And although one of them also sells other sorts of meat (mostly pork, I think), clearly the two food items are a common combo. Do they sell seafood with vegetables here because Shanghai is on the coast? Anyway, it feels a little odd to see row after row of eggplant, celery, beans, carrots, squashes/gourds, other various unidentifiable (to me) greens, etc. accompanied by row after row of big crab, medium crab, little crab, big shrimp, medium shrimp, little shrimp, big fish, medium fish, little fish, etc. There's a shop across the street that sells only eggs. Why not have separate seafood and vegetable shops? Somehow, for me, the smell of slightly off fish doesn't make me want to buy cabbage.

I take a few photos, eliciting a few unkindly looks. I get it. I mean, seriously, does anyone (other than kids) like having their picture taken?

Arriving back at the hotel, I return to the heat of my room. Heat?

Yes. Like many hotels outside America, you insert your key card into a sleeve near the door to activate electricity in the room. It has to be a key card, too. No other cards work. So, if you take your key card with you on a Sunday walk, as I did, the air conditioning has no power and shuts down. So does the power to your computer, your second cell phone, and anything else you have plugged in. Somehow, I always seem to forget this until I return home to a hot room. Regardless, unlike most hotels I frequent, the air conditioning is really good, and quickly restores the temperature.

**STOREFRONTS IN SHANGHAI**

**COMBINATION SEAFOOD AND....**

**...VEGETABLE SHOP**

# FRUIT OF THE CACTUS

I am particularly enjoying the diversity of fruits in China. True, we have many of the same fruits in America, likely thanks to international commerce. Grapes, pears, oranges, apples, bananas, and grapefruit are common. Huixia tells me there are also peaches, plums, figs, and apricots in the shops, but I haven't happened to eat any yet. She sent me some cherries and blueberries the other day.

But there are many other fruits that are super common here in China, but pretty rare in America. Kiwi and dragon fruit come to mind.

I lack standard WCDs (weapons of culinary destruction, especially a knife), so I was a little baffled at how to tackle a dragon fruit. These are the large pink and green fruits with fleshy, floppy "leaves" on them that you can find in bigger grocery stores in the US. They're pretty expensive at home, but they're common here. I guess their skin is supposed to look a little like dragon skin. I don't have firsthand experience with dragon skin. If it's this soft (easily pierced by, say, a pencil), it might explain why there are no dragons today. But I don't think so: Smaug would have been DOA when he attacked the dwarves, Bilbo wouldn't have found the ring, the whole *Lord of the Rings* trilogy would never have happened, and my whole adolescent fantasy world would fall apart. I'm not going there. Real dragons must have much tougher skin.

Anyway, Wikipedia tells me dragon fruit comes from a CAM plant (Crassulacean acid metabolism), specifically a cactus. In the world of carbon isotope geochemistry, we often talk about how there are "two" types of plants in the world that have quite different isotope compositions: C3 and C4 plants. Their photosynthetic processes create compounds that contain three carbon atoms and four carbon atoms respectively (that is, a C3 plant makes a compound with three carbon atoms; a C4 plant makes a compound with four carbon atoms). This naming convention demonstrates once again the amazing creativity of scientists! Actually, however, there's a third group of plants, which are the CAM plants. These engage in photosynthetic processes that are intermediate to C3 and C4 plants. They're commonly succulent (often have fleshy leaves), can be very drought-resistant, and include the dorm-room-favored jade plant (doesn't die if you forget to water it for a couple months). Other CAM plants include the monstrously evil (invasive) ice plant, yucca, pineapple, and cactus. Dragon fruit comes from the cactus *Selenicereus* sp., although I'm glad to report it doesn't have spines. The inside is absolutely riddled with tiny seeds (you just swallow them), and the variety we have here in China is a brilliant magenta.

How do you eat a dragon fruit? In the US, I cut it open with a big knife. But I have no big knife here. I ended up peeling off some of the outer leaves to expose the soft edible part (shaped a little like an American-style football). Then I spooned it out. It's a little messy, but effective. Just don't drip any juice on your shirt. It stains something awful.

But I already knew about dragon fruit from the US. So, an exciting discovery for me has been all the other fruits. Here are some examples:

Chinese dates. Are these really dates? I guess so, but they don't look or taste like any dates I've ever experienced. They're tiny brown-and-green-mottled spheres, about the size of a large cherry, and their texture and taste strongly resemble apples. At first, I thought they *were* tiny apples, until I realized the seed structure is totally different (one single elongate seed, just like a date!). Also, apples upset my stomach and these don't.

Grapes. These are pretty similar to the grapes we get in America, except they still bear seeds, and one variety tastes a little like scuppernongs. Scuppernongs are a type of wild grape, indigenous to the southeastern US, and they taste awesomely awesome. They were one of the true pleasures of living in South Carolina. It's hard to explain the flavor, but it somehow tastes "wilder" than other grapes. I get a little of that flavor from some grapes here.

Mangosteen. These are dark purple fruits about the size of a large plum (like a black plum, not like an ornamental or Italian plum). Their stem ends have four petals, so I thought they might be like persimmons (my favorite fruit): after all, both have fourfold rotational symmetry, just like the tetragonal crystal system (had to slip in a little mineralogical geekiness). Unfortunately, in that mistaken correlation with persimmons, the first thing I did was bite into one. That's how I found out they have thick, dry, extremely bitter rinds. The best way I found to open them is simply to squeeze them in a couple different directions. The rind cracks, and you can pull it off. This reveals the edible fruit in the middle, which bears a disturbingly close resemblance to large white grubs. Except they don't wriggle. Thank goodness.

Once you get past that first shock, you can pull the grubby parts out. They're shaped like sections of an orange or grapefruit, and are the size of a very small mandarin orange. The flavor is even more awesomely awesome than scuppernongs. Sweet, like mango or persimmons, but with a citrusy sour flavor. You can eat most of the sections completely, but there's always at least one that has a gigantic seed in it. Apparently, mangosteens have a short season, so I'm lucky to try them.

I looked at them again later, and noticed that they don't actually have fourfold symmetry to their petals, it's twofold. Plus, there are six petals on the other side. So, they must be orthorhombic, not tetragonal, and can't possibly be related to persimmons.

Longan. I receive a handful of these for breakfast every morning from the hotel. These are spherical, cherry-sized fruits that look a little like puffballs (light yellowy-brown color). I thought they might be related to pears, so I first tried to take a bite out of one. Will I ever learn?

Longan is covered by a thin, leathery skin, a little like flexible eggshell. True, the mistake of biting a longan doesn't rise to the level of a mangosteen, but it's not pleasant. Once you peel them (not too difficult), the fruit appears gelatinous, but has a texture a little like grapes, only chewier. The flavor is sweet and (again) a little like grapes. There's a big, beautiful, dark brown seed in the center.

Assuming all goes well with visa extensions, I'm looking forward to trying more through the late summer and fall. I hear persimmons are coming soon . . .

**DRAGON FRUIT IN SHANGHAI. EACH FRUIT IN THE FOREGROUND HAS INDIVIDUALIZED FOAM PACKAGING.**

**MANGOSTEEN**

# TESTING, TESTING ... THIRD TIME'S A CHARM

To leave Shanghai, I had to be tested a third time. After the joys of my previous testing, it was with some trepidation that I attended a different center (the one I used before wasn't open on Tuesdays). The taxi delivered me at 8:00 a.m., just as the testing trailer opened, in the parking lot of a big hotel. Employing my trusty translation app, I ascertained from the decidedly laconic (or possibly suspicious) guy ahead of me in line that, yes, I was at the right place for the test.

Fortunately for peace of mind, I could see the testing windows and people getting tested. I'm not from Missouri ("The Show-Me State"), but I was relieved not to have to deal with this "Just walk behind those bushes where people seem to disappear but never emerge."

True, registration was laborious. The two apps that Xiaochi and I found still didn't work on my phone (surprise!). However, one of the medical staff found a *third* app, filled it out for me, and I got my test. I laughed at the address she listed ("1"). I guess the app needed some kind of text there. I'm not quite certain what phone number she listed. Was it her own? Someone she dislikes? The Chinese CIA? For all I know, she works for the Chinese CIA, and they share the same number. Anyway, the phone number worked, and I got my test. And it took only half an hour, not the one-and-a-half hours of my test last Friday, or the three hours in Dallas. I count that as a major victory!

I calculate that, with a decrease in test time of a factor of two to three, any tests I might require in Beijing should require only ten to fifteen minutes!

Anyway, that left a long walk back to the hotel. Xiaochi offered to call a taxi, but it was only 8:30 a.m., and cool by Shanghai standards (82°F, 28°C). Walking gave me a chance to experience a little more of the city, and make a few more observations before I move on to Beijing, tomorrow.

I will never understand how the most populous city of the most populous country on Earth can have such wide and spacious boulevards. I assumed the streets would be narrow and congested, like I see in India or Nepal, or in old movies. But they're not. They're beautiful. Other than a bridge over a freeway, sycamores line the sidewalks, and many corners feature outdoor sculpture. The bike/moped and car lanes are wide enough to accommodate some pretty heavy traffic, too, so it feels spacious. And there's ample room for bike racks on the street side of the sidewalks.

I will also never understand why such a well-regulated traffic system demands so many traffic cops. Most intersections seem to have one. A guy in uniform, wielding a baton, stands at the corner and eyes everyone suspiciously. I studiously avoid looking at him. Why is he there? Are the traffic light and crosswalk signals (which are the same as in the US) so confusing? Maybe China thinks so, because they've added a countdown system: when a traffic light is approaching its time to change (either green to red, or red to green), it counts down the number of seconds you have to wait. I think everyone understands that, because all I ever saw the traffic cops do was point at people occasionally and (once) toot a whistle. They weren't actually directing traffic. I never saw one reading a book or checking a cell phone either. So at least they take their jobs seriously, pointing and occasionally tooting.

I will also never understand how bicyclists and (especially) moped riders ("mopedists"?) appear so thoroughly dismissive of the basic principles of physics. Newton's first law implies that two objects on a collision course will, in fact, collide unless at least one object changes its trajectory or speed (through an applied force). Similarly, it is not possible for one relatively massive object (me) and another relatively massive object (rider plus moped) to occupy the same physical location at the same time. The approach of two such bodies on said collision course generally recommends one object change its speed and/or trajectory. At minimum, I recommend reducing velocity, or Newton's third law (the one about equal and opposite reaction) might smack you upside the head. Yet, it seems like, in every block, a moped or bicycle rider comes to a screeching halt right in front of me (or right next to me in the crosswalk), seemingly baffled about how I could possibly have been about to occupy the same space.

At least Shanghai isn't like the southeastern US, where whoever has the bigger vehicle assumes the right of way. In South Carolina, I've had cars swerve toward me when I was crossing in a crosswalk, partly to scare me a little, but also to "remind" me that the car has the right of way (which it doesn't, legally; it's a cultural thing). In the rock-paper-scissors game of roadway intersections (except there it's called pedestrian-car-truck), the written rules (aka "laws") don't matter, truck always wins. Unless you drive something bigger, like a bus. Or a tank. I think everyone makes way for tanks there. That's definitely not true here in Shanghai. Well, I haven't seen a tank, so I can't be certain about that, but I've seen plenty of cars and trucks and even buses give way to pedestrians in crosswalks. It's not like California either, where traffic comes to a standstill if you venture within fifty feet of a crosswalk and (God forbid) actually glance in its direction.

Maybe the screeching halts reflect a philosophy of "let's not worry about something until it actually happens." Or, perhaps, a different perspective on personal space. Maybe Americans obsess so much about maintaining their space that they start acting long before it's really necessary.

It's not only drivers who seem unaware of pedestrians, other pedestrians do too. Many times, people who are standing off to one side have moved directly into my path as I approach, then stop dead, so I have to walk around them. Why would you do that? The entropy of the universe is increasing fast enough, you don't have to move it along a little faster. I had one guy slowly wheel his bike from its parking spot next to the sidewalk until it completely blocked my way (actually, the entire sidewalk), timed exactly for when I arrived.

For two reasons, though, I'm convinced people are simply oblivious, it's not a deliberate "let's annoy the white guy" action.

First, just before the collision, everyone acts so surprised to see me. What? How did you get here? I know I saw you walking directly toward me, but I can't believe you actually continued walking. And, OMG, at the same rate, too? I've actually had people apologize for nearly hitting me.

Second, it happens to Chinese pedestrians, too.

Actually, there's a third reason, which is that people in China have been uniformly kind and polite. Maybe I'm naive, but I can't believe anyone here would do this intentionally.

My interactions with pedestrians on my walk home (and other walks) also tell me that China and the US do not share car culture. In the US, when someone approaches you from the opposite direction on a sidewalk, you move to the right. That's because that's how we drive, on the right side of the road. Everyone drives, so everyone does this. The opposite occurs in England, of course, because they drive on the left side of the road. I've actually had people in a park in Boise lecture me that I shouldn't walk on the left side of a path (which I was trained to do as a kid, so I could see oncoming cars)—it was "wrong." Here in China, cars drive on the right, just like in the US, but there's no rhyme or reason to any pedestrian movement. Pedestrians on mutual collision course seem to drift about vaguely until some accommodation is made at the last minute. Sometimes someone ends up on the street. I guess that makes up for the fact that bicycles and mopeds also use the sidewalks.

Well, assuming all goes well, I won't be walking around Shanghai much longer. I have a train ticket to Beijing for tomorrow. Then I'll find out if pedestrians in Beijing behave differently than in Shanghai.

**SURPRISINGLY WIDE BOULEVARD IN SHANGHAI**

# LEAVIN' ON A JET TRAIN

The Chinese railway system is incredibly easy to navigate . . . after you've navigated it already, that is. The first time, it's a little confusing.

The train station that I departed from (Hongqiao) is huge—easily as big as Hongqiao International Airport, which is right next to it. There are so many entrances, it's not altogether clear where you should enter, but I doubt the specific entrance actually matters.

Still, it wasn't altogether clear where I was going or what I was supposed to do when I passed through the vertical plastic strips of doorway number eight. These are the same plastic strips that American grocery stores use in meat lockers to separate cold meat from warm store. Some Shanghai grocery stores use them at their entrances too. Was I actually entering a grocery store/meat locker, rather than a train station? It did feel a little cooler than outside. That's not saying a whole lot in Shanghai, though.

Fortunately, the cousin of Huixia's husband (an affable guy named Mingkun) arranged to pick me up at my hotel, and he guided me through nearly all the steps. In fact, anticipating that there might be some extra hurdles, he hired a staff person at the station to escort me through check-in and onto the train. Without them, I probably would have succeeded, but I also would have stressed much more. I'm so lucky I have friends here.

Anyway, first things first. How do you catch a train in China?

First, I had to pass an entrance exam, consisting of finding and displaying a screenshot of my ticket (which Xiaochi had sent me two days prior) and my passport. The examiner spoke no English, so it was Mingkun who translated for me. Good thing, too, because that's when I realized my translation app wasn't working. Wi-Fi connectivity in China is not super reliable.

While I was fixing Wi-Fi and firing up my translation app, I had to pass my next test: X-rays of my luggage to make sure I wasn't trying to smuggle a crate of thermonuclear devices to another province. This makes sense when you think about it—you want to protect the local economy, right? If everybody shipped their thermonuclear devices around, the price would drop, and what would happen to the local thermonuclear device industry?

Anyway, they didn't seem to pay much attention to the small bicycle pump that I inadvertently left in my pack, the blocks of electronics that were also in there, or all the metal in my suitcases. I glanced at the images, and couldn't see much of anything. I probably could have slipped a small thermonuclear device past them. Too bad I inadvertently left mine at home.

After passing the metal detector (which everyone sets off with their cell phones) the safety officer seemed most concerned that I remove my hat. Her wanding was perfunctory at best, and didn't even register my zipper.

Or the Glock G43 handgun I had stashed between my butt cheeks. *Just kidding!* I don't own a handgun. I had to look up a make and model to crack this joke.

We pick up our bags from X-ray, and the next thing I know, there's a guy with a red shirt and empty luggage cart. He asks us something. I assume he's offering his services, but with two of us and only two suitcases, it seems excessive. I make a dismissive gesture (I've practiced this in India and Nepal about 42,617 times), but Mingkun takes him up on his offer (if that's what it was), and we put our suitcases on the cart. I decide it's OK to be lazy, especially if I'm on sabbatical.

It turns out this was a very smart move of Mingkun. The red-shirt guy knows exactly what needs to be done, and where to go. And (more importantly), Mingkun can't go with me to the train. Red-shirt guy, however, can take me anywhere.

Next stop: a desk where a woman scans my ticket and hands Mingkun three slips of paper. I'm not positive what they are. His translation app says something about . . . receipts? Maybe he's placing bets for her at the local dog track. They also check my passport.

Then on to a window. It's hard to tell what it's for. I mean, I have electronic verification of my ticket. What more do I need? Everything else is electronic. Fortunately, I had my translation app working by then, so Mingkun and I are conversing using both mine and his.

> Matt: What are we doing here? What do I need to do?

> Mingkun: Here you get your ticket.

> Matt: OK, what do I need to provide?

> Mingkun: The image of your reservation [from Xiaochi].

I hunt down the scanned image on my phone, and hand it over to the railway agent. Hurdle number one overcome!

She enters some information into her computer.

The agent then says something incomprehensible to me. [Actually, the speaker connected to her microphone is sufficiently loud and clear that I could probably have used my translation app easily at this point. But Mingkun was already here.]

> Mingkun: And she needs your passport.

I hand over my passport. Hurdle number two overcome!

She scans it, and hands it back, with my phone. Then she hands me my ticket. Easy peasy. Once you know how it works, that is. I'm not sure I would have known what window to approach. And if I didn't have translation? Travel in the past must have been *much* harder.

The last stop is to check in and board the train. We spend several minutes with the gate agent. She's looking for my "all clear" health code. Once you've proven you don't have COVID-19, you're supposed to receive a green QR code. All the Chinese passengers in line have them out already on their phones.

But I don't have one. Why not? Probably because I don't have a Chinese phone number.

She tries her best to coerce WeChat to scan a QR code and run the mini app that would generate the code for me. Of course, it doesn't work. Same old spinning wheel of death. Why? Because Wi-Fi isn't working. Eventually, I put her in a headlock and wrestle the phone away (not really, she gives it up willingly—I'm just exaggerating). I then use my translation app to let her know that most apps don't work on my phone. I don't try to explain about bank accounts and telephone numbers.

She immediately hands Mingkun a paper form and explains something to him. Unlike every other official I've encountered, she's obviously dealt with this before. Often. Mingkun uses his translation app to tell me that we have to fill out the form instead of submitting a QR code. I knew there had to be alternatives! It's only now that one has actually materialized.

I scan the form with my translation app (am I signing away my secondborn child now? What if I have only one child?), and find it's essentially an affidavit that I'm not lying about being healthy. I don't know what happens if someone discovers me with the sniffles later, and I just about faint with fright when I sneeze on the train an hour later. But obviously I'm not getting on the train until it's completed. And signed.

We fill out the form and give it to the gate agent. She asks me for something. I'm not quite sure what she wants—my ticket? They keep asserting something in Chinese. Then I realize—oh, they're just saying "passport" with a Chinese accent. How can I be so dense?

She scans my passport and returns it, and the next thing I know, red-shirt guy and I are walking through the gate to an area populated by about thirty other passengers. We all stand around, studiously avoiding looking at each other. What are we waiting for? It's not clear.

Red-shirt guy and I are standing next to a tiny elevator. Every once in a while, someone on staff either enters the elevator or exits it, so I know it works. Are we waiting for someone to push the down arrow? I start to edge closer to the elevator.

I'm starting to sweat—I knew the humidity would find me eventually.

A suspiciously pale-skinned woman elbows her way to the front of the group at the elevator. She eyes the button and pushes it assertively. Many times. With increasing force. Nothing happens. I guess we're not going anywhere soon.

Suddenly, there's a shift in the crowd, and about twenty people spill out of the area and down some escalators. Although I couldn't see it, we were blocked from exiting this area, and we're only now allowed to leave (by escalator, anyway).

Lo and behold, the elevator button works now, too!

Red-shirt guy and I let others take the elevator ahead of us (they were there first), but eventually we cram five of us in there, with luggage, and descend one floor to the level of the train. We wheel the cart to the correct car (number four). Red-shirt guy stows my luggage, shows me my seat (12F, a window seat), and shoots a short video of me sitting on the train. He then sends the video to Mingkun, who sends it to Huixia, who sends it to me.

I'm on my way!

I'm afraid I didn't see much scenery from the train. It rained heavily during the first part of the trip, plus there was too much mist and fog. It was dark before I arrived in Beijing. I did see some pretty hills in a couple places (for example, approaching Nanjing), but otherwise everything seemed just flat, and wet, and green. After a couple hours of watching this, the penny dropped—of course it's flat (you dolt)! You can't put high-speed rail through mountain ranges!

And this is definitely high-speed rail. The total trip from Shanghai to Beijing takes only four-and-a-half hours. A streaming text message at the front of the car informs me the standard "cruising" speed is 344 kilometers per hour (214 mph). I read online that speeds can reach four hundred kilometers per hour (250 mph). That's faster than the express train between Geneva and Paris that I took once (maximum of 320 kph) and it's takeoff velocity for a jet. It's my first trip on a jet train.

# TESTING, TESTING . . . WHAT AGAIN?

Almost as soon as I arrived in Beijing, Xiaochi informed me that I have to be tested for COVID-19 again, the next day. Although unanticipated, this was maybe not as big a surprise as you might think. Besides the fact that there had been lots of twists and turns (things don't surprise me quite like they used to), China was freaking out about their approximately one hundred daily cases of COVID-19.

Now, to put this into perspective, last week my county in Idaho had a similar daily rate. But my county has less than five hundred thousand people. China has almost 1.5 billion. I'm much safer here in China (with respect to the pandemic) than in the US. In fact, by the numbers, I'm about three thousand times safer.

Given the trend of decreasing time per test, I also wasn't too concerned about sweating in the heat too long. Plus, I knew that Xiaochi would be along to smooth any bumps.

I was completely wrong about one thing, though—the amount of time. Now *that* was surprising.

I had predicted the next test would take ten to fifteen minutes (two to three times less than the previous test, right?). In fact, it took only four. Seriously. Four minutes. After the taxi dropped us off at the corner, it took us longer to find the testing site than for me to get tested. After the test, we waited even longer (seven minutes) for the taxi to arrive to take us back to the Academy.

Once you get the system working, dang, it works well!

In my experience, medical staff who administer COVID-19 nasal swab tests fall neatly into two camps: the merciful ones who rotate the swab quickly around the front of your nostril, and the merciless ones who assiduously attempt to scratch the back of your eyeball.

Unfortunately, this woman fell into the second camp.

As we waited for our return taxi, and for my eye to stop watering, the aftereffects of her probing got me thinking about the bizarre anatomical convergences around human eye sockets. It's not just nasal cavities back there. For example, there are your "eye teeth."

Ever wonder what eye teeth are, or why we have them?

An anthropologist once explained them to me. Your "eye teeth" are your cuspids, and they have very long roots that extend way upward to just below your eye sockets. With such long roots, they're difficult to remove. So, when you say "I'd give my eye teeth for that," it essentially means "I'd undergo major surgery for that." A little slip up there, and—whoops!—you're not seeing out of that eye any more.

Now, why would such a dinky little tooth like a cuspid need such a long root?

Well, *your* cuspids don't need them. But a few million years ago, when our ancestors were knuckle-walking around Africa, those cuspids were nice long pointy canines. Apes back then likely used those canines for more than just impressing their neighbors, and long roots kept them from snapping off at inopportune times. You know, like when you're chomping on the back of some big carnivore with ten of your buddies, trying to protect a member of your tribe.

Darwin's Law (aka the Theory of Evolution) argues that there must have been some evolutionary pressure to prefer shorter canines over time. For example, when climate change converted closed forests into open grasslands, horses and camels (and many other animals) evolved longer legs. Long legs don't necessarily serve you well in forests, but they sure do help you run away from predators on the open plains. Among social animals like us, there can be other non-physical reasons for evolution, for example "Oooh, look at that guy with the cute little cuspids—Hey there, sexy!"

A less well-known corollary to Darwin's Law is that a feature that causes no *dis*advantage (like a long tooth root) can simply be retained. So, if there's no pressure to evolve shorter tooth roots (what difference does it make?), they stick around.

So, some kind of environmental or social pressure favored shorter cuspid tooth crowns, while there was no reason for their roots to change length. Voilà! "Eye teeth."

As long as I'm on the subject to dental idioms, I'll point out that the phrase "long in the tooth" (meaning "old") refers to gum recession. I wore braces as a kid, and the way they were installed (metal sleeves around the tooth crowns back then, rather than cemented posts today) induced gum recession. The same thing happened to my friend, Tom.

I guess we became old before our time.

# NOW WE'RE TALKIN' MONEY!

Recently, Xiaochi and I went out to get me a cell phone SIM card and a bank account. We both assumed it would take hours. After all, I set up a new bank account and cell phone service in the US before leaving for China, and that took about two hours. Why would it be any simpler here? No surprise—it's not simpler.

First, the cell phone. If you haven't upgraded your cell phone plan recently, or purchased a new phone (or SIM card), then perhaps you've forgotten the pleasure of receiving a steady stream of incomprehensible jargon, ultimately culminating in a profound feeling of having been cheated. For me, the minute-by-minute excitement of purchasing a SIM card ranks right up there with baseball, which I sometimes comment consists of ten minutes of action packed into three hours of game (5.5 percent fun).

Actually, that's not fair. A study of games in 2013 found that it's a little less than eighteen minutes of action packed into three hours of game (almost 10 percent fun!).

Regardless, my experience with cell phone service providers mostly involved sitting around while they fiddled with their computers, and answering their occasional question. In terms of time, purchasing a Chinese SIM card for my phone took only about an hour, which is less than in the US. But—you guessed it—while at first it appeared to work in my phone, ultimately it didn't.

A big part of the problem is that I have a Verizon phone, and Verizon is notoriously incompatible with other systems. Thanks, Verizon.

But there were other problems as well, and Xiaochi solved the problem (the next day) only by giving me an old Chinese phone. It's a Huawei phone, so knowing the US government's affection for Huawei, I'll probably have a long conversation with the Department of Homeland Security when I get home. But at least it works. I can't say the same for US technology here.

Technological incompatibilities aside, there is still a surprising amount of red tape in the Chinese system. For example, just to enter the building, Xiaochi had to scan a QR code and type personal information into an app. Because my cell phone doesn't work with these QR codes, we filled out my information on a sign-in sheet.

Then we had our temperature checked. Twice. Once by heat-seeking camera, a second time by a guard-operated, handheld sensor.

I originally scoffed at the accuracy of these sensors, but I think I've been unfair. Thermometers at various institutions register my skin temperature at 36.1°C–36.4°C (97.0°F–97.5°F). Normal body temperature is 37°C (98.6°F), but of course, your skin should be a little cooler. So, the temperatures could be accurate. I might as well get used to the checks, anyway, because they're required everywhere we go in Beijing (although shops didn't routinely require them in Shanghai).

After temperature checks, we waited a couple minutes for a salesperson to become available. Then we sat down, and Xiaochi started explaining the situation.

I'll spare the details. Xiaochi and I ended up spending 90 percent of our time on our phones, texting other people, or otherwise amusing ourselves, while the salesperson entered information in her computer, scanned documents, and frowned pensively. Actually, "salespeople." Most of the time, it took two people working together, sometimes even three. I don't know what they were doing, but I had to sign documents twice. Did I sign away rights to my firstborn child *and* secondborn child? Or the title to my car and my Swiss bank account? I'm still not sure, although I closed my Swiss bank account eight years ago, after my mini-sabbatical there.

They also scanned my passport twice, and engaged in two conversations with Xiaochi about the significance of its expiration date (a little over four years distant). Apparently, if I get a new passport, I'm supposed to spend upwards of one thousand to three thousand dollars to fly back to Beijing to get it re-scanned, otherwise they'll terminate my three dollar per month cell phone plan (oh no . . .). They also talked with him three times about my name. Same old story: "what's his first name, what's his last name, why does he have two first names?" Thank goodness they didn't have to deal with my friend Caroline, who has three first names!

The salespeople seemed especially anxious that I choose exactly the best phone number. They gave me ten choices. I didn't try to see what would happen if I said I didn't like any of them, I simply chose the first one. However, because I waited two minutes to peruse all ten numbers (to see whether someone's birthdate might be hiding in there somewhere), it was already taken. I now have the second number.

They took my photo. Why? I don't know, they just do that.

Last, they checked to be sure the SIM card worked in their phones, then installed it in my phone. Xiaochi called my phone—which rang! Awesome!

Seriously, all things considered, it was relatively painless. For me, anyway. Until we got outside.

> Xiaochi:  OK, start WeChat.
>
> Matt:  Right. Hmmm . . . it doesn't work. That's odd, my phone doesn't seem to know its own phone number.
>
> Xiaochi:  It worked in the store.
>
> Matt:  I know, it doesn't make sense. Oh, it doesn't recognize the cell system either. I thought it did in the store.
>
> Xiaochi:  Can you log into WeChat?

> Matt:  Hmmm . . . no. I think I might need to buy a new phone here.
>
> Xiaochi:  Maybe. Let's go back to the institute [Chinese Academy of Sciences, Institute of Geology and Geophysics] and see if we can get it to work.

It never really worked. Still, Xiaochi invested another three hours resuscitating WeChat. That one little task alone required logging into the institute's Wi-Fi and changing all the phone's system settings. It's clear now that an Android phone from Verizon does not work reliably on the Chinese cell system. This is how I ended up with an old Huawei phone (the next day). And (probably) a date with DHS when I get home.

In contrast, the bank proved much more successful. Well, OK, not at first. But, third time's a charm.

At the first bank, as expected, to get in the door, Xiaochi scanned the QR code and entered his information while I registered my presence on paper. Upon talking to a bank officer, however, we learned that I could not get a bank account there.

Why not? Because banks don't create accounts that they think have lifetimes of only three months.

Now, in all likelihood, I'll keep my Chinese bank account for many years. Without an account, I can't pay for anything. If I can't pay for anything, I can't arrange for a hotel while I'm being quarantined and observed. And if I can't arrange for quarantine and observation, I can't enter the country. I mean, yes, it's possible (I did it, right?), but it's also a royal pain. So, if I ever return to China, I'll want to keep that bank account. But my visa is good for only ninety days, and the bank thinks I might close my account when I leave. So, the bank didn't want to risk that, and turned us away.

I read later that this is standard bank policy, but different branches do different things. If you're persistent enough (for example, if you try five to ten branches of the same bank), even Americans on three-month visas can get a bank account.

But there was a different bank only a block down, so we decided to try them. The second bank was definitely more encouraging. Basically, yes, I could open an account. But I had to provide additional documentation that said I would be collaborating in China long-term. Please gather some extra documentation and come talk to us later.

So, we returned to the institute (which turned out to be right around the corner), and Xiaochi wrote some documents indicating that I would be working in China for the next thirty-seven-odd years (it's so convenient when your colleagues can write official documents whenever you need them). OK, I don't really know what the letter said, but I assume it asserted (correctly) that I wasn't some fly-by-night tourist. And, that afternoon, on our third try, the bank opened an account for me.

It did take two hours, and the forms were quite impressive. I took a picture of one form, simply because I'd never seen one that was so long.

Unfortunately, at one point, I wrote my last name in the wrong space (kind of off in a margin). So, we wrote it again where it belonged. It was only a little extra ink. But, oh, what a shitstorm that created!

Well, that's not fair. The bank was very polite, so it was more of a "storm of relatively odorless, nonstaining fecal matter."

After a ten-minute discussion with three bank officials (seriously, this is what it took) the verdict was returned: Nope, no dice. Fill out the entire form all over again.

AND IN CAPITAL LETTERS ONLY. So, we did.

They took my picture again (although maybe they were comparing my real mug to my passport photo). And scanned my passport again. And again. And again (third time's a charm).

And there was the regular discussion of what the hell my name was. Three discussions, actually. No, I'm not kidding. Three discussions.

But I walked out of there with a viable bank card, and a balance of one yuan (about fifteen cents).

In reflecting on my whole experience with the phone and the bank (and my COVID-19 tests), what impresses me is not the bureaucracy. Getting medical tests, communications hardware, or financial services is never going to be easy, regardless of where you live. Think what it's like to register your car or see your doctor for the first time in the US. Now imagine that you don't speak any English, and the staff doesn't speak your language. Do you think it would be any easier? Probably not.

Instead, what I noticed was all the monitoring. For example, my local community here in this sector of Beijing knew exactly when I would be arriving, and called Xiaochi to alert him that I had to be tested. This wasn't his initiative—they called him.

Maybe I shouldn't be surprised. I mean, there's a major worldwide health crisis that China is seriously trying to keep at bay (even if many Americans are not). I had to inform the authorities of my every move. I didn't have a choice about my first hotel either—they knew exactly where I was. A sensor was activated every time I opened my door.

But there are also cameras everywhere, and even the simplest of tasks (buying a SIM card) documented my face. I'm not super libertarian, and I generally trust government. But it's a little uncomfortable to know the Chinese government monitors me so closely here.

Of course, some Americans claim the US government does the same thing, we just don't know about it. Maybe Homeland Security and I can discuss that when I get home.

**THE FORMS IN CHINA OFTEN HAVE
ENGLISH TRANSLATION (IN TEENY-TINY TYPE)**

# A DAY IN THE LIFE

So, what is a day in the life like for an American scientist in pandemic China? Of course, every day is different, but some things are consistent, and consistently a bit different from the US. Let's start with the bathroom.

First, my apartment actually has a bathroom. I'm not sure how many of them do here—there's a communal bathroom right across the hall from me. But I'm glad I have privacy.

My bathroom has a sit-down toilet, like we use in the US. The bathroom across the hall has both a sit-down toilet and a standard Asian toilet. Sit-down toilets in India, Nepal, and Bhutan are very rare; normally you get a hole in the floor with two corrugated steps on either side for your feet. You squat there to do your business. This type of toilet (I call it the "squatty potty") is actually more effective anatomically—kind of a straight shot for your GI tract. Plus it's more sanitary. But you need good knees to use one. I admit the other toilet (a "sitter shitter"?) is more comfortable, and I'm glad I have one in my bathroom.

Now, in many places in Asia, there's no toilet paper. Rather there's a bucket of water. You wash yourself with one hand (the *left* hand), reserving your right hand for eating and shaking other people's right hands. But I'm living at one of the most advanced scientific institutes in one of the most advanced cities on Earth. They have toilet paper here. I'm glad for that too.

Now, the shower—this is fairly standard for Asia. There's a hot water tank mounted on the wall. This is good because other people can't use up your water, and you don't have to wait for your water to get hot. Well, you do have to remember to turn on your water heater ahead of time (or leave it on).

Like most bathrooms, there's no bathtub or shower stall. Rather the whole bathroom is open tile, and the shower water floods the floor. The shower head itself is connected to a long hose, so you can send that shower water wherever you want, for example onto yourself, all over your towel, or into the toilet. I don't know why I'd ever want to wash my toilet at the same time I'm washing myself, but it's an option.

The water is supposed to exit the bathroom through a small drain in the floor. And like most drains I've encountered in Asian bathrooms, it's located at what's supposed to be the lowest point on the floor, but actually isn't. No, a huge lake of water accumulates on the far side of the room. There's also a squeegee mop for drying out the floor. So, taking a shower consists of five minutes of showering, followed by ten minutes of trying to persuade a large pool of water on the far side of the room to transfer around the toilet and down a tiny open drain. A byproduct of showering is a very clean bathroom floor!

For most meals, I've been eating at the institute's cafeteria around the corner. The food is OK, nothing to write home about in terms of quality, but it's fine.

For breakfast, I recently tried a large purple pancake, and for dinner I had noodles. Those experiences have helped me understand a little more about styles of eating. First, the pancake.

I think the purple ingredient is purple yam, and scrambled egg is layered into it while it's cooking. It has the consistency of dense crepes, only a little thicker. It's all folded up for eating into a shape similar to a blintz that's been folded crosswise. And it's huge. I didn't try to unfold mine, but if I did, I think it would warrant its own zip code.

So, how do you eat this massive folded thing? There are no forks or knives, just smooth ceramic soup spoons and chopsticks. Clearly, it's a job for chopsticks.

I grab the thing and start lifting it, but it's very heavy (because crepes are dense, especially if they're made with yams). So, all I can do is get one edge sticking up in the air. Nothing else for it, I drop my head down close to my plate and bite off a rubbery chunk.

Now, psychologically this is not an easy thing for me to do. Flashback fifty-odd years:

> Mom:  Matt, don't put your face down in your plate. Sit up straight and lift your food to your mouth.
>
> Matt:  But the peas keep rolling off my fork.
>
> Mom:  You just have to learn how to eat. It's rude to put your face down like that.

I've noticed Chinese people have no problem lowering their faces close to their plates or bowls as they eat (or raise their plates and bowls up to their faces). In the past it made me a little uncomfortable (thanks, Mom). Now I know better.

I briefly consider finding some yoga exercises for my fingers to strengthen them sufficiently to sit up straight when I eat a large purple pancake. But then I remember how the nineteenth-century composer and pianist, Robert Schumann, mangled his fingers in a misguided attempt to improve his piano playing. At least for now, I'll stoop to conquer.

The pancake is pretty chewy, and, strangely, it's interleaved with lettuce and a "meant-to-be-crispy-but-isn't" layer of flakey . . . something. I'm not sure what that extra layer is. Piecrust? Am I actually eating some kind of pancake-lettuce pie? The flakey layer is probably flour-based, but I'm not positive. It does add a different textural component. I could do without it. Actually, I do "do without it" (at least some of it), because I'm sufficiently inept with chopsticks that the flakey layer tends to slip out.

My first noodle dinner was similarly challenging and educational, although in a different way. I received a large bowl with an assortment of "main item" blobs—steamed greens, fried potatoes, blanched bean sprouts, pork something-or-other—encircling a central mound of noodles.

I start eating a bit of this and a bit of that, occasionally (successfully!) pulling up a wad of noodles fairly high in the air and biting off a chunk. Mom would be proud.

Xiaochi politely suggests a different approach. As he makes his suggestions, many things start to click.

The different items around the outside are all very salty and highly flavored. In contrast, the central mound of noodles is pretty bland, dry, and sticky. He suggests I mix in the different items with the noodles to balance out the salt and flavors.

This is how lunches are served, also: there are several highly flavored "main item" kinds of foods served separately on small dishes (see "Fish Heads" chapter). There are also bowls of plain, steamed rice. You're supposed to pick up a chunk of "main dish" food with chopsticks, dab it into the rice, then grab up a hunk of rice plus "main dish" food with chopsticks, and eat them together. Everything balances out.

What he says makes sense, so I stir everything up. I'm not sure I'll do that again, or at least not in the same way.

The bottom of the bowl is filled with (very tasty) liquid, which coats my noodles. They now become much tastier (which is good), but also slipperier (not so good). As soon as I start to raise a bit of noodle towards my mouth, it slides out of my chopsticks.

I look over at Xiaochi, who is eating noodle soup, and see that he copes with this by—you guessed it—putting his face close to his bowl. So, I do the same. It's not very elegant, but it gets the job done.

I also notice that the wet noodles kind of flop around a bit, slapping my face with tasty wet liquid. Maybe I'm still too inept with chopsticks, but it could also be one reason Asian men tend not to adorn their faces with whiskers. I need several napkins to repair the damage.

Napkins in China also baffle me. They're tiny, about half the size of a small facial tissue, and roughly as (in)substantial. If you work in chemistry labs, they're very similar to a small Kimwipe. Don't assume these will protect your clothes from floppy wet noodles—they won't. They're solely for mopping noodle juice off your face. That's what I use them for, anyway. Until I find those yoga exercises for my fingers.

**PURPLE PANCAKE WITH LETTUCE AND . . .?**

**NOODLES**

**MY BATHROOM. THERE'S A HUGE PUDDLE, DEEPEST NEXT TO THE RADIATOR, WHICH HAS TO BE SWISHED AROUND THE TOILET INTO THE FLOOR DRAIN.**

# INTERIORES, BEIJING STYLE

When I was a graduate student, one of my first field projects was to investigate rocks in southernmost Chile. In fact, it was a place called Cordillera Darwin[4], named after Charles Darwin, who first described the rocks there during the voyage of the Beagle. The Beagle Channel (named after Darwin's ship) borders Cordillera Darwin on the south.

To get there, you first fly into Santiago. That's where the leader of the project, a guy named Ian Dalziel (pronounced almost exactly like four letters: E-N D-L), met us. The night before we left for Cordillera Darwin and the end of South America, Ian took us out for a special dinner. This was essentially an asado (grilled meats), and in addition to some memorable appetizers (including sea urchin eggs), he ordered several plates of beef: two or three plates of "exteriores" and one plate of "interiores."

Exteriores are the muscle meats that we eat most in the US—steaks, ribs, and roasts.

---

4. "Cordillera" in Spanish means "mountain range," so, in English, we might refer to it as the "Darwin Range." Occasionally you'll find an old Anglo-American map with that name. But scientists today generally try to refer to places using the country-specific official name (converted to the Roman alphabet, as needed), rather than translations.

Interiores were something I had never really eaten much before: liver, kidneys, tripe, and blood sausage. I tried a little of each, and remember thinking the blood sausage was OK, but it was too rich to eat much of.

I was reminded of Santiago when Xiaochi took me this evening for a Beijing specialty soup, down the street. To me, the restaurant looked like any other hole-in-the-wall place. Little did I know . . .

Now, Xiaochi keeps paying for all our meals, so I told him I would pay for this one. But QR codes at the door bested me. Again.

I think I mentioned that, to enter a restaurant, you have to certify that you've passed health inspection. First, I fumble with my US phone. Surprise! Even though it has worked perfectly a half dozen times in the last two days, today the certificate fails to appear. All I get is the spinning wheel of death.

I roll my eyes, pull out the treasonous Huawei phone, login again to WeChat and successfully pull up my health code. On the first try, no less! Damn, I'm good!

Unfortunately, the sour-looking guard lady at the door either doesn't like my looks or doesn't like my certificate (which isn't a QR code). Or both. She says something to me very sternly. A guy in the restaurant volunteers his translation skills (Chinese people are so generous!), and quickly punches through a series of screens on my WeChat app that I didn't know existed. This scans the restaurant's QR code, which brings up exactly the same certificate that I showed the woman two minutes prior. She says something in a gruffly conciliatory tone and waves me through.

However, the delay at the door costs me the opportunity both to pay for the meal and to find out what the hell we're going to eat. So, when the soup arrives, I'm a little surprised.

> Xiaochi:  This is special soup. That is liver of mutton.
>
> Matt:  OK, I like liver. [Well, it's not exactly my favorite, but it's OK. Regardless, I'm here to learn, and this is the first time I've had liver soup.]

> Xiaochi: Yes, it is a Beijing specialty. This restaurant is famous for its soup.
>
> Matt: Great! Thanks for bringing me here.
>
> Xiaochi: Yes, this is the inside of mutton.
>
> Matt: Oh, OK.

So, this isn't just liver, it's other stuff, too. This is where I start to remember Santiago . . .

There's mostly liver (I think it's liver), but then I find a skinny strip of something that looks a little like a multi-legged sea worm. Most of it is white, but the wiggly parts are black. OK, they don't actually wiggle, but they look like they could. Or did when it was alive. Maybe it comes from a zebra?

> Matt: Xiaochi, what is this?
>
> Xiaochi: It is stomach of sheep.

This makes sense. I've eaten beef tripe, but never mutton tripe.

As I poke around the soup, I find some things that might be intestines, or maybe rings cut from blood vessels (there are not very many of them). I thought I might find some bits of heart, but never do see anything that looks like it.

There's a poster on the wall with an empty plate, bowl, and glass. They're overprinted by a circle with a slash through it.

> Matt: Xiaochi, what does that poster mean?
>
> Xiaochi: It means eat all your food.

This is a little strange when you think about it. Usually the slash means "don't." So logically the poster says "Don't leave completely empty plates." I've been told it's impolite in Asia to completely clear your plate. Leave a little, so your host knows you got enough to eat. In this case, it's easy for me to be polite—it's a huge bowl of soup. I eat all the protein bits (I think it might be insulting not to). But I leave behind most of the liquid and noodles. Then we leave. I hurry, so I won't have to interact with the sour guard lady again.

All in all, it was more of a textural rather than true gastronomical event, because everything was cooked to the point of near-flavorlessness. Mostly I focused on anatomy (what's that?).

More generally, the longer I live here, the more impressed I am at all the different things that Chinese people eat. They don't waste a thing!

For example, one of the items we turned down during a Sunday brunch was duck foot webbing. The picture looked about like you would imagine—flat, triangular pieces of something-or-other. If the caption hadn't said webbing, I would have thought it was pita triangles. Or tortilla chips.

That makes sense, right? A high class restaurant in Beijing, and one of their dishes is Doritos? Duck foot webbing makes much more sense. In a weird sort of way.

In Shanghai, I saw a guy walk out of a market carrying a bag of chicken feet. I don't think they were for his dog.

Still, in the spirit of adventure, I try to pick out things to eat that look unfamiliar. I've had a couple successes, so far, in addition to mutton guts soup.

For example, my "tofu" the other day turned out to be duck blood pudding. Kind of like blood sausage, but with a different texture and in slab form. I can't say I'm glad Xiaochi told me, though. Pickled eggs: interesting texture, kind of like ricotta cheese, but much tastier. The famous purple pancake.

I did go back and buy those dried duck tongues in Shanghai, and I managed to eat a couple.

But two were plenty.

**THE DARK GLISTENING LIVER-Y LOOKING SLABS JUST BELOW THE SAUSAGE AT THE TOP OF THE BOWL ARE DUCK-BLOOD PUDDING.**

# DOING THE LAUNDRY

Doing the laundry in China is pretty easy. Of course, it's always easy if you don't have too many clothes to wash. And I can never bring *that* many clothes when I travel, especially when this time I need three wardrobes: everyday clothes for . . . well, every day; moderately formal clothes for giving talks and for meeting high muckety-mucks; and field clothes.

I've met only one muckety-muck, and haven't done any field work. So, I've employed only one-third of my wardrobes.

Still, laundering shocked me with its simplicity. First, I gather my clothes and pull out my two phones—the traitorous Huawei phone for paying for things, and my patriotic US phone for translating.

After putting the clothes in the washer, I scan the QR code on the machine using my WeChat app (big surprise there, eh?).

That brings up a screen asking me what kind of wash I need (including little pictures of clothes with radio buttons next to them). This also lists prices, which range from (roughly) thirty to eighty cents. I choose the seventy-cent option. More expensive means it'll be cleaner, right?

There is a radio button that (translated) asks me if I want to start now or schedule a later start. I leave it on "Now."

I press the "Continue" button, and am taken to a screen that I've seen only about thirty-seven times now, asking for a pin number on WeChat. I type in my pin and hit the green button on my screen.

Immediately the machine starts beeping angrily like a son of a bitch. There's an error code. Crap! What did I do wrong?

I get out my phone and translate the message. Oh, I left the top open. Well, *yeah,* of course I did. After all, it was gonna take me ten minutes to get the damn washer going, right? Assuming I could even get it going. And I didn't want concentrated laundry detergent sitting on my clothes too long.

I did that once (and only once) in college. I put all the laundry in the washing machine, threw some liquid laundry detergent over it, closed the door, inserted my money, pressed the start button, and left. Except, I either didn't push the start button hard enough, or I actually forgot to close the lid, because my clothes just sat there with concentrated laundry detergent on them until I returned half an hour later. For the next two years, I had an oddly colored pillowcase, sort of like homemade camo with variegated light and dark mottles. I didn't want to repeat that. It probably wouldn't have mattered for my tie-dyed T-shirts, but I have only two pairs of decent shorts.

I quickly measure out some detergent, dump it in and close the lid. Immediately, the machine starts filling with water and humming contentedly.

Dang, that was easy! Easier than the average laundromat in the US, anyway. No coins, no laundry card . . . But wait, it gets even better.

As it happens, my apartment is kitty-corner to the laundry room, so I can readily bounce over there and check on stuff. I do that a couple times, while I'm WeChatting with Huixia about future dinner plans. My conversation with Huixia distracts me from the messages I'm receiving via WeChat. Translated, these read:

> 4:06 p.m.:    "Master, your washing machine has failed."

Apparently, I received this message when I tried to start it with the lid open. By the time I see the message and check on the washer, it's already halfway through its cycle.

> 4:42 p.m.:     "Master, your clothes are ready in five minutes."

> and,

> 4:47 p.m.:     "Master, your clothes are finished."

How sweet is that?

I mean, first, who doesn't like being called "Master" by an app? Sure, if I heard this from a person, it would freak me out. But after being jerked around by all those other apps, it's nice to know that this one thinks I'm in control.

Second, I didn't have to set a timer or take responsibility for keeping track of time. The app did it for me automatically. True, I'm right across the hall. But if I lived down the hall, it would be pretty darn handy.

Drying the clothes is a little different because there are no clothes driers. Instead, the laundry room is filled with racks of other people's stuff, drip-drying. Drip-dry is fine with me, but I have only a half dozen clothes hangers for an entire load of laundry. So, some of my stuff goes back in my apartment, draped around the room. A public laundry isn't quite as convenient as hanging stuff out to dry on a 100°F (38°C) summer afternoon in Boise, with a clothesline in your backyard and 5 percent relative humidity. On those days, by the time I've finished hanging up the last bit of clothing, the first things are already dry. But hey, for travel, the Chinese system is pretty darn nice.

OK, true confessions—I was kind of putting this off, partly because I was dreading another QR/app fiasco, and partly because I was afraid of getting in someone else's way. I chose a time (Friday afternoon), when I thought no one would be around. In fact, I haven't seen or heard a soul. Still, this was *so* easy! What was I worried about?

I just hope no one makes off with my tie-dyed shirts. How else will people know I'm American? Oh, right, the accent . . .

**THE WASHING MACHINE AND LAUNDRY ROOM NEAR
MY APARTMENT**

# BIDDEN TO THE FORBIDDEN

One Saturday morning, Xiaochi and his wife, Summer, took me to the Forbidden City, which is essentially a national historic park. Because it was a little late in the morning and warm to ride a bicycle, we took a taxi.

Few people drive in Beijing, at least in proportion to a typical American city. If you have the money or need to keep a strict schedule, you take a taxi. Otherwise, you ride a moped or bicycle, or take the subway or bus. The public transportation system is good here. And the number eleven bus is always running (or, rather, walking).[5]

Why don't people drive? Part of it is convenience (it's always a pain to deal with parking in any densely-populated city), but it's not as much a question of finances as Americans might think. With China's economic growth, many people have sufficient money to buy a car. No, the reason is because the government restricts the number of license plates.

Now this is completely different from the US, where, if you have enough money, you can usually buy whatever you want. What's that you say? You want to buy your own personal submarine and explore the Pacific coast? Hey, if you have the money, be my guest. I'll put you in touch with a guy who makes and sells them.

---

5. My friend in India, Dr. Sudip Paul, explained to me that "taking the number eleven bus" means to walk. The two ones in the number eleven represent your legs.

No, seriously, I know a guy who runs a personal submarine business. His card is in my office. You may need to apply for some permits and licenses to anchor it, but it's not like you have to ask permission to buy one.

True, you can't buy cruise missiles or fighter jets in the US. But there are very few restrictions.

Not so in China. It's too densely populated. If you want a car, you have to apply for and receive a license plate first. And China doesn't issue many license plates in places where traffic congestion is bad (for example, in Beijing and Shanghai). Last year Beijing received about three million applications and approved only thirty thousand (so one percent success). Some people wait for years to buy a car. If you're unmarried or don't have kids . . . well, keep on taking the number eleven bus. Or a taxi.

So, we took a taxi and enjoyed the congestion of street traffic between 8:00 and 9:00 a.m. on a Saturday morning in Beijing. And, yes, there is a lot of traffic in Beijing, even on a Saturday morning.

Entering the Forbidden City is a little like taking the train:

Hi, here's my passport and health code. Yes, there's my visa. Yes, the metal detector is squealing loudly because you told me not to put my two cell phones on the belt of the X-ray machine. You look surprised, is it because of the squealing? I doubt it because everyone is hand-carrying a cell phone and is setting off the detector. Maybe it's because I have two phones? Or because I'm the only white guy in a crowd of 2,714 tourists. OK, sure, wand me to your heart's content. Back and front, side to side. See, no nuclear warheads or handguns.

The external entrance takes you underneath a gigantic poster of Chairman Mao. So, you pass beneath a gigantic symbol of communism to gain sight of a gigantic symbol of imperialism. I'm sure the irony is not lost on China's political leaders.

After that:

Hi, here's my passport and health code. Yes, there's my visa. OK, I'm glad you found our reservation. Thanks for the entrance ticket.

And we're good to go. Or . . .?

Hi, here's my passport and health code. Yes, there's my visa. Yes, the metal detector is squealing loudly because you told me not to put my two cell phones on the belt of the X-ray machine. OK, sure, wand me to your heart's content. Back and front, side to side. See, no nuclear warheads or handguns.

Now, you might be thinking I made an editorial error here and accidentally duplicated text from a previous paragraph. Surely, in the space of five minutes, they didn't screen me twice for weapons and three times for my health status and nationality, right? They don't even do that at airports.

Well, it's true I duplicated the text, but I did that to make the point that it's exactly what they did. I went through exactly the same procedures, multiple times. In fact, these same "entry fees" occur throughout the Forbidden City. True, the Chinese medicine museum cost only a health code. Period. And not even that, because my health code didn't scan properly, and they still let me in.

But the Hall of Clocks and Watches cost ten yuan, one health code, and one passport scan to get the ticket, then one health code, one passport scan, and one temperature check to enter the exhibit building. The exhibit building is about fifty feet from the ticket booth.

I guess officials want to ensure that in the time it takes me to walk across a couple plazas (or, in the case of the Clock and Watch Museum, around the corner), I don't either emigrate to Brunei or develop a raging fever and trigger a super-spreader event.

Fortunately, once I was in the city proper, I didn't have to run any more metal detector gauntlets. I guess officials weren't worried that I might try to stash a four-foot-tall, two-ton, bronze statue of a lion down my shorts.

I don't think any written description can do justice to the Forbidden City. The place is *huge.* Gigantic buildings front gigantic plazas. If you ever watch *The Last Emperor* [which—spoiler alert!—is about China's last emperor], it seems like the guy is constantly running through plaza after plaza, and huge entryway after huge entryway. I rewatched the movie while I was in Shanghai, and I thought "Geez, did they make a mistake? How can there be more than one gigantic building and entryway like that?" But, just like health and passport checks, there really are multiple (not quite "duplicate") gigantic buildings and entryways. As you progress through the complex from south to north, the buildings become older and smaller. But nothing is small, and there's always a sense of grandeur.

As a geologist, I'm required to report that much of the marble (and it's everywhere) comes from the same region as Xiaochi. Well, actually the marble was there first. Xiaochi comes from the same region as the marble. And it's quite beautiful—a clean, white calcite with folded lenses and stringers of quartz. A little heat and water, and it would make a fantastic calc-silicate. OK, lecture over.

Some commentary about the city:

Different buildings have different numbers of beasts decorating the ends of their roofs. The more beasts (up to eleven), the more important the building.

Huge metal cauldrons adorn the interior (older) courts. These once held water in case of fire. Many were gilded, but when the city was ransacked in the 1900s, most of the gilding was scraped off. A couple kilograms of gold might have coated a single cauldron.

Why did the emperor need so many clocks? I guess if you have a lot of rooms, and you want a clock in every room, you end up with a lot of clocks. Come to think of it, we have a lot of clocks at home, too, sometimes several in one room (like the kitchen). Another cultural parallel . . .

I've seen a stork, and I've seen a lion, and I've seen a turtle, but this is the first time I've seen a dragon turtle.

The thresholds all stick up well above the ground. I'm not positive why—to ensure you couldn't run through an entryway without falling flat? But it's caused no end of effort to build ramps to ensure wheelchair access for the most popular areas.

The "tiles" in the Imperial Garden are constructed of tiny pebbles arranged and cemented into beautiful designs. And there must be thousands of tiles. The amount of effort is jaw-dropping.

The main doors all have eighty-one semispherical knobs (nails) in a rectangular nine-by-nine array. Why nine by nine? Nine was a number reserved for emperors. So, nine by nine was impressively imperial.

The nine-by-nine imperial arrays take me back to Kathmandu twenty years ago, when Heather tried to cash a traveler's check at a local bank. For some reason, she was carrying a green pen. And when she was asked to countersign our last check, she signed it in green. OMG, was that ever a problem!

At the time, only government officials were allowed to use green ink to sign documents. A lowly peon foreigner was supposed to sign in either blue or black ink. Green?! Impossible!

It took several minutes of continuous hard-core arguing, but eventually the bank teller backed down and cashed the check. Reluctantly. And good thing, too, because it really was our last bit of funds. Back then, an untenured professor and mom with a two-year-old toddler weren't exactly rolling in dough. And you wouldn't put your bank card into a cash machine in Nepal.

The thresholds take me back to field work in central Oregon. One summer, I met a guy there who had worked in the Peace Corps in central Asia. He commented that we were committing cultural faux pas in how we entered his house. Why? Because we paid no attention to whether we actually stepped on the threshold or over the threshold, and also whether we stepped with our right foot or left foot.

Apparently, this is common in some Muslim cultures—right is good, left is bad (sorry, southpaws). Looking at the thresholds in the Forbidden City, you wouldn't ever step on a threshold. That requires too large an increase in gravitational potential energy. You'd take an elevator first. But whether you stepped over it using your right foot or left foot—that didn't seem to matter to anyone here. I'm a scientist, and I checked.

The clock museum at the Forbidden City was a real trip. Here are some thoughts:

Wow, this is the first time I've actually seen a bird in a gilded cage.

Where's the clock? Oh, it's that tiny thing at the bottom.

Wow, they really had a thing for elephants.

And boats.

Are all those colored bits gems? That would be a lot of gems. It must be glass, right? (I'm still not sure.)

This doesn't seem to have much to do with keeping track of time, it's more about wealth and appearance.

I've got to show some pictures of these clocks to folks back home. [I took many pictures, but there are something like two hundred clocks there.]

Would I visit the Forbidden City again? Sure, happily. Some specific museums were closed, and it probably takes a couple times to get a true sense of scale. Plus, my electronic guide stopped working halfway through, so I missed most of the stories. However, attendance was sparse because China isn't issuing tourist visas right now. I was the only white person I saw. If I'm going to visit again, I should do it during this trip.

But first I'll watch *The Last Emperor* again.

**A "DRAGON TURTLE"**

**IMPERIAL GARDEN**

**NINE-BY-NINE ARRAY OF KNOBS/NAILS ON EACH DOOR**

**BIRD IN A GILDED CAGE CLOCK**

**MIND THE STEP! (BOTH OF THEM)**

# DESSERT MIMICS

After visiting the Forbidden City, Xiaochi and Summer took me to lunch. This afforded me another opportunity to commit further cultural atrocities with chopsticks.

They chose an upscale restaurant. This one seemed like a preferred locale for toddler birthdays, because there were lots of toddlers, and the birthday song— broadcast over the restaurant's speaker system, first in Mandarin, then in English—played at least five times during our lunch.

It took me only a couple minutes to realize I was out of my depth.

Why do I have two sets of chopsticks? Is it like having two forks—an outer one for your main meal, and the inner one for your dessert? What am I missing here? And why does one have gold filigree and the other one has silver?

Unfortunately, I had already committed cultural faux pas before I figured out the mystery of the double chopsticks. After carefully (but surreptitiously) spying on Xiaochi, I saw that:

The outer chopsticks are for serving—you use them to transfer food from a central plate onto your plate. Preferably without dropping that food all over something else.

The inner chopsticks are for eating—you use them to pick up food from your plate. That way, your mouth touches only the inner chopsticks. And the outer chopsticks remain uncontaminated by your spit.

I don't know whether two sets of chopsticks are an upscale restaurant norm, but it seems like a good idea during a pandemic. Even if you're good friends with all the members of your dinner party, do you really want even a little of their spit on your food?

Of course, I had already contaminated my outer (serving) chopsticks with my mouth before I figured this out. So, I switched them.

But now—oops—had I committed further cultural faux pas? After all, now my serving chopsticks had silver filigree, and my eating chopsticks had gold. Well, it was too late to fix that now.

The food, of course, was delicious. I'll spare the details of the main courses, except to note that I found it a little challenging to dissect a whole fried fish with chopsticks. Mostly, I celebrate my success in not slopping burnt sugar glaze all over my face (not excessively, anyway), or permanently staining my clothes. But this is all variation on a theme.

The desserts were something new. First, the presentation was stunning. There were five different desserts, each with four pieces stacked in a neat tetrahedral pyramid, beautifully arrayed along a linear tray. Not to be too geeky, but it crossed my mind that if they represented silica tetrahedra, our dessert tray would be classified as an orthosilicate.

Anyway, from left to right (from my side of the table), they looked like: vanilla fudge, a fudgy petit four, a creamy chocolate roll, pecan puffs, and chocolate fudge. Well, 0.75 correct out of five isn't so bad, right?

The creamy chocolate roll really was kind of creamy and chocolatey, although I expect it didn't actually have cream in it. Half a point for that one. A quarter of a point for the pecan puffs, for reasons I'll explain later.

The bounding "fudge" and "fudgy" petit four, though? Nope, not even close. I should have known better, because milk doesn't rank high up there in Chinese cooking. I can't quite explain what these things were, but I would guess they contained some kind of fruit puree or were fruit-flavored rice/bean/pea flour puree. They tasted a little like fruit (although not super fruity or sweet), and had a texture a little like jam. But, not as sticky, and they maintained their blocky shapes, even at room temperature. Now that I think about it, the texture reminds me a little of cold cornmeal mush. Not quite what you expect for dessert.

The "pecan puffs," though—wow, that was different! Pecan puffs are a traditional dessert in Heather's family. They consist of sugar, flour, butter, and ground pecans, molded into balls, baked, then rolled (twice) in powdered sugar. Superficially, dessert number four on the table looked almost exactly like them. True, these balls had little indentations that I hadn't seen in pecan puffs before. But otherwise, my subconscious expected something similar in texture and taste.

Well, it turns out these are glutinous rice flour, somewhat sweetened, with ground nuts (a quarter of a point for Matt!). However, powdered sugar doesn't dust the outside, rather it's either corn starch or rice flour. Deep down, I knew these couldn't be pecan puffs, but my subconscious kept insisting they were. And let me tell you, it's a little surprising to put something in your mouth that you think is coated in sugar, but that actually turns out to be nearly flavorless desiccant. It's almost as surprising as biting into a blob that you think will fragment into little cookie crumbs, and have it squash into a soft gooey ball.

Finding the nuts was a relief. At least something was familiar. True, I don't know if they were pecans (maybe only an eighth of a point?), but the texture was right.

Now, I hope this doesn't sound like I'm complaining about Chinese desserts, or that I think Euro-American desserts are better. Not at all—I like Chinese desserts! I'll eat them again in a heartbeat.

No, I merely marvel at my capacity to misjudge appearances so completely. A couple desserts looked something like fudge. So, in my mind, they were fudge, despite all the evidence to the contrary. Of course I knew better. I knew before I ever sat down that fudge is extremely unlikely in China. And the texture as I picked them up was obviously different. And still I expected them to be sweet and fudgy.

And, not having learned my lesson (twice), I did it again with the "pecan puffs." Ha!—when will I ever learn? Well, there's only one solution to this problem: I just have to keep eating Chinese desserts at every opportunity! With the gold chopsticks.

**DOUBLE THE CHOPSTICK PLEASURE!**

**FIVE DESSERTS (PLUS A TOWER OF SWEETENED PEA SPROUTS)**

# DOING THE LAUNDRY, INTERNATIONAL EDITION

Brrrriiiiinnnngggg!

What the heck? Who's calling me with a Chinese phone number at 8:30 on a Sunday night?

Brrrriiiiinnnngggg!

I'm in the middle of watching the movie *Fargo*. I paid Bilibili the princely sum of twenty dollars for a year's subscription, so I can watch a higher class of movies. I haven't seen this one in a long time.

Brrrriiiiinnnngggg!

Action in the movie is picking up. The funny-looking guy just got shot as he's taking the ransom money. I'm not going to pick up the phone for an unknown caller during this scene.

Silence. I wait for the alert that tells me they left a voicemail message. More silence. Then . . .

Brrrriiiiinnnnngggg!

Same number. Wow, this person is persistent. OK, pause the movie.

Matt: Hello?

Caller: Hello. May I speak with Matthew Kohn?

Matt: Yes, speaking. [Strange, I was expecting to have to engage in another lengthy and frustrating attempt to use my US phone to translate Chinese from my Huawei phone. At least tonight I'm spared the embarrassment of being just another ignorant American. Or, rather, being immediately identifiable as another ignorant American.]

Caller: Hello, I'm calling from ICBC, the Industrial and Commercial Bank of China. [ICBC is the bank where I have my bank account. So, it's probably not a crank call. But at 8:30 on a Sunday night?]

Matt: Oh, OK. What's up?

ICBC: We wanted to inform you that Chinese law prohibits selling or renting your bank account to outside users. If you do this, you will be prosecuted, fined, and potentially imprisoned.

Matt: What? I don't understand. Can you say that again?

ICBC: Yes. We want you to know that you are not allowed to rent or sell your bank account.

Matt: Uh, OK. Why would I want to do that?

ICBC: Some criminals launder money by renting or purchasing other people's bank accounts. So, it is illegal for you to rent or sell your bank account to other people.

Matt: Oh, OK. That never occurred to me. Thanks for letting me know. [I guess.]

ICBC: You're welcome. Goodbye.

Wow, was that ever strange.

I think ICBC called me because, a few days prior, Xiaochi received my stipend from the Chinese Academy of Sciences. He had to transfer roughly ten thousand dollars to my bank account, but there's a daily transfer limit of about three thousand on his app, so it was taking him a few days. Transferring all that money over several days may have tripped some flag in the Chinese banking system.

Still, would this ever happen in the US? Would a US bank call me up on a Sunday night to give me new ideas about how to cheat the system, or engage in illegal activities? I mean, just imagine (*No!* This has not happened—it's hypothetical):

Here I am, sitting at home in my living room in Boise on a Sunday night, watching a movie. I get a call from an unidentified caller with a 202 area code.

Because I call my legislators, I happen to know that 202 is Washington, DC (interesting), so . . .

I pick up and hear:

> *Hello, this is the US Federal Bureau of Alcohol, Tobacco, Firearms and Explosives. We're calling you this evening as a service to let you know that it is illegal to mix ammonium nitrate with fuel oil to create a bomb (generally referred to as ANFO). Please do not mix these two materials together, especially in small ratios of fuel oil to ammonium nitrate. Such materials are highly dangerous. The US government will view any attempt to create such materials with great suspicion.[6]*

Do all institutions in China call you to help you learn how to commit crimes? I'm about to apply for an extension to my visa, so I can stay in Beijing until December. Will the police call me to let me know how to become an illegal immigrant?

The imaginary ANFO conversation about explosives reminds me of when I was a teenager, and one particular sixth of July. When I still lived in Ohio, a very large

---

6. Note: I'm no expert on making ANFO, but it's used for legitimate purposes, so it's possible to find instructions on how to make it. Getting the ratios exactly right sounds tricky though, and you definitely need permits to make and use it.

park near our house had a large fireworks display every Fourth of July. Actually, maybe they still do—I haven't been there on the Fourth of July since I was nineteen. These were the big, beautiful aerial displays with large explosions that look like flowers and showers and streamers, etc. Lots of different colors.

At some point, I learned that, back then, explosives in these fireworks don't always ignite. So, if you hunt around the fields where they shoot off the fireworks, you could sometimes find small packages of explosives. Some were spherical, and the largest were about the size of a ping-pong ball. Others were cubes. If you tear open the packages, you can access the explosive, which was either simply a powder or a mixture of powder and small compact pellets.

Well, one year, a couple days after the Fourth of July, I tore open a couple of these packages and piled all the powder and pellets on a rock or slab of concrete (something nonflammable, anyway). I think I put a plastic toy on top to see whether it would burn or just melt. Then, I tried lighting it all with a match:

Hmmm . . . this isn't lighting very well. I'll try again. Nope. Try again. Nope. And—whoooomph!! The whole pile flashed up in my face.

If I hadn't been wearing glasses (fortunately with glass lenses, not plastic) I might well have been permanently blinded. As it was, I gave myself second-degree burns across my nose and lips. The heat was so intense that even behind my glasses it curled my eyelashes. For the next week or so, blinking was super annoying because my upper and lower eyelashes kept linking, kind of like Velcro.

This was the last time for the next thirty years that I completely shaved (to even out the distribution of hair—it was completely gone from the middle of my lips and chin). The next time was for field work in Mozambique, when I needed to wear a gas mask in a cave. Bat guano gives off noxious fumes, and gas masks don't make air-tight seals if you have facial hair.

I suppose future circumstances might possibly lead me to try lighting a small pile of explosive powder again. Carefully. From a distance. With a face shield. And long tweezers to hold the match.

But I'd be bat-shit crazy to think about money laundering in China.

# PAL-ING WITH SUMMER AT THE SUMMER PALACE

Fortunately, the day that Xiaochi, his wife Summer, and I chose to visit the Summer Palace was relatively cool and dry. The next weekend poured rain (again).

Maybe it was crowded by modern COVID standards, but it was pretty empty of tourists. In fact, this is the only place I've been in China where nearly everyone was barefaced—no masks! I was a little shocked, actually. But there were so few people, it's not like we got close to anyone. It's mainly an outdoor park.

There's certainly a palace at the Summer Palace. Or, I should say "Palaces." Like the Forbidden City, there are many beautiful buildings. You're not allowed inside most of them, but you can peek through the windows and see the Thousand-Hand statue of the Buddha, and the furniture and knickknacks of the emperors and empresses.

Actually, the "Thousand-Hand Buddha" has only twenty-four hands. I'm not sure how you get to one thousand from there. OK, yes: add one and multiply by forty. Don't be such a smartass. No, I mean, how is twenty-four equivalent to one thousand? Couldn't they count?

Then again, art is rarely literal. And that's still a lot of hands. More than I would know what to do with.

Come to think of it, I suppose it's a good thing the Buddha was so serene. Can you imagine if the Thousand-Hand Buddha were fidgety? What are you going to say: "Sit on your hands?" Maybe that's why there are only twenty-four.

Anyway, the statue stands on a pedestal with 999 bronze lotus petals, arranged in nine rows. Although it's still not quite one thousand, the number makes sense, because nine is reserved for emperors. The number 999 arranged in nine rows must be super-imperial.

There's an interesting story about that particular temple. One of the empresses had it built to sleep in, but she fell ill the first night there. She determined that the building didn't belong to her after all, it belonged to the Buddha. No, I don't know how she figured that out, I think it's one of those spiritual things. You know, like how twenty-four is equivalent to one thousand. Anyway, she had it converted into a temple to the Buddha. She celebrated her birthday there once per year, and that was the extent of nondivine activities.

But most of the park isn't buildings, it's . . . well, a park.

Kunming Lake occupies most of it. Walkways along its edge border vast swamps of lotus plants (similar to water lilies), which were still blooming when we visited. However, China is very particular about its parks. You're supposed to walk on the paths, and nowhere else. So, don't think you can trot across the lawn and down to the lake shore to pose for a closeup with a lotus blossom. Well, I suppose you could, but it would definitely be a foreign faux pas. If I tried it, the government would probably deny my request for a visa extension next week (we don't want this guy. He walks on the grass and poses with water lilies). No, you just have to hope that your cell phone has sufficient pixel resolution that you'll get a pretty good picture from fifty feet away. Either that, or bring a real camera.

Now I kind of wish I'd snagged the camera that someone left on the jetway back in Dallas.

The walkways are connected with bridges with an unusual shape, a bit like a Gaussian (bell-shaped) curve. While these definitely satisfy a visual aesthetic, they're miserable for walking, at least for humans.

Now, I know it's not easy to design stuff ergonomically, even stairs. In fact, I know a little about stairs because Heather and I have built them before. Well, mainly Heather has succeeded in building them, despite my best efforts to muck up the measurements. One of my problems (among several) is that I keep forgetting about the thickness of the tread, which is the flat part of the step. So, my steps are all perfectly matched until the last one, which is always one tread height too short. Or too tall.

The boards that support the treads are called stringers, and that's where my special talent for miscalculation really shines. After one ill-fated project, my miscut stringers constituted a major component of the firewood that we took on camping trips for the next year or two.

Ergonomic guidelines for stairs specify how high up you step ("rise") compared to how far forward you step ("run"). An ideal rise/run ratio should be around seven/eleven—a seven-inch rise to an eleven-inch run. I guess in metric, the "seven/eleven rule" would be the "17.8/27.9" rule. Although maybe there's an "eighteen/twenty-eight rule"?

Anyway, the bridges at the Summer Palace do an impressive job of violating every principle of good stair design. At the bottom and the top, the rise is so small, you feel like you're trying to skate, but without the advantage of frictionless movement. The experience ranks right up there with the joy of slogging up a sand dune, where you keep stepping up, sliding back down, and getting nowhere. Or like walking down an inclined plane. [Which is no fun. Try looking up the video of Donald Trump creeping down the ramp at West Point Academy in June, 2020. Sure, the guy obviously has poor balance, but that's not the only problem.]

Halfway up one of these Gaussian bridges, where the slope is steepest, you feel like you might well fall over backward.

Were the bridges created to teach architects how not to build stairs? Possibly, although they are truly beautiful. I suppose art doesn't have to be practical. Or mathematically accurate either—look at the "Thousand-Hand" Buddha.

Bordering the edge of the buildings is the world's longest corridor. It has a particularly catchy name, too: "The Long Corridor." Now, when I say longest, I mean that *Guinness World Records* lists The Long Corridor as both the "Longest covered wooden corridor" and the "Longest covered promenade" in the world. I didn't think to bring a tape measure to check (maybe next time?), but Guinness reports the length as 728 meters, or almost half a mile. (I'll be sure to bring my one-kilometer tape measure) This dwarfs the "Infinite Corridor" at my alma mater, the Massachusetts Institute of Technology. The Infinite Corridor is only 251 meters long, or almost three times smaller.

The name "The Long Corridor" is grammatically appropriate because, while it may be the longest wooden corridor, it isn't technically the longest corridor. For example, the "Death Star Corridor" at a Royal Air Force complex in the Falkland Islands (Islas Malvinas) is made out of concrete and paces out at eight hundred meters.

Did the Brits make it eight hundred meters so it would be a little longer than "The Long Corridor"? International politics has played sillier games.

Also, India claims an even longer concrete corridor, specifically a 1,019-meter-long "corridor" at a mental health clinic. Sorry, India, I disagree because it's not one continuous length, rather the total includes cross-corridors. The farthest you could walk from the end of one corridor to the end of another, without backtracking, would be "only" about four hundred meters.

Anyway, none of these dry statistics really matters that much to me because what makes the Long Corridor so spectacular isn't its length. After all, it curves a bit, so it's not like you can look down a straight three-fourths-kilometer-long corridor and see a little tiny dot in the distance at the other end.

No, the beauty of the Long Corridor is that it's made out of wood. So, to protect it from the weather, every bit of it is covered with spectacular paintings. My electronic guide told me that many images derive from classical stories, including *Journey to the West*, which I happened to read during my COVID-19 brain-stupor last year. There are also many landscapes and details of flowers, insects, birds, etc.

I snapped a few photos, but with more than fourteen thousand paintings, it would take a lifetime to begin to grok the full beauty. I mean, the Louvre is a gigantic museum, but it exhibits only about half that many paintings. True, the paintings here show less variety stylistically. But the entry fee for the Summer Palace is also four times lower than the Louvre, and there are far fewer people. Plus, it's outdoors—how awesome is that! I suspect the guards at the Louvre would frown on people picnicking in front of the Mona Lisa too. Not so, here.

And then, of course, there's the lake itself. Xiaochi told me that Kunming Lake is the main water supply for Beijing. If so, Beijing must have a hell of a water treatment plant, because the lake is disturbingly yellow-green—like split-pea soup laced with virulent yellow curry. Or old baby poop. I winced when I saw people swimming in it. On the other hand, you can rent a paddleboat to toodle around the lake. There was a bit of a line for rentals, so we ended up walking the whole perimeter. But the paddleboats do look like fun. As long as you don't get any accidental splashes of baby poop lake water in your mouth.

You certainly won't risk accidentally ingesting lake water on one paddlewheel boat at the park. That's because the boat is made out of marble. Fortunately, my electronic guide clarified that it's not meant for sailing at all. It's only a pavilion constructed to look like a paddlewheel boat.

Now I know this is a real shocker, but I can affirm that the Chinese do not normally make boats out of rock. I know because I've made numerous careful observations on each waterway I've encountered, and never seen one. If the Chinese do build rock boats, they're either very rare, or they're subject to strict national security controls.

I confess, part of me hopes there actually is a top-secret rock-boat program here. I mean, it makes sense, right? Rock is as common as . . . well, dirt. If everyone knew how to build boats out of rock, everyone would have boats. And China would lose its technological and market advantage in the rock-boat industry.

To test my theory, I plan to return to the Summer Palace to take a closer look at the marble boat. Maybe it could float. But I'll wait until after I get my visa extension.

**A "GAUSSIAN" BRIDGE**

**MARBLE BOAT**

**THOUSAND-HAND BUDDHA WITH TWENTY-FOUR HANDS**

**PALACE BUILDINGS**

**THE LONG CORRIDOR**

# VOUCHING FOR TREES —AND ROCKS

One thing I noticed at both the Summer Palace and Forbidden City is that every tree is cataloged. Yes, each one has a little metal label with a number. In the Summer Palace, the lowest numbers are at the main building complex. One of my pictures includes tree number 2615. So, the park has thousands. In the Forbidden City, there are fewer than two hundred because they're limited to the Imperial Garden, but each is hundreds of years old. Every tree is spectacularly beautiful. This attention to cataloging beautiful trees got me thinking about science, scientists, and collections.

Now, one (sometimes annoying) characteristic of scientists is that we like to organize things. True, our personal offices may look chaotic, but we're ultracareful about observations and data. Microsoft Excel is our friend. So, the Chinese approach of numbering each tree in a park strangely appeals to me. I wouldn't want to be in charge of keeping track of all those trees myself, but I'm glad someone does.

Another characteristic of scientists is that we're all terrible skeptics. Just because someone says something doesn't make it true. Of course, that's a foundation of the scientific method—observations have to be repeatable and/or independently verifiable. So, scientists are constantly checking up on each other, far more than other professions. One reason "cold fusion" was rejected over thirty years ago is because no one could replicate the original experiments. Sure, the popular press talks about the triumph of science in creating a vaccine for the COVID pandemic in record time. I agree. It is a triumph. But so was disproving cold fusion—a mistake of colossal proportions was identified and dismissed in a matter of months. Science isn't all just about harvesting discoveries. It's also about separating wheat from chaff.

Because of these characteristics (organize and repeat), scientists classify species in reference to something physical that can be observed over and over. These include "type specimens" (which define a species) and "voucher specimens" (which are other exemplary specimens that serve as references for understanding what a species looks like). These physical examples have to be housed professionally and made accessible to researchers, so they can serve as the reference for the species. There are type specimens of everything, including trees.

I suppose *Homo sapiens* must be my favorite species, but I also appreciate *Equus simplicidens*. Yes, I'm biased. I've analyzed *E. simplicidens'* teeth to learn about paleoecology and paleoclimate in the Pacific Northwest and also how fossil teeth absorb rare elements like uranium. This animal—"Hagerman horse"—is Idaho's state fossil, and the best-preserved fossils come from what is now Hagerman Fossil Beds National Monument in Idaho. But the type specimen is housed at the Texas Memorial Museum. Why there? That's because a guy named Edward Drinker Cope discovered the first *E. simplicidens* fossils in Texas almost thirty years before a rancher found them in Idaho. Those first fossils in Texas were the basis for naming the species (being first matters for naming conventions). And because Cope chose to deposit them in Texas, that state has the type specimen, even if it's not the best preserved. Voucher specimens from Idaho are housed elsewhere.

You might have heard the name Cope before, and not just for "Cope's Rule" (which says that lineages tend to evolve to larger body size over geologic time—the ancestors of elephants, hippos, and whales were originally small and got bigger during evolution over the last tens of millions of years. Our *Australopithecus* ancestor, Lucy, was smaller than us). Rather, in the late 1800s, Cope engaged in a "Bone War" with another guy, named Othniel Charles Marsh to discover and name new species of dinosaurs. Most of the basis for the "war" was ego trips. If you name a species, articles that reference those species are supposed to credit you. So, by nineteenth century convention I should have said "*Equus simplicidens* (Cope 1892)." Fortunately, we don't do that anymore (or not much). Among other reasons, it keeps down conflict over naming species. But, basically, these guys were looking to discover type specimens that would be linked to their names forever.

Type specimens and voucher specimens are all dead, of course. Standards can't keep changing. Observations and measurements have to be repeatable, and strictly speaking that can't be done only on living things.

But sometimes type specimens or voucher specimens get destroyed. Buildings burn down or collapse during disasters, invading forces loot museums, etc. It's rare, but it happens. Then scientists have to look for new examples so that scientists of the future have something to compare against.

If anyone ever needed another voucher specimen for a tree, I might recommend looking in the parks in China. Each tree seems so spectacularly tree-like. Then again, how would you choose? There are so many beauties.

In that respect, it's probably a good thing Monet grew up French and not Chinese. It's one thing to paint twenty-five canvases of haystacks, or thirty-odd views of Rouen Cathedral from exactly the same vantage point. It's another thing entirely to capture the distinct beauty of ten thousand individual trees. He'd have gone crazy.

It does seem like the Chinese care more about trees than Americans do, at least in public spaces. Each tree is identified and treated as a special individual. Many trees, especially the oldest ones, have massive poles to help prop up their limbs. Sort of like a walker, if trees walked. There are spectacular examples in the Forbidden City. The poles aren't always sufficient, and I've seen scars where limbs have broken off. But there's a fundamental cultural difference in how we treat our trees. I get the feeling that they're considered more like equals here in China. I've certainly seen that same cultural bias in India, where people sometimes choose to plant a tree to ensure their legacy, rather than to have another child.

Of course, the flip side of reverence is that the gardens and parks here are ultramanaged. Climbing trees is forbidden in the Forbidden City.

It's not only trees, many Chinese revere rocks too. Both the Forbidden City and the Summer Palace have large individual rocks exhibited as pieces of art. Natural statues, I suppose.

I suspect most people do this. I certainly have unusual bits of wood and rocks on my windowsills. But it's different here. Some people search out especially large and statuesque (some might say grotesque) rocks to display in their gardens.

There are many examples at the Summer Palace. The most famous one is the Blue Iris Stone. Personally, I don't think it looks particularly blue. The emperor who put it in the Summer Palace persuaded his reluctant mother it was OK to stick it there by claiming it looked like a special type of healing fungus. I'm no expert on funguses, but I don't see the resemblance to that either.

The Blue Iris Stone is absolutely huge. To transport it, the original owner (not the emperor) borrowed a page from that classic bestseller, *How to Build the Great Wall of China*: he hired workers to construct a road and pour water on it in the wintertime. After the water froze, the stone could slide on the ice. Unfortunately, the guy went bankrupt while the stone was still being transported. Maybe movers charge extra to transport "blue" stones (rather than gray or brown stones) or stones that resemble funguses. I would, if I were them. Anyway, apparently none of them was searching for a giant rock to put in his own garden, so they left it by the side of the road. Around one hundred fifty years later, the emperor saw it, took a fancy to it, and paid big bucks to have it transported to the Summer Palace.

I read that it's the largest decorative rock in a Chinese garden, and I believe it. Judging from its dimensions, my rough calculations put it on the order of twenty-five tons, possibly closer to forty.

It's not just emperors who exhibit rocks on their property. The Institute for Geology and Geophysics here in Beijing, Peking University, and China University of Geosciences all do too (and probably many other educational institutions and parks). The intent is basically the same—some rocks are naturally beautiful, so why not display them as works of art?

And, of course, I have a couple hundred rocks displayed around my office, mostly ones I collected during field work. Each has its own unique beauty and story. Heather and I have a few rocks in our garden, too, although nothing so massive as the Blue Iris Stone. At least not yet.

All these rocks tell me that it doesn't really matter where you come from, or how you grow up. In some respects, people are the same the world over. Or, at least, I'm convinced that shared interest in rocks can bring people together. If I didn't, I guess I wouldn't be here now.

**PINE TREE, SUMMER PALACE. NOTE ALL THE SUPPORTS**

**ROCK, SUMMER PALACE**

**ORBICULAR GRANITE, INSTITUTE FOR GEOLOGY AND GEOPHYSICS, CHINESE ACADEMY OF SCIENCES**

# SEPTEMBER

# JAWBONE OF AN ASS

"Do Chinese people eat dogs?" That's a question that Huixia fielded when she was in Boise. Apparently, many Chinese people are asked that. Her answer didn't really surprise me: "Very few and not regularly. But there are some Chinese people who do eat dog. Occasionally."

Eating dog in China goes back several thousand years. Well, it might not have been called "China" then, but Chinese ancestors have been eating dog a long time. More generally, in China (and many other parts of the world) anything that provides nutritional value, and that doesn't carry diseases or pathogens, and that isn't legally protected, is likely to be eaten. Humans are omnivores in the very *b r o a d e s t* of senses.

I think one of the main reasons we don't eat armadillos so much in the US (at least, not since the depression) is because they carry leprosy. And while the French eat their snails as a delicacy, people in the western Pacific don't eat their snails—they carry meningitis.

Now, don't imagine that occasional dog eating is singularly Chinese. The Norwegian explorer, Roald Amundsen, planned the nutrition for his expedition to the South Pole to include eating his sled dogs. He left for the South Pole with fifty-two dogs, and returned with eleven. Other cultures eat dogs, too (for example, some Native Americans), and not only under desperate circumstances.

I don't know about eating dogs myself, but I'm definitely omnivorous and generally game to try almost anything. Raw clam? Why not? The kids on Yap (island in the western Pacific) sure were enthusiastic. They're the ones who showed me how to twist your heel in the sand until you uncovered a clam, then pull apart the shells and dig out the little salty protein blob. How could I say no?

Sheep stomach? Yes, a few times now. Donkey? Uh . . . sure. And that's how Xiaochi and I ended up at the donkey restaurant.

Yes, there's a restaurant just around the corner from the Institute that specializes in donkey meat. And when I say donkey, I'm not using some euphemism for another animal. I mean bona fide *Equus asinus*. There are images of cute-looking burros on the menu, which lists bulk meat (essentially like going to the butcher), as well as various prepared dishes.

I admit I felt some slight hesitation, mostly because I read *Brighty of the Grand Canyon* (by Marguerite Henry) when I was a kid. I watched *Shrek* too. And I have a general fondness for equids.

But I was willing to give it a taste. So, in addition to seaweed-and-egg soup and cucumber-and-peanut salad, I ate donkey sandwich. The meat is reddish and looks surprisingly like corned beef. It tastes a bit like corned beef too. It was generally more tender than other meat I've had here, but that's not saying much. The cafeteria at the Institute wasn't exactly fine dining, and I was constantly digging tough meat fibers out of my teeth. Ironically, the shape of the sandwich closely resembles the lower jawbone of horses and burros. The jaw widens for a set of (typically) six large teeth, then tapers toward the front. The jawbone of an ass takes on a whole new meaning here.

> Xiaochi: Do people in the US eat donkey?

> Matt: No. We generally don't eat donkey or horse.

Strange, when you think about it. We kill our horses and donkeys to make food for our dogs. And we don't eat dogs. So, that means a whole food chain in the US exists because of humans, but independently of us. The difference in China (and many other countries) is that their food chain is a little less chain-y and a little more mesh-y.

The bottom line for me on donkey is that I wouldn't go out of my way to eat it again (hard to get *Brighty* out of my head), but I might eat it in a social setting. I'm glad I tried it.

Back to dog, though—would I eat it? Well, I've never been offered the opportunity, but I think I'd turn it down. I admit to feeling a little conflicted, though, because I think I could eat a coyote, and they're basically wild dogs. Yes, technically they're classified as a separate species—*Canis latrans*, rather than *Canis familiaris*. But coyotes look like dogs and can crossbreed with dogs. So how different are they, really?

I couldn't eat a wolf, though. They're too scarce and protected. To borrow a line from *The Princess Bride,* I would sooner destroy a stained-glass window than kill a wolf. Coyotes, though, they're like rabbits—no shortage of them.

And what about cats? I'm not likely to eat a house cat (too many happy memories of pets). Still, I'm reminded of a story from Euell Gibbons about trying to live off the land in the Canadian backwoods.

If you're old enough, you may remember Gibbons from his Grape Nuts commercials in the 1970s. If you're not, you can find them on YouTube (unless you're in China; I haven't found them in China yet). He's the health food and outdoors advocacy guy with a couple memorable lines, like "Ever eat a pine tree? Many parts are edible." And the taste of Grape Nuts "reminds me of wild hickory nuts." Of course, no good deed goes unpunished—the Federal Trade Commission banned the commercials because it was scared that little kids would run outside, start eating any old random plant, and get sick. Thus ended an early advance in the health food movement. But not before Gibbons became the good-natured butt of many jokes:

Q: How do you know Euell Gibbons in the nude?

A: By his golden rod and hickory nuts.

Anyway, Gibbons and a friend grubbed along several days in the Canadian woods without finding anything to eat, until finally in desperation they shot a bobcat. When Gibbons asked his friend what he thought of the meat, his friend replied that the "bob" part was pretty good, but the "cat" part was a little hard to swallow.

Thinking about other species, I definitely couldn't eat a primate. Not unless I was really desperate. Think Donner party, or *Alive!* (Piers Paul Read).

But did you know that some Neanderthals were cannibals? I learned this only last week. In deposits in Europe that predate "our" arrival (*Homo neanderthalensis* was wandering around Europe for a hundred thousand years before *Homo sapiens* showed up), Neanderthal bones have cut marks and tooth marks identical to those on other animal bones. Only people (in the broad sense) use knives, so it must have been Neanderthals doing the cutting. And the eating. Of each other.

And lots of other animals too. Neanderthal chemistry indicates they were hypercarnivores (like cats and polar bears), so they obtained most of their calories from meat.

Actually, archeologists have known about Neanderthal cannibals for over twenty years, but I was ignorant of those studies until now. It's not clear if Neanderthals commonly practiced cannibalism, or if archeologists got lucky in their discoveries. Only a couple sites show this.

On the other hand, there are fewer than one hundred Neanderthal sites, and only the richest ones could preserve that kind of information.

Actually, it's not fair to say "Neanderthals were cannibals." It's not like we're all that different from them. Other than people from sub-Saharan Africa, nearly everyone's genetic code has at least a few percent Neanderthal. So, it's really "We were cannibals." I suppose some of us might still be. But not me. And not people in China either. You can trust me on that one.

**MEAL AT THE DONKEY RESTAURANT. I NEVER DID FIGURE OUT WHAT KIND OF SEAWEED MAKES UP THE DARK BLOBS IN THE SOUP ON THE RIGHT. THE DONKEY IS THE MEAT IN THE SANDWICHES TO THE LOWER LEFT, WHICH ARE SHAPED SOMEWHAT DISTURBINGLY LIKE JAWBONES.**

# VISA IN, VISA OUT

Getting a visa extension in China isn't that hard. True, I had to amass more paperwork, especially a letter from the Institute saying that they desperately needed my input into fourteen different projects, otherwise the Institute's entire science endeavor would founder. That's what they told me it said, anyway. And I had to visit the police station to register an address with them. And a telephone number.

Now, a couple weeks later, Xiaochi takes me to the visa office where the guards verify my passport and (uninfected) medical status, and Xiaochi and I fill out an app that requests my local telephone number. I don't know what they would do if I lacked a local phone. Deny my visa extension request? Make me stand in an extra-long line?

Anyway, Xiaochi navigates that mud puddle at the front door, and we go upstairs.

> **Xiaochi:** Hi, this guy wants to request an extension to his visa. We have all the paperwork. What do we do?

> **Clerk:** First he has to have his picture taken. Go to that office, get a picture, pick up a set of codes, and come back to me.

So, we go, stand in line for about ten minutes, and I have my picture taken. The photographer hands me some verification codes, and we head back to the first desk.

> **Xiaochi:** Here are our codes. What do we do now?

Clerk:     Your number is forty-one. Wait until it's called. So, we sit down and wait.

I'll be honest—this is eerily like waiting for a window at the DMV. You know what it's like, right? All the excitement of meeting a new friend in government, filling out forms that you didn't know you needed, trying to explain a complication to someone who deliberately yawns in your face, learning that all your payment methods are unacceptable. I'm practically wriggling on my seat! So are the kids. But I don't think it's quite for the same reason.

Anyway, our number gets called after fifteen minutes, and we . . . move to another line?

This is different. Here, instead of sitting in relatively comfortable chairs, we sit on backless little stools and wait for a window.

I spend the next fifteen minutes reminding myself how the spin rate on stools can be used to illustrate conservation of angular momentum. Start rotating with your legs out straight, then draw them in. Your speed increases because you're moving your moment of inertia closer to the spin axis. That's what ice skaters do. I spend the next several minutes pretending I resemble an ice skater. I hope I'm amusing everyone else, but they studiously avoid looking my way. I'm sure they're thinking:

"Those American troublemakers. Always spinning on stools and pretending to be ice skaters. Even in the summertime. Why can't they just sit still? Harumph!"

Finally, a clerk calls me to her window and starts talking with Xiaochi. Everything seems to be going smoothly, until a scrum of other clerks shows up for a confab with her. The more reasonable half of my mind thinks she's a more senior clerk, and they have some complication. Probably some American down the line is asking for a visa extension, and doesn't have a local phone number. The other half of my mind suspects all the clerks spontaneously gather to discuss the daily frog races as a way to break up their monotony. And to see if any of the people waiting to talk with them will crack.

Anyway, she finally returns to us. She takes my passport, reads through the forms, asks a couple brief questions of Xiaochi, then hands him a bright yellow card with some stuff written on it. She does not return my passport.

Xiaochi:  OK, let's go.

Matt:     Uh, what happens now?

Xiaochi:  We leave and come back in ten days. You pick up your passport next week on Wednesday.

Matt:     Wait, I won't have a passport for over a week?

Xiaochi:  Yes, it's OK. Just pick up your passport next week. I will be out of town, but I will find a staff member to help you. This yellow card is the receipt. You bring it, pay the fee, and pick up your passport.

Matt:     OK . . .?

No, I wasn't super happy about roaming around Beijing without a passport. I mean, besides all those pesky Chinese federal laws that say you must never ever go anywhere without it, your passport has that QR code sticker on the back with a stern warning to never ever remove it. And if you don't have a QR code in China, man, you're barely human. It's almost as bad as not having a telephone number. But, there's nothing I can do. For ten days, anyway.

Unless . . .? Hey, maybe I can find a tattoo parlor that's willing to tattoo the same QR code onto my butt. Now, there's a thought! Anytime an official asks me for ID, I could drop trou, just like in that Tom Hanks movie. Oh, except I don't have a picture of the QR code. Damn! No, I'll just have to sneak around the city pretending I have a passport. I won't have any trouble getting into places, right?

Fast forward ten days to Wednesday. One of the faculty at the Institute, Jiamin Wang, calls a taxi and we inch our way back to the passport office. Not surprisingly, traffic is stiff in Beijing on a Monday morning at 8:30 a.m. But it's not like all twenty-two million inhabitants are trying to get to the same passport office. So, the fifteen-minute ride takes thirty minutes. Not surprising, all things considered.

Same deal at the door—health code, extra QR code linked to my phone. No passport, but I have the receipt to say we're here to retrieve it. And we're in! Sixty seconds flat.

I swear, we should have asked the driver to wait for us, because the rest of the visit takes about five minutes. And most of that is figuring out which windows to go to. First, I pay for the visa. Not super cheap—US$150 (the exchange rate is a little down compared to two months ago)—but hey, it could be worse. Remember, I paid nearly a thousand to a company to get the first one.

Then we go to another window with our payment receipt. There must be a couple hundred passports, all lined up in a drawer, waiting for people to come claim them. I briefly consider vaulting over the retaining window, grabbing a bunch of passports, and making a run for the exit, just for a little excitement. Pushing that thought to the back of my head, I instead pass over my payment receipt, the woman there finds my passport, and—voilà!—I have my passport back. With a new visa through January of next year.

Easy peasy. If I had a lemon, I'd squeeze it. Some bureaucratic nightmares morph into pleasant dreams. DMV, eat your heart out.

Then again, even when Chinese bureaucracy fails in its quest to impede scientific collaboration, the US can sometimes step into the breach. And that's exactly what they did. But not for me.

No, I received my visa extension on a Wednesday. Two days later, a student here in China, who received a fellowship last month to come to Boise State and work with me for a year, had his visa application rejected by the US embassy, without any option of appeal.

As I understand it from the student, the in-person conversation went like this:

> Official:  What's your name?
>
> Student: Wangchao [last name]
>
> Official:  Where do you study?
>
> Student: Sun Yat-sen University

Official:  What's your major?

Student: Geology

Official:  [Scrolls through a screen on his computer, then stamps "Rejected."] Goodbye.

Why? Former President Trump's proclamation 10043, of course.

You see, in June, last year, Trump issued a proclamation (which is still in effect) that denies travel visas specifically for any student in China who engages in STEM (Science, Technology, Engineering, and Math) research. The reason for the ban is that China funds military and espionage research at some universities, and the Chinese military can recruit students and postgraduates in some of these sensitive fields as potential spies. There's evidence this has happened a couple times, although clearly spies represent a miniscule fraction of Chinese scholars.

But what exactly constitutes "STEM" fields? Who gets in and who gets the door slammed in their face?

Fortunately, the US visa office provides its rejectees with its list of nearly five hundred individual subdisciplines that define STEM fields. Wangchao sent the list to me. These fields do include things like Information Technology, Robotics Technology, Nuclear Engineering, and Nuclear Physics. Now, I'll be honest, I can see why the US might want to be careful about those fields. At least, a visa officer should want to look into the specifics of what an applicant in those fields does before approving a visa.

But Wangchao studies continental collisions, and somehow I don't think either the Department of Homeland Security or the Chinese military cares about what was going on in the Himalayas twenty million years ago while the Indian subcontinent was colliding with Asia. No, the problem is that the list also includes *all* things scientific, for example mycology (mushroom research), veterinary physiology, reproductive biology, and (of course) geological and Earth sciences/geosciences.

So, what does that mean? That means if you're a Chinese student who studies snail sex, or shelf fungi that form on trees, or (heaven help us) what was going on in the Himalayas twenty million years ago, the US visa office will summarily deny your application. Of course, it's all in America's best interest, right? Who knows, a sneaky reproductive biologist could compromise all our military secrets about snail sex.

The visa office should be checking the support letters to see if students are eligible for exemptions from the visa ban under the conditions of Proclamation 10043. But at least this visa officer doesn't. It's highly hypocritical, but they get away with it because no one wants to look soft on China.

Actually, I can't resist telling you how stupefying the geological categories are. Here are the five in the list that Wangchao sent me that are relevant to him (he studies geochemistry and petrology, which are subdisciplines in geology):

1.  Geological and Earth sciences/geosciences
    - [OK, that encompasses anything anyone might care to do. Period.]
2.  Geological and Earth sciences/geosciences, other
    - [Huh? Does that mean "Anything anyone might care *not* to do, but does anyway"?]
3.  Geology/Earth science, general
    - [So, "geological sciences" and "geosciences" aren't sufficient any more, we have to say "geology" too? Or is the government trying to distinguish "Earth science" from "Earth sciences"? SMH (shaking my head) . . . ]
    - And . . .
4.  Geochemistry
5.  Geochemistry and petrology
    - [Doesn't "geochemistry and petrology" include "geochemistry"? Does that mean someone who studies just "petrology" is OK?]

Anyway, at this moment, Wangchao is thoroughly stuck—there's no appeal process. And—surprise!—it doesn't look like any geology student from China has applied for or received a visa to come to the US in the context of a temporary fellowship in over a year (Chinese students studying in US PhD programs have received visas). Sound familiar? So, we're currently trying to identify what documentation we need to convince some faceless drone here in China that a guy who studies continental collisions does not constitute an imminent threat to US security. Once we figure that out (if we figure that out), we can pay that application fee and try it all again. And keep our fingers crossed.

# I SEE SOME SEASUM

According to Eliza Doolittle (*My Fair Lady*), the rain in Spain stays mainly in the plain. I wouldn't know because I've never been to Spain. Actually, I don't think she knew firsthand either. Nonetheless, I can assure you that the rain in China does *not* stay mainly in the plain. No, during our last three days of field work, while it did rain in the plain, it rained even more in the mountains, hills, and valleys. In fact, based on nearly two months' experience so far, the rain in China falls everywhere and everywhen. It's very egalitarian in that respect. We had one beautifully clear day in the province of Inner Mongolia. But mostly it was overcast, slightly drizzly, and one day it poured constantly.

Maybe I was fortunate that outcrops of rocks are few and far between out there, so most of the rain fell on our rental cars rather than our heads. Yes, we spent a lot of time driving, and that was good, because I saw a lot of the Chinese countryside.

Matt:     Xiaochi, what are they growing in that field?

Xiaochi:  Seasum.

Matt:     What?

Xiaochi:  Seasum.

Matt:     I still don't understand.

Xiaochi:  Wait. [He looks it up and spells the word.] S-e-s-a-m-e.

> Matt:      Oh—sesame!
>
> Xiaochi:  Yes, seasum.

Of course, how is the guy going to know how to pronounce an absurd English word like sesame?

If only he had attended my seventh grade English class. My teacher was very strict about spelling and pronunciation. For example, she posted a banner above the blackboard that read "Neither leisured foreigner seized their weird heights"—all violations of the "i-before-e, except-after-c" rule. And other than "their," each also violates the rule's extension "or when sounded like 'a' as in neighbor and weigh."

Sesame. What a bizarre word. I'd recommend the alternative, except the Gullah-based word, "benne," is pronounced like "Benny." Not much help there.

I grew up in Ohio, so I'm pretty familiar with different crops. But two were a mystery: Xiaochi's "seasum" and some droopy-eared wheat-like plant. "Seasum" actually turns out to be sorghum, not sesame. Sorghum grows tall stalks, a little like corn. There were lots of corn fields around too. If the valleys hadn't been ringed by mountains, it would have felt like Ohio.

Sorghum and corn are both grasses, so it's maybe not surprising they resemble each other. But unlike corn, with its straggly tassel of flowers, sorghum forms brown clusters of seeds, tightly bunched at the top of the stalk. Sorghum also has the lovely tendency to accumulate (hydrogen) cyanide when it is water stressed. Cattle have died from eating too much sorghum. And, let's not let good enough alone, it can also accumulate toxic levels of nitrate. Lovely little plant . . .

Besides making it into noodles, people in this area of China ferment sorghum and distill it to make clear liquor, called baijiu, which we drank at every dinner. I guess when you're traveling in sorghum country, you drink baijiu. Kind of like drinking bourbon in Kentucky. Or champagne in France. Or gin in the bathtub.

Fortunately, sorghum liquors have harmlessly low levels of cyanide. Drinking a lot of baijiu might poison you, but not from the cyanide.

The droopy-eared plant turns out to be millet. Millet is also a grass, so I suppose that's why it looks like wheat. I hardly ever see millet in US stores or restaurants, but it's common here. We had it in some form with practically every meal.

In the field, we also encountered "sea buckthorn." Yeah, I had never heard of this thing before either, but we drank sea buckthorn juice at lunch one day. The shrubs grow about 10 feet (3 meters) tall and bear small orange fruits, mostly filled with big seeds. How producers manage to extract sufficient juice from such thin pulp impresses me. They taste a little like apricots. Same color, too. The fruits form right up against the branches, and can cover them like orange bubbles.

We also encountered a couple people hunting mushrooms. The field area in Hebei Province (between Beijing and Inner Mongolia) must be a mycologist's Mecca. Or a chef's Mecca, anyway. The sidewalks in the town of Womakeng, where we ate lunch, were covered in drying mushrooms. Of course, lunch that day included mushrooms.

I've heard that mushrooms are the closest that vegetables come to making meat. [Yes, I know mushrooms are fungi, not plants, but they're still considered "vegetables."] I believe it, at least for these mushrooms. The stuff we get in the US doesn't really resemble meat in either taste or texture, but at first glance I thought the mound of slightly purplish mushrooms on our plate was liver. They had much better texture, though (like tender meat). And they tasted better than liver, too. I suppose if I drank enough baijiu, I'd probably think they *were* meat. On the other hand, with the kick that baijiu packs, it wouldn't be too hard to convince me of just about anything.

**MOUND OF COOKED MUSHROOMS**

**DRYING MUSHROOMS IN WOMAKENG**

**FIELD TRIP PARTICIPANTS IN INNER MONGOLIA**

# NO, NO, AFTER YOU!

Chinese people can be exceedingly polite. And when I say "exceedingly," I mean yes, it's charming, but to an American (well, this American) it can be so polite it feels a little uncomfortable. Take, for example, the group dinners.

Some of these are huge affairs, almost twenty people, all seated around a large circular table. In the middle is a motorized lazy Susan, slowly rotating clockwise. All the different components of the meal [pitcher of hot water or tea, other drinks, fish dish, shellfish dish, beef, pork, unidentifiable vegetable number one, unidentifiable vegetable number two, second type of pork, seafood soup, mutton stew, fried pork pancake, and (seriously) seven or eight other different dishes] drift past at a sufficient dawdle that you can grab something with your chopsticks and pop it in your mouth before the next dish slowly drifts by. Assuming you're proficient with chopsticks.

The politeness arrives with the toasts that involve minute glasses of baijiu. There is a group toast at the beginning, and a concluding toast (or acknowledgement that we're done) at the end. In the middle, though, are the awkward toasts. It's here that members of the group get up out of their seats, spend several minutes in view of everyone else, hiking around the vast expanse of table to approach the guest of honor (me). Once they arrive, they say how honored they are to be allowed into the presence of such an illustrious individual. Oh, if only I would clink my glass with theirs, stare deeply and meaningfully into their eyes, and take a sip of whatever is in my glass, their lives will be complete. Now, they can die peacefully, preferably right there at my feet or (second-best option) perhaps later that night. Oh, and the rim of their glass has to be lower than the rim of my glass.

OK, it's not that intense, and actually it's a sweet gesture. But it does feel a little awkward.

Take the students on our last field trip. Most came up in small groups (safety in numbers) and said how they appreciated that I came to China and on their field trip. But one small group of guys came up and thanked me for all they had learned from me. Really? I had spoken maybe three times during the whole field trip, and mostly it boiled down to "Wow, these are really interesting rocks. I don't know anything about them, but I sure do appreciate being allowed to participate!"

What did they learn from me? Probably not science. Maybe it was humility. I didn't have much to be proud of on that trip, that's for sure. The students knew more than I did. I'm sure I demonstrated my comfort with ignorance multiple times.

Or maybe they learned about laughing. I was so happy to be outside and looking at rocks again. First time since the pandemic . . .

As I think of it, I would be proud to teach them that lesson—that science is a joy, and we should appreciate every moment, especially when we can spend those moments with other scientists. I hope they learned that from me.

I'll drink to that!

A TOAST WITH HUIXIA'S FATHER. THE TWO-HANDED CUP-HOLD IS NORMAL. BUT, WHILE HIS EYES WERE TURNED TO HUIXIA'S HUSBAND (WHO IS TAKING THE PICTURE), I SNEAKILY ENSURED THE RIM OF MY GLASS WAS AT THE SAME LEVEL AS HIS. ANOTHER DEPARTURE FROM TRADITION, WE'RE NOT LOOKING LONGINGLY INTO EACH OTHER'S EYES. USUALLY SOMEONE ISN'T LAUGHING IN THE BACKGROUND EITHER.

# OCTOBER

# STINKO GINKGO

Many of us are familiar with the ginkgo tree (*Ginkgo biloba*), with its characteristic fan-shaped leaves that turn bright yellow in the autumn. There are lots of ginkgo trees here at the Institute, and since it was the beginning of October, they were starting to turn their characteristic golden yellow.

Ginkgos are interesting trees, geologically, because leaves nearly identical to today's modern species go back 170 million years. That's a long time, even for geologists. Knowing where ginkgos can grow today (temperature, precipitation, etc.), we can learn about past environmental conditions, all the way back into the Jurassic.

Ginkgos are additionally important because, like all land plants, they have little holes on the surfaces of their leaves that allow carbon dioxide inside for photosynthesis. The holes are called stomata (an individual pore is called a stoma). I once confused stomata with stigmata. Don't do that. Stigmata are holes, too, but they don't occur naturally—the Romans added them to Christ's wrists, feet, and side. They let blood out, not carbon dioxide in.

The density of the ginkgo leaf's stomata broadly correlates with the concentration of atmospheric carbon dioxide. Some fossil ginkgo leaves are so well preserved, you can count the numbers of stomata and estimate past concentrations of atmospheric carbon dioxide. Think about it, you can actually see individual cells on the surfaces of fossil leaves, and use them to learn something about atmospheric chemistry. How cool is that?!

These fossil ginkgo leaves are one way geologists know what's normal for carbon dioxide and what isn't. I work in paleoclimatology, so at this point I'm required to digress and tell you that today's levels of carbon dioxide are not normal. But that's another story for another day. Let's get back to ginkgos.

Like humans, an individual ginkgo is either a male (produces pollen) or a female (produces fruit). The technical term is "dioecious." As an ornamental tree, nearly all ginkgos in parks and gardens are male. That's because the fruit smells like dog shit. OK, yes, you'll find less graphic descriptions of the smell, such as "pungent," or "like ripe camembert cheese or rancid butter." Yeah, right. I know what those things smell like, and ginkgo is *much* more fragrant and *much* less appealing. No, whenever I walk within ten meters (thirty feet) of a female ginkgo tree, I start checking the bottoms of my shoes. Whew!

Anyway, I learned this week that Chinese people eat the fruit of the ginkgo. Seriously. A postdoc here told me that cooking kills the stink.

I looked this up, and actually it's the nut of the ginkgo tree that is consumed, rather than the fruit. Heating does drive off the smell. But remember how I said that people in many parts of the world will eat basically anything that has nutritional value, doesn't carry diseases, and isn't poisonous or protected? Ginkgo definitely pushes the boundary.

Besides the fact that the seed contains cyanide (hey, so do almonds), the outer coating of the ginkgo seed contains a compound that can cause Stevens-Johnson syndrome. Stevens-Johnson produces severe skin blisters and rash, far exceeding even poison ivy or poison oak. Actually, it's called Stevens-Johnson only if blistering and rashes affect less than 10 percent of your body surface. If more than 30 percent of your body is affected, it's called toxic epidermal necrosis ("life-threatening skin death"). I don't think I'm likely to start harvesting ginkgo fruit here or anywhere else.

And the fun doesn't end there—even after cooking, eating the nuts destroys essential vitamin B6 in your body. Why care? Well, your brain and immune system need B6 to function properly. So, don't eat too many ginkgo nuts, or you'll catch some disease (maybe Stevens-Johnson) and be too stupid to do anything about it. In fact, children are advised to avoid ginkgo nuts altogether.

Who figured out you could eat this stuff, anyway? Was it the same visonary who figured out that peeing into a vat of indigo catalyzes the dye-making process. If not, it must have been someone equally desperate.

Yeah, I'm interested in trying out different experiences here in China. But I'll pass on the ginkgo. At least for now.

**GINKGO LEAVES**

**GINKGO FRUIT—LOOKS LIKE CHERRIES BUT . . .**

# PAWPAW AND PAPAYA

I have carefully stocked two books in my office at Boise State, just in case I'm on the phone or temporarily occupied with something, so students have something to read while they're waiting.

The larger book is a parody of junior-high science textbooks and is titled *Science Made Stupid: How to Discomprehend the World Around Us* (Tom Weller, 1985). A vertebrate paleontologist named Eric Scott, who has a good sense of humor, recommended it to me. The cover shows a flaming meteor smacking a T. rex on the back of the head, a hairy caveman playing tic-tac-toe solitaire (X is about to lose to O—how can you lose to yourself?), and a ball-and-stick model of a molecule, labeled "Acme," no doubt in reference to the *Looney Tunes'* Wile E. Coyote and Road Runner series.

Inside, the text provides invaluable (mis)information, such as how to build a nuclear reactor in a garbage can to heat your hot tub, various (non)elements of the periodic table (chlorox, irony, pandemonium . . .), and the general structure of the Earth—a light flaky outer crust and an inner dense filling, which is further divided into the mantle (toward the outside) and a hot fireplace underneath it. For a scientist, there's just enough science to be recognizable. And hilarious. The book is out of print, but it's still possible to find copies.

In 1986, *Science Made Stupid* won the Hugo award for a nonfiction book related to science fiction or fantasy. Obviously, the judges took a *broad* view on what constituted "nonfiction" that year.

The smaller book on my desk is a charming set of poems and woodcuts, first published in 1907, titled *How to Tell the Birds from the Flowers, and Other Wood-cuts: A Revised Manual of Flornithology for Beginners* by Robert W. Wood. The author was a well-known physicist who investigated the physics of the propagation of sound and light waves, and his book prompted a review in the journal *Nature*. That's pretty impressive because *Nature* is one of the two leading journals in science. The other journal bears the stunningly creative title: *Science*.

I reproduce one of Wood's verses below, so you can get a sense of his wit.

## TITLE: THE CLOVER. THE PLOVER.

> The Plover and the Clover can be told apart with ease,
> By paying close attention to the habits of the Bees,
> For En-to-molo-gists aver, the Bee can be in Clover,
> While Ety-molo-gists concur, there is no "B" in Plover.

The woodcut of the plover plausibly depicts a bird with a black head, black bill, and round feathery body, standing on one leg. The woodcut of the clover mimics the plover, such that the single leg becomes a stalk, the round body becomes the clover blossom, and the black head and bill become a bumblebee with black antenna.

Actually, scientists long ago noticed that some plants closely resemble animals. This gave rise to the "doctrine of signatures," or belief that these resemblances weren't coincidences, they represented some innate characteristic. If interpreted correctly, such plants could provide special power to the user, usually as medicines. So, for example, parts of the palma Christi plant ("hand of Christ," aka castor-oil plant, *Ricinus communis*), were supposed to help your joints, while the root of the aconite plant ("wolf's bane," genus *Aconitum*), which somewhat resembles a scorpion's tail, was supposed to alleviate effects of scorpion stings. Both these plants are highly poisonous (the castor-oil plant is the source of the poison ricin, while *Aconitum* is also known as queen of poisons), which makes me wonder: was it considered a success if a medieval doctor killed his patient with castor bean extract? The patient's joints sure wouldn't hurt anymore.

The doctrine of signatures applied to minerals too. Powdered hematite (iron oxide) is bloodred (geologists would say it has "red streak") and was supposed to be good for treating problems with your blood and liver. Amethyst (purple quartz) was supposed to prevent drunkenness. In fact, the root words for both these minerals come from Greek: "hema" means blood and "methys" means "drunken. Get it?—if "atypical" mean's "not typical," "amethys" means "not drunk."

Beliefs linger on in names.

I suppose crystal healing may be a modern form of the doctrine of signatures.

Dr. Wood's *How to Tell* . . . reminds me that I once had a student who was extremely talented in drawing. I pitched a new book to her on minerals, patterned after Wood's. Something like "How to tell minerals from everyday objects." I would write the poems. She would sketch the images. Examples might include:

Barrel and beryl.

Olive and olivine.

Horn and hornblende.

Nephew and nepheline.

There's no shortage of possibilities.

Scapula and scapolite.

Serpent and serpentine.

George and georgeite.

See what I mean? Anyway, we never got our act together. But I always wanted to work on it.

In truth, I've written several Earth-science-centric poems, including one song about my PhD research (*Ballad of Cordillera Darwin*), a few haikus to encourage proposals for science sessions at meetings, and a biography in verse. None would rank up there with old Dr. Wood. But we can all dream, right?

*How to Tell the Birds from the Flowers* also reminds me that, in both China and the US, there are two edible fruits with extremely similar names, the pawpaw (*Asimina triloba*) and the papaya (*Carica papaya*). In fact, both use the same Chinese characters, even though they're completely different fruits. Not to confuse things even further, but papaya is sometimes called pawpaw. Although papaya has several variants, all produce a similar, large fruit with dense flesh and a huge pile of seeds in the middle. It's pretty easy to find dried papaya in grocery stores in America, usually sort of pink-orange in color.

The pawpaw is something altogether different. Native to eastern North America, it produces smaller, flattish fruits (almost like a small mango in shape), with gooey yellow flesh and dispersed seeds. The flavor is described as a cross among banana, pineapple, and peach.

I had eaten papaya before coming to China, both fresh in India and preserved in America. But I had never tried pawpaw, despite living in the southeastern US for quite a few years, both as a child and later as an adult. So, I thought I should compare them here.

Papaya is easy to find at the grocery store, so I thought to remind myself of what it tastes like. Easy peasy—I bought a big one for a buck or two, brought it back to my apartment, and let it ripen for a couple days.

OK, now what is it with fruit flies? I didn't have any before I bought that papaya, and they weren't flying around in the store. Now I have half a dozen. Do they lurk in dark corridors, smoking gnat-sized cigarettes, waiting for a hapless American sap to bring home fragrant fruit? Were baby flies somehow hiding in the packaging? Was Aristotle right, and they generate spontaneously from inanimate matter? And why are such tiny flies so hard to swat, and why do they have such gigantic chromosomes? Bizarre little creatures.

Sorry, where was I? Oh, what did it taste like?

Well, thinking carefully as I ate it, the texture reminded me of ripe melon, only less grainy, and it tasted a bit like cantaloupe, too, but with the slightest hint of acidity. Maybe a little like cantaloupe with a twist of peach. A little dull, frankly. If I had had a lemon, a good squeeze would have done the papaya good. Or some salt.

Now, what about pawpaw?

Alas, no luck so far! My friends are scouring the larger stores and online for any sources. But, even though I did see one at the Summer Palace in late August (oh, why didn't we grab it?), I'm not positive it's in season. The problem, of course, is that the name is the same as for papaya, but the fruit is much smaller. Can you imagine if Xiaochi ordered a half-dozen pawpaws online, and I ended up with a half-dozen cantaloupe-sized papayas?

My apartment would become fruit fly central!

# RAIN, RAIN, GO AWAY

I've been in China over two months, and I swear I can remember only three days that it definitely didn't rain:

The day we visited the Forbidden City in late August.

The first day of our geological field excursion in mid-September.

Last Friday, October 1 (the national holiday).

Otherwise, it seems like every day has been at least a little drizzly. It has certainly always been cloudy.

All these clouds—am I suffering from vitamin D deficiency again? It happens every winter in Boise. Regardless, I'm looking forward to the next few days, when the forecast calls for sun! Or, at least, only partly-cloudy skies.

Popular reports in China say this year has had the most rain since 1959. Back on July 20 (the day I arrived!), over twenty-five inches of rain (almost 650 millimeters) fell in a single twenty-four-hour period in the city of Zhengzhou, the capital of Henan Province, in central China. Almost eight inches (a little over two hundred millimeters) fell in a single hour. That's like eight months of Boise's precipitation condensed (pun intended) into an hour, or two normal years into a day. It was reported as the heaviest rainfall in one thousand years.

I saw the impacts up close because, during the national holiday, a postdoctoral scholar here, named Lishuang, went home to help harvest corn on the family farm. They also live in Henan Province, and she sent me a video of the fields.

Now, I grew up in corn country, and I've seen wet years in the US, when fields were so deep in mud, many farmers couldn't drive their tractors. That was a disaster.

The fields in Henan, China, are beyond anything I've ever seen. But they're not muddy. They're lakes. And when I say "lakes" I mean the video shows one of Lishuang's in-laws, wading through a flooded field in fishing waders, piling ears of corn into a washtub. She floats the washtub over to a high point, where the corn is off-loaded onto a cart. It's slow, and tedious, and heartbreaking to watch, at least for someone who knows the efficiency of machine harvesting and what a full day of hand labor feels like. On the other hand, the persistence of humans in the face of disaster is inspiring.

The popular reference to 1959, though, is a little chilling. Now that was a disaster my mind can't quite comprehend. Called the "Great Chinese Famine," the number of people who starved between 1958 and 1962 is estimated at around thirty million. Although China first blamed the famine on an unlucky combination of drought and flooding, they later admitted that it was mostly bad government policy. The government imposed drastic changes to farming practices, and people were encouraged to kill sparrows, which they were told would eat their grain. Sparrows do eat grain, but they also eat insect pests. So, when people killed the birds, the insect population boomed, helping to deplete the already ailing fields.

I could find only two events in the history of human-induced tragedies that exceed the sheer carnage of the Great Chinese Famine. World War II killed about seventy-five million people, and the Native American genocide may have killed one hundred million people. True, a large proportion of Native Americans died from disease, which spread without direct contact, and the "event" stretched over several hundred years, not four or five. But, fast or slow, directly or indirectly, western European occupation killed something like 90 percent of Native Americans—many times deadlier than the Black Death.

Of course, many other countries have adopted deadly policies, either intentionally or by mistake. Besides all the deliberate acts in history, like genocides (Armenians, Ukrainians, Jews, Cambodians, Rwandans, Chinese in Nanjing . . .), and wartime airstrikes (Hiroshima, Nagasaki, Dresden . . .), Great Britain's mismanagement of India killed about eight million people between 1876 and 1878. The myth that "rain follows the plow," promoted by American officials (and hucksters) in the late 1800s helped contribute to the misery and ecological disaster of America's Dust Bowl in the 1930s. I suppose all big countries eventually make big mistakes.

Ironically, the myth about rain and the plow has a little bit of truth to it. Not in the sense that Charles Dana Wilber meant in his 1881 book *The Great Valleys and Prairies of Nebraska and the Northwest.* He claimed that increased crops would induce precipitation on a continental scale by lowering temperature. True, plants are very good at evaporating water, and evaporation consumes heat. So, vegetated areas do tend to be a little cooler during the day than unvegetated areas, at least in the lower forty-eight states. But a hypothetical cornfield can't survive if the plants need an extra liter of water from the soil (relative to what's available), but lower temperatures induce only half a liter of precipitation. The water cycle has to balance on a regional scale—gaining water in one area means losing it somewhere else, so planting crops doesn't increase net precipitation regionally.

But Wilbur was correct that precipitation had gradually increased during settlement of the Great Plains. As the "plow" moved west, precipitation increased.

The problem is that correlation doesn't imply causation.

Take, for example, global temperature and piracy: both have increased over the last fifty years. So, what, do pirates cause global warming? Do higher temperatures increase pirate fertility? Sure, the social, political, and economic impacts of global warming and climate change could influence piracy—that's worth thinking about. But temperatures in the Arctic are increasing faster than almost anywhere on Earth. Should we start calling up our Air Force buddies in Point Barrow, Alaska? "Hey Dana, better keep a lookout for ol' Cap'n Jack Sparrow (or Johnny Depp, or both), I hear he may come swingin' in off some yardarm and steal your cutlasses." I don't think so.

Or, if pirates aren't your thing, here's another: between 1998 and 2003, the Dow-Jones Industrial Average rose and fell in sync with the Wolf Sunspot Cycle.

Does one cause the other?

No.

Scientists disproved any correlation between economic cycles and sunspots long ago (even though you can still find advocates on the internet). It's simply a fact of probability that any two things that have oscillations of similar duration are going to line up sometime. That's what happened around Y2K with the Dow Jones and sunspots. It doesn't mean that one causes the other.

No, Wilber, and Gilpin (Governor of Colorado), and Hayden (US Geological Survey), and other American influencers of the 1870s and 1880s simply fell into the correlation-causation trap. Their mistake didn't matter much at the time because precipitation trended upward for a while. But fifty years later, when precipitation trended downward, the idea that "rain follows the plow" killed people in Kansas, Colorado, Oklahoma, and elsewhere. Another 2.5 million moved away.

An especially sad part to the Dust Bowl tragedy is that one of the world's largest sources of fresh water—the Ogallala Aquifer—lies just below the worst-hit areas. But the Ogallala wouldn't become a major source of water for the region until after World War II. Too late.

So, were there really droughts and floods in central China around 1958 to 1962 that triggered the famine? Was rainfall super high in 1959, as implied by at least one popular report? Or am I hearing echoes of long-dead politicians who wanted to blame the famine on nature, just like some people still want to correlate beef futures with sunspots?

Here's what I've found:

On the one hand, there's no question that rainfall in 1958 was high, and the Yellow River flood of 1958 was serious. Nineteen fifty-nine was a wetter than average year too. Nineteen sixty was drier than average. That does support a climate effect.

On the other hand, none of those years appears that extraordinary in terms of yearly averages or extreme events. If anything, 1964 looks like it was a killer year for precipitation—possibly the highest in the region until now.

Now that I think about it, nineteen sixty-four was the year I was born, and I arrived in China on the day of the heaviest rainfall in one thousand years. And it hasn't stopped raining since I've been here.

Hmm . . . China might not be so sorry to see me go. Except the mushroom farmers in Hebei. They might miss me.

# MUSINGS ON MUSEUMS

One day, Xiaochi and I visited the Geological Museum of China, in Beijing. How cool is that? China actually has a national museum devoted specifically to geology! Most other countries don't bother. They put their rocks, minerals, and fossils in more general museums (usually museums of "natural history"). You have to squeeze past the emerald boas and diamond-back rattlesnakes to get to the real emeralds and diamonds.

And while China's Geological Museum doesn't rank with major museums, they have some nice stuff. Plus, it's just down the road from the Institute, so it's easy to get to.

Oh my, it was crowded, though! It was a holiday, so maybe that's not so surprising. But it's nice to know that people in China value geology.

I think all museums should have a wow! factor, and a few of the exhibits at the Geological Museum definitely deliver. I'll get to fossils later, but gems include carved tourmaline seals (although who would want to seal a document with one of these beauties?), aquamarine (beryl) crystals that are appropriately water-clear, large chunks of rose quartz carved into lion statues, a carved bas relief made out of lapis, a wall of azurite, and gigantic carved green serpentine.

I confess, though, I don't quite understand the layout of the exhibits. Yes, the gems are in one area, rocks/minerals in another, and fossils on the floor upstairs.

That makes sense. But what rhyme or reason (or curator) organized some of these gems together? One gem case has brown and white scheelite from China, yellow danburite from Tanzania, blue tanzanite from Tanzania, and varicolored fluorite (but I don't remember the locality).

It's a pretty exhibit, and that tanzanite is spectacular. But, it's a geologic dog's breakfast—the colors don't coordinate, the minerals belong to wholly different groups (tungstates, salts, and silicates), and the causes of the colors are totally different (for example, charge-transfer in tanzanite, defects in fluorite).

I guess I expected the curators to sneak in a little more education on the sly. Maybe something like, "Why do minerals have colors?" with examples of how the same principles form color in several minerals. Or, "What processes form metamorphic rocks?" with progressions of rock types in different settings. China has some spectacularly beautiful metamorphic rocks, but they didn't appear here, or in a logical sequence. I can't remember how the Smithsonian and other museums arrange Earth materials, but I think there's more logic to the organization.

The fossils collection? Quite the experience, in more ways than one. China has some eye-popping, jaw-dropping fossil localities, for example the Precambrian Doushantuo Formation, the Cambrian Maotianshan Shale, the Jurassic Yixian Formation (Jehol biota), etc. These all represent sedimentary deposits with extraordinary fossil preservation. There's a technical term for this, "Lagerstätte," which is a German word that, roughly translated, means "sedimentary deposits with extraordinary fossil preservation."

OK, not really. Actually, Lagerstätte means "storage place." For example, lager beer is beer designed for storing. But, hey you Germans, what useful information does the term "storage place" convey? All sedimentary rocks store stuff. Aren't they all Lagerstätten?

Anyway, the three localities I listed for China aren't just Lagerstätten, they're "Konservat Lagerstätten." That means their fossils are extraordinarily well-preserved (conserved). The incredible preservation reveals some incredible details about extinct animals.

For example, the Jehol biota includes *Confuciusornis* and numerous other early birds, along with dinosaurs and many other animals. Preservation includes delicate beaks, bones, feathers on birds, feathers on dinosaurs, and even color organelles. One fossilized bird occurs with its fossilized egg. These extraordinarily well-preserved fossils allow us to answer some pretty basic questions that you wouldn't think we could even try to answer. Take, for example, *Confuciusornis*.

Could it fly? Yes. It had the correct bone and muscle structure, in addition to correctly shaped and distributed feathers. What scientists discuss now isn't whether it could fly, but how well it could engage in flapping flight rather than soaring flight.

What color was it? Gray, red/brown, and black. Yes, really, you can tell that.

Who ate it? *Sinocalliopteryx*, for one. How do we know? Bird fossils in its stomach.

That *Sinocalliopteryx* is an interesting critter too. It was a compsognathid ("elegant-jawed") dinosaur that stood upright and sported fluffy feathers. Good for insulation, not for flight. Back in the late 1860s, when Thomas Henry Huxley was intellectually bludgeoning other scientists about the importance of Darwin's Law (the Theory of Evolution), he argued that compsognathids could have evolved into modern birds via early intermediary "lizard-birds" like the famous *Archaeopteryx* (preserved in another Konservat Lagerstätte: the Solnhofen Limestone). He was basically correct that birds did evolve from dinosaurs, although it took over a century of research to demonstrate that definitively. In fact, it was the opening up of research on fossils from the Jehol biota in the 1990s that convinced the skeptics. He was also right in proposing that compsognathids might have had feathers. Once again, the Jehol fossils show that.

I guess being related doesn't always keep you from eating one another, though. *Sinocalliopteryx* didn't just eat its distant bird relatives, it also ate other feathery dinosaurs, like *Sinornithosaurus*.

I don't feel so sorry about that, though, because *Sinornithosaurus* was related to the nasty velociraptors in Jurassic Park. We all know they ate humans. If you can believe Hollywood.

Anyway, with all these Lagerstätten in China, I thought the museum would have some pretty spectacular fossils on display. True enough.

They have several slabs with *Confuciusornis*, the famous "Dave" (a *Sinornithosaurus*), various frogs and bugs, a Cambrian shrimp-like critter that preserves the oldest cardiovascular system, and many other incredibly well-preserved fossils. Really spectacular stuff!

But what astonished me most wasn't just that you could see spectacular fossils. No, some of these you could touch. These fossils were all bigger and more robust, not the delicate or super-important ones. But I never thought I would ever run my hands over a slab of exquisitely-preserved 450-million-year-old sea lilies, or determine directly whether my head could fit in the jaws of an ichthyosaur. That truly distinguishes a Chinese museum from an American museum. And it must inspire young geologists, too. Even if it is a little hard on the fossils.

Maybe that's why China has so many geologists, whereas the American Geosciences Institute is projecting a US workforce shortage of more than one hundred thousand (out of approximately three hundred fifty thousand) in five years.

Isn't it Lehman Caves (Great Basin National Park) in Nevada that has a "sacrificial" stalagmite for people to touch before entering? That way they're less likely to touch the preserved ones. Touch is important, and maybe American museums should try to provide more opportunities. After the pandemic . . .

**SEALS MADE OUT OF TOURMALINE**

**LIONS CARVED FROM ROSE QUARTZ. THEIR HEADS ARE THE SIZE OF VERY LARGE ORANGES.**

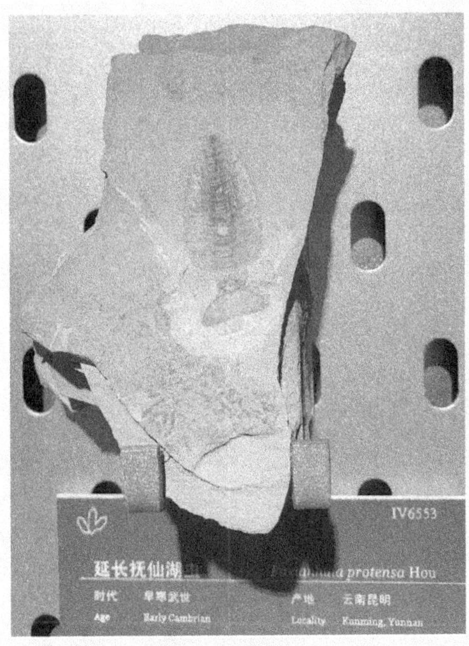

**CAMBRIAN "SHRIMP" (*FUXIANHUIA*)**

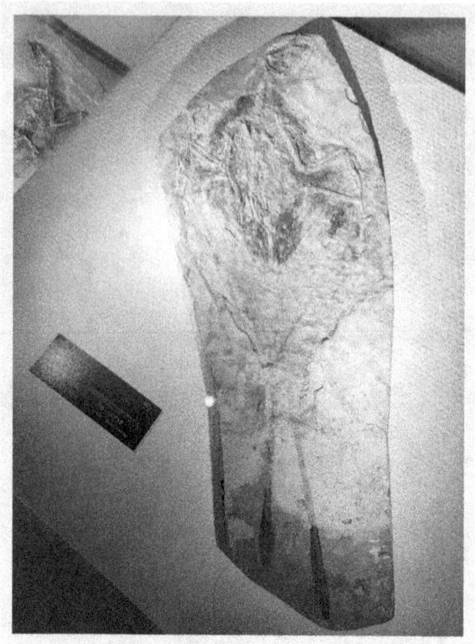

**CONFUCIUSORNIS (AN EARLY BIRD)
PROBABLY IT CAUGHT WORMS**

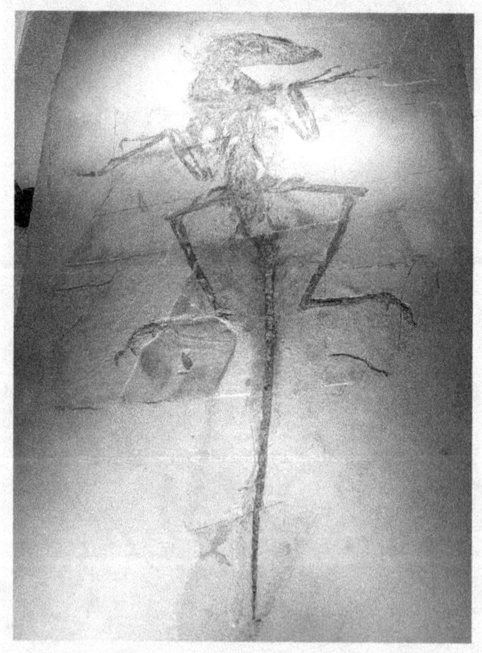

**SINORNITHOSAURUS**

**YOU CAN GET UP CLOSE AND PERSONAL
WITH THESE AMMONITES**

# EVERYBODY WANTS BARBECUE!

One of my favorite bands is Mumbo Gumbo, based in Sacramento, California. They played at the wedding of my friends Dan Orange and Bonnie Holmer, and I attended a couple of their gigs with Heather when I was a postdoc. We still play their music on road trips. One of their earlier songs, "Barbeque," celebrates folks getting together for a cookout party.

> Hey, open the gate
>
> Come on through
>
> Everybody wants barbeque.

Now, we do a fair bit of grilling in the summertime in Boise (it's too hot to cook in the kitchen). So, when offered dinner options at a gigantic mall near Olympic Park, I passed over the KFC, Subway, hot pot, noodles, and three fish restaurants, and opted for barbecue. And discovered that Chinese barbecue is not quite like American.

Here's how it works. You sit at a small table for four. An electric heating coil is recessed below the surface, with a dome-shaped steel mesh (or grid) above it. You order whatever you want to grill, and after the heating element has warmed up, you put the food on the grid and grill it yourself. Yes, that's right, you do the cooking.

We ended up buying many different things to grill, including chicken, a couple kinds of steak, shrimp, a couple kinds of pork, mushrooms, thinly-sliced potatoes, and dough. Yes, dough. I think my presence made it more of an experiment in grilling—hey, let's try this!—rather than a normal meal with fewer options. Naturally, the quality of the cooking depends on your skills as a cook (or the skills of your companions).

Once you've cooked something, you dip it into a powdery topping (two varieties: one very spicy, one moderately spicy), and/or a thick (peanut?) sauce, and/or vinegar, maybe add a little cauliflower or carrot for crunchiness, and pile it into a large lettuce leaf. The lettuce acts like a wrap, and you eat it that way. Sort of like southeast Asian spinach-leaf wraps. Or Pacific betel nut. Of course, you don't have to use the lettuce, but fresh vegetable options are limited. I advise letting the meat cool a little before flavoring, wrapping, and eating, otherwise you burn your fingers.

Is it barbecue? Speaking as an American, a barbecue restaurant for me implies grilled (usually smoked) meat and some kind of barbecue sauce. But there are lots of different sauces that might qualify for barbecue. I lived in the southern US for many years, and although I'm definitely no authority on barbecue, I'm at least modestly familiar with different sauces.

For example, in South Carolina, there are three types: white (vinegar-based), yellow (mustard-based), and red (ketchup-based). Curiously, people's preferences for these types broadly parallel the state's soils: vinegar-based is found only along the coastal plain, where white sands dominate. Mustard-based is traditional inland (the Piedmont), where the soils are yellow. Ketchup-based prevails towards the Appalachians (the mountain range that runs along the eastern US), where rocks weather red.

Actually, there are barely any mountains in South Carolina. So, we should probably call it the Appalachian (singular) there, rather than the Appalachians (plural). In Scandinavia, the geologist's joke is that Norway and Sweden split the Caledonides (another mountain range), while Finland has a Caledonide.

We lived on the edge of the Piedmont in South Carolina, and I grew to prefer mustard-based barbecue. I suppose every place imprints itself on you in ways you never anticipate.

Nothing like any of these sauces was at the restaurant, though, and the meat wasn't smoked. So, an American like me might not refer to the Chinese version as barbecue, rather as grilling. Maybe the powdery topping could qualify as barbecue-encrusted grilling.

But why be so parochial? In Australia, the grill itself is generically called a barbie (short for barbecue), so any kind of grilling is barbecue. And Australia's a hell of a lot closer to China than the US.

Barbecue it is!

The staff at the restaurant doesn't quite leave you to your own barbecuing or grilling devices, though. Periodically, someone wanders by, puts all the stuff you're grilling into a bowl, replaces the grid, and dumps your food back on. Trust me, though, they do this only to prevent sticking and charring (this is not asado). Food safety and health don't enter this equation, and no one will check whether you're cooking your pork or chicken thoroughly. We were careful, but regardless, we didn't sterilize the tongs between picking up raw meat and removing materials that were already cooked. Trichinosis is rare these days, but if the chicken has campylobacter or salmonella bacteria, there's some slight chance you'll get food poisoning.

Then again, I contracted food poisoning twice off a particular brand of bottled beer in South Carolina, as well as from Nepalese food in Texas. You always take a chance.

Anyway, I think it's worth the slight risk. The food is some of the best I've had, even for a restaurant from a mall food court.

I can't exactly rave about the grilled dough, though. Shaped like little pillows, the yellowish outside was dry, tough, and nearly flavorless, while the inside was gooey with even less flavor, and a consistency similar to pudding (and lots of other, less pleasant things). Grilling browns the outside, and heats the inside goo to scalding. On a scale of "comforting" to "terrifying," I would rate the hot gooey surprise as "threatening." A little bombshell in every bite.

You definitely want to let those pillows cool a bit first before eating. And you'll wait awhile because dough has high heat capacity, and atmospheric convection doesn't cool solids (or other viscous substances) very effectively.

So, would I go again? Absolutely! Maybe not for the dough, but definitely for everything else. I might even fire up the music app on my phone to play some Mumbo Gumbo while we're eating.

**BARBECUE SETUP. ALL THE STUFF TO COOK IS AT THE TOP OF THE PICTURE. THE GRILL IS THE CIRCLE IN THE MIDDLE AND LOWER RIGHT. THERE'S AN ELECTRIC HEATING COIL BELOW THE COOKING GRID. THIS PICTURE SHOWS AN ASSORTMENT OF CHICKEN, STEAK, SHRIMP, BEEF, AND TWO TYPES OF PORK. THE LITTLE BOWLS CONTAIN SAUCES AND COATINGS. THERE'S ALSO LETTUCE FOR MAKING WRAPS, OFFSCREEN.**

# HITTING THE WALL

After many delays, Huixia and I hit the Great Wall on an ideal day—after the national holiday (relatively few visitors), on a beautiful sunny day (what a miracle), and before any ice or snow.

We did struggle a bit the week before, deciding where to go. At least a half-dozen sections of the Great Wall are accessible from Beijing. Most tour guides say "Go to Badaling." Badaling is super-well restored, has a variety of different attractions (causeways, guard towers, etc.), is easy to get to (direct train), and has handrails (good if field work and backpacking have damaged your knees).

On the other hand, my sister-in-law Heidi warned me that Badaling is also where sellers will mercilessly and tenaciously accost you with their junky wares, every step of the way between the train station and the wall. She knew I had forgotten my taser at home, so she recommended a different section, either Mutianyu or Jinshanling. Neither of those is quite so overrun.

Any of these places sounded great to me, but ultimately what decided us was time. For Mutianyu or Jinshanling, Huixia would need four-and-a-half hours of travel, *each way*. With an infant at home, she didn't want to inflict that much misery on her family. The regular train to Badaling takes only twenty minutes, and the express train is only fifteen. So, it was off to Badaling, hawkers and all.

I'll be honest, too, I was a little curious to see how aggressive the sellers might be. After all, I trained in Kathmandu, and those folks are serious professionals. It's a little-known fact, but before hitting the streets, sellers in Nepal and India must complete marketing degrees with a specialization in "persistent-aggravation-of-tourists-to-point-of-purchase-just-to-get-rid-of-you" and additionally receive certification in "how-to-judge-the-ideal-markup-of-cheap-goods-based-on-buyer's-clothing-and-apparent-nationality." Even then, bigger cities provide licenses only to those who score above 90 percent in both skills. And the local cops rough up any sellers who don't have the correct credentials. If you've traveled to Nepal and India, you may know the "how-to-judge . . ." certification by its more common name—the "Whitey Tax." This is the skin-color-based 50–200 percent markup on everything from bottled water and camping supplies to taxi service and hotel rooms that I so enjoy with every visit.

But would my training in Nepal and India protect me from the bloodthirsty Badaling sellers? I itched to find out.

First, though, we had to get there. Traveling by subway in Beijing at 9:00 a.m. was standing room only, but not as squashed as I thought it might be. Huixia planned it to avoid the real rush. There was a bit of a mix-up at our rendezvous point at the intersection of two subway lines, but ultimately we made it to the Badaling train with seven minutes to spare. It needed only a little running. Plus two health code scans and a passport scan. Of course.

After twenty minutes, we exited into glorious sunshine (at last!!) in the hills to the north of Beijing. The landscape reminded me of Colorado. Big granite cliffs poke out of pines and other trees. The vegetation is a little thicker, but it felt familiar. The main difference, though, between Badaling and places I'd visited in the Rockies was . . .any guesses?

Well, true, the ages of the granites are completely different—the Badaling Batholith (batholith equals ginormous intrusion) is ten times younger than the 1.4 billion year-old granites in the Rockies. But that's not the difference I was thinking about. Rather, it's this ginormous wall looming over everything.

Now, this thing isn't just tall, it's massive! You could drive a bus down the causeway at the top of it. If you had a bus that could handle stairs and sharp bends. Or if Sandra Bullock (heroine Annie in the movie *Speed*) were driving.

If it were up to me, though, I wouldn't call it The Great Wall. I'd call it something like "The Magnificently Behemothic Towering Wall of China that Dominates the Landscape from Here to the Horizon." That's probably why no one ever lets me name things.

Most of the wall is faced with large granite blocks, which also make up the guard towers. That makes sense. After all, the local bedrock is granite. The top of the wall is made of brick.

Now, when I read last week that parts of the Great Wall were made out of brick, I naively thought of bricks like we see in America. You know the type: little dinky "brick-red" blocks? The kind your parents combined with some spare boards to make bookcases? The kind your neighbor maliciously heaves at squirrels and skunks? The kind that fire stations are made out of so they don't burn down?

I didn't even recognize the Great Wall bricks as bricks until Huixia told me what they were. I thought they were quarried blocks of sandstone. Who the heck makes bricks this big? People in China, I guess. These slabs are several inches thick and 16" x 16" (40 cm x 40 cm) across. There must be millions of them in the wall. OK, I just looked it up—over three billion. In China, the color would be called "brick gray."

If China ever decides to dismantle a section of the wall, do you think it might consider repurposing the bricks as pizza stones? They're big enough. The cost of shipping might be prohibitive, though. Also, I question combining iconic Italian food with an iconic Chinese relic. They're not only different culturally, they're totally asynchronous, too. The Badaling section of the Great Wall was completed right around AD 1500, before more than a handful of Europeans even knew about tomatoes (native to South America), and at least a couple hundred years before Italians started squeezing them on pizzas.

Anyway, we trekked up and down these pizza stones along the north section of the Badaling Great Wall. Measuring via Google Earth, that section is only approximately two-and-a-half kilometers long (one-and-a-half miles). But it took us over two hours to walk it. There are so many interesting views to take in.

The stairs alone are fascinating. It finally dawned on me that of course the builders placed the pizza stones to ensure each step is the same width. They just made no attempt to normalize the pitch of the slope. So let me tell you, if you find the steps on the "Gaussian" bridges at the Summer Palace a little annoying (shallow pitch and dinky stairs at the bottom and top; steep pitch and tall stairs in the middle), you'll find the steps along the Great Wall absolutely maddening. Every little variation in hillslope is matched by differences in step height. You'll be tripping over one step that's a couple inches high, and two steps farther hauling yourself up some monster with the aid of a handrail. One spot was so steep and the stair steps so high, a few less steady folk used both hands and feet to crawl upslope. One woman, anticipating this, wore gloves.

I knew I should never have left my jetpack at home.

Why does the local slope matter to a builder when you're twenty-five feet (eight meters) up in the air? Why couldn't some sections be twenty-six feet tall, and all the steps be the same?

I guess someone really wanted a constant height. Perhaps some ancient military scholar calculated the ideal height of the wall by balancing the kinetic energy of a dropped boulder (higher is better, up to a point) versus energy expenditure against gravity (higher is worse), and published the result to the nearest tenth of an inch. Or perhaps the calculation was based on the fractional decrease in velocity versus distance through moist air at an average elevation of eight hundred meters and temperature of 25°C (77°F) for an arrow drawn by an archer of average height and strength. If some engineer went to that kind of computational trouble, I could perhaps understand why no one would want to deviate too far from their calculations. Engineers can be pretty persnickety.

Back at the wall, the granite seems pretty well-preserved, even after five hundred (or more) years of exposure, but some of the bricks are distinctly worn down, in some cases almost all the way through. Others are nearly constant thickness. Of course, the parks may have replaced some, but I wonder: did medieval China have "Friday bricks"? You know, workers were looking forward to partying all weekend, so their attention flagged during the week. The bricks they made on their "Friday" (whichever day of the week that actually was) weren't quite as robust? I kind of like the idea, but I don't know how to test it. I doubt the bricks are stamped with the day that they were molded or fired. And who knows? Maybe brickmaker Mary's bricks were always good, and brickmaker Marty's always sucked. Maybe I'm just noticing Marty's bricks.

And let's be serious. It took five hundred years to wear down these bricks. If someone stepped on me for five hundred years, I'd be pretty worn down too.

Until now, I had visited only small walls, so I thought I should read up on how other so-called "Great Walls" compare with the Great Wall of China. Short answer? No comparison. The Great Wall of China dwarfs them all in every way.

For example, the "Great Wall of Europe"—encircling the city of Ston, Croatia— is about seven kilometers long. For comparison, on Google Earth, the Great Wall at Badaling measures out at a little over eight kilometers long. But that's only the restored section in that one location. I could easily trace the Great Wall southwestward another thirty or forty kilometers on Google Earth. And all the sections of Great Wall over all time periods span more than twenty thousand kilometers, or enough to make a couple thousand Great Walls of Europe.

What about Hadrian's Wall? That's pretty big, right? I have a bit of Scottish ancestry, which gives me a passing interest in it. Not that it's in Scotland, or built by the Scots. Actually, it's in England and was built by the Romans. But it was meant to keep the Scots as far away from Rome as possible, so I think of it as "Scots-inspired." At a little over one hundred kilometers long, Hadrian's Wall still doesn't rank up there with the Great Wall of the Ming dynasty (which is what I visited), but it does begin to compare with the original continuous Great Wall of China—the Great Wall of Qi. True, construction on the Great Wall of Qi started five hundred years earlier (approximately 400 BC), and it's six times longer. But at least they're within an order of magnitude of the same length.

Otherwise, the Great Wall of Gorgan in Iran, at nearly two hundred kilometers long, twenty-five feet (eight meters) wide and twenty-five feet high, is closest in scale. Builders used similarly-sized bricks (10 x 40 x 40 centimeters) too. Did Persia and China have some ancient trade agreement in bricks? I don't think so, because Persian bricks are red, not gray. Still, even that underappreciated but spectacular wonder of the Near East is pretty small compared to the Great Wall.

Returning to Beijing from the Great Wall, we missed our normal train, and took the express train forty minutes later. So, the ride back took fifteen minutes, rather than twenty. There were relatively few commuters at 4:00 p.m. headed into the city, too, so the subway was easy. Spectacular day, all round.

But wait! What about the street sellers? How persistent were they?

We don't know. We never encountered any!

There are shops along the avenue from the exit point on the Great Wall's north section toward town. And the salespeople there were pretty loud. But everything is loud in China. In the train station, the echoes of the announcements drown out the actual announcements. So, I never got to test my Kathmandu field shopping skills. At least, not this day. I guess I didn't need my taser after all. But a jetpack, now . . .

**UP AND DOWN AND UP AND DOWN. BAD-GUY SIDE ON THE RIGHT. GOOD-GUY SIDE ON THE LEFT.**

**THANK GOODNESS FOR HAND RAILS!**

**HUIXIA ISN'T WATCHING TOO CAREFULLY FOR BAD GUYS. BUT THIS GIVES YOU A SENSE OF JUST HOW FAR DOWNSLOPE THEY'D BE.**

**"MARTY" BRICKS AND "MARY" BRICKS
WHO PLANNED STEP HEIGHT?
THICKNESSES OF THREE, ONE, ONE, TWO, TWO . . . BRICKS?**

**CAUSEWAY ("ALLURE" IS ITS TECHNICAL TERM)**

# BEIJING HOSPITAL-ITY

If you want to travel around China, sometimes you have to get pretested for COVID-19. Otherwise, you can't take a train or plane, stay in hotels, etc. Previously, I had to make an appointment at a local clinic (well, Xiaochi did that for me), show up more or less on time (managed by Xiaochi), scan some documents (again, Xiaochi), and get tested.

Not this time. This time, to take the train and stay in a hotel for field work in the Dabie Mountains of central China, I had to go to a hospital for testing.

If you've never visited a Beijing hospital, you haven't missed out on any of life's important pleasures. Not unless you enjoy crowds, confusion, bureaucracy, and very loud people. Maybe other hospitals aren't quite so mobbed, but Beijing Anzhen Hospital on a Monday morning at 9:00 a.m. sure was. Now I understand better what it means to live in a country with nearly five times the population density.

Xiaochi's student, Shaoxiong, took me there. Good thing, because I don't think I could have managed this on my own.

We've just gotten off the bus, and have turned down Anzhen Street.

Shaoxiong (pointing): The hospital is that building down there.

Matt:             OK, that doesn't look so far.

Maybe not, but on the way, we walk past the physical exam building, cardiovascular and pulmonary building (good to know if I ever have a stroke), gynecology and obstetrics, venomous bite clinic, nonvenomous bite clinic, clinic for bites if you're not sure whether they're venomous or not, clinic for teeny-tiny bites and stings . . . where the heck are we going? We've long since passed the building that Shaoxiong pointed out. How many buildings are there? Finally, we arrive at . . . Outpatient Services. Perhaps predictably, people are standing around outside, in clumps, holding their cell phones in front of various poster-sized QR codes.

> **Shaoxiong:** First scan this code using WeChat.
>
> **Matt:** OK, no problem.

Or is there? Ugh, what a lot of information, all in Chinese characters, no English options.

> **Matt:** Can you help me?
>
> **Shaoxiong:** Sure. That's your name, first and last.
>
> **Matt:** OK. M-a-t-t-h-e-w K-o-h-n.
>
> **Shaoxiong:** What's your phone number?
>
> **Matt:** Just a sec, I'll look it up. [I find it and we enter the number.]
>
> **Shaoxiong:** Passport number?
>
> **Matt:** Just a sec. [I get out my passport and we enter the number.]
>
> **Shaoxiong:** OK, I'll fill in the rest.

He fills in the street address and other information (dang that guy is fast!), checks all the right boxes (I guess) hits enter, and . . .

> **Shaoxiong:** We have to go talk to someone.

Somehow, after living here for three months, I thought the apps on my phone would start working. Nope. Not yet, anyway. Maybe in another couple months, around the time I leave.

So, we go stand in another "line." It's not really a line, though, it's a splodge of people clumped around a terminal. People keep pushing in front of us, so it takes a little while to behave sufficiently aggressively to reach the terminal. There, I see people insert their identity card. Their faces come up on a screen, they sign their names on the screen, and an attendant prints out a receipt. I don't know what the receipt is all about, but this looks pretty easy. Except I don't have an identity card. What do we do? Scan the QR code on the back of my passport?

Shaoxiong talks briefly to the attendant. She explains something, and hands him a paper form. It's the same information that was in the app. This must be the option for troglodytes who lack cell phones. Or for Americans. Or for troglodytic Americans whose cell phone apps don't work. We fill it out, the attendant takes it, puts it somewhere out of sight (into a paper shredder?), and hands us two slips of paper. They allow us past two sets of attendants and into the Outpatient Services building. No one pays attention as my cell phones set off the metal detector.

Shaoxiong pushes through a mob of people to talk to an attendant behind a desk. She says something to him.

What is it with the people in service jobs here? Does China require them to train at the Grating Voice Institute first? Do they take special classes in "harsh-tone speaking?" I don't know what this attendant says, but the tone still reverberates inside my skull.

| | |
|---|---|
| Shaoxiong: | We have to go to the second floor. |
| Matt: | OK. |

This is where the tests will be, right?

Another line, but this time I don't need to scan a code.

| | |
|---|---|
| Shaoxiong: | We need your reservation information. Can you give me that? |

| | |
|---|---|
| Matt: | Uh, I don't have any reservation information. Xiaochi just told me to come to the hospital. |
| Shaoxiong: | Check on WeChat. |
| Matt: | No, I'm sure Xiaochi didn't send anything to me . . . Oooooooohhhhh . . . |

Now I understand the significance of the message I received this morning. In some defense, I get about ten messages every day from various apps trying to sell me things, or warn me there might be rain this afternoon in a neighboring province. I ignore them. Fortunately, I don't delete them. This one was pretty important.

Shaoxiong relays some information to the attendant behind the window. That guy enters information into the computer and hands over a card the size of a credit card. I guess I'm not getting tested here.

| | |
|---|---|
| Matt: | What's this? |
| Shaoxiong: | You need this for medical services. |
| Matt: | OK, but what does it do? |
| Shaoxiong: | You have to have it for any kind of treatment. You use it for paying. |
| Matt: | OK. [Well, I say "OK," but I'm clueless. I have two payment apps plus a bankcard. I'm not sure why I need another card. This one does say "Bank of Beijing" on it, but I don't have an account with that bank. Whatever.] |
| Shaoxiong: | Now we go back to the first floor. |

We're standing in front of another terminal. I insert my new card. Shaoxiong punches through a set of prompts (dang that guy is fast!), a screen comes up saying I have to pay . . . zero yuan. Thank goodness I have my new payment card! Shaoxiong punches a prompt, causing the machine to return my card and print out a receipt, which we take.

Now where are we going? Oh, outside. We need to go to another building? OK, whatever. I've given up thinking I'll be tested anytime soon. Now I'm mainly curious how many lines and computer programs I have to navigate before a Q-tip is shoved up my nose.

Instead of walking back up the street to the exit—approximately a block away—then back down, we casually step over a low barrier, and—oops!

Now that guy definitely trained at the Grating Voice Institute! I think he must have specialized in peremptory speech too. Surprisingly, he turns out to be mild-mannered, and he lets us take the shortcut.

Now we enter a "building" that used to be a parking area, but is currently enclosed in plastic. We both sigh in relief because this place has heating. Beijing shuts down all heat starting October 1, and doesn't turn it on until November 15. I wear a coat and hat in my office. But the hospital installed space heaters here, so we're pretty comfortable. I take off my hat for the first time since getting out of bed.

We snake through a slow line for a few minutes. As we get to the front, Shaoxiong slips past the guard lady, but she stops me and says something very sternly. Wow! Was this woman class valedictorian of the Grating Voice Institute? Or, more likely salutatorian. I actually wince as she speaks. I wince even now as I think about her.

Shaoxiong explains that we're together. And probably mentions that I'm a troglodytic American who doesn't speak Chinese and whose apps never work. She gruffly allows him to return to the line with me.

Eventually she lets us through, where we approach . . . another terminal? What the heck is this for? Oh well, third time's a charm, right? I insert my card, and Shaoxiong punches through several prompts (dang that guy is fast!), which brings up a QR code.

| Shaoxiong: | You need to scan and pay using WeChat. |
| --- | --- |
| Matt: | OK. |

I scan and pay using WeChat. It costs eighty yuan (about $12.50). I guess I had to pay after all.

The machine spits out my hospital card and another receipt. We take the receipt over to a window. The woman there takes it and—glory be!—sticks a label on a vial and hands it over to me. I know what this is—this is the vial that the test swab goes into. I must be at the testing center!

We take the vial over to another open window. I sit and the attendant there reintroduces me to the joy of having a Q-tip stuck down my throat. Her perfunctory swish means I don't gag.

I sit there a second or two. Is that it? I spent forty-five minutes standing in lines, punching in codes, and being lectured in harsh tones for a three-second throat swab? Somehow I feel let down. But at least it's done.

> **Shaoxiong:** On WeChat, you can access your health code and see the results of your test. It's easy.
>
> **Matt:** Oh, yes, that sounds simple. Thanks!

We walk back out to the street, scan a couple bikes, and ride them back to the Institute. Fortunately, traffic is relatively light, and we don't end up returning to the hospital in the back of an ambulance.

Thank goodness for Shaoxiong! If it weren't for him, I'd still be at the hospital. Waiting in line. Or, more likely, in the cardiovascular and pulmonary building, being treated for stroke. While the class valedictorian of the Grating Voice Institute is being treated in the nonvenomous bite building, next door.

# TAKING A SHORTCUT

I've been getting a little shaggy, so I thought I should cut my hair again. The first time I cut my hair in China was in quarantine in Shanghai. I used my beard trimmer. I brought the fittings we use at home, and it worked reasonably well, except I couldn't see the back of my neck to ensure it was even.

This time I decided I should visit a real barber shop. Not that I use one at home. Heather normally cuts my hair. At this point in my life, it takes only about ten minutes. But I thought the experience might prove interesting.

Huixia offered to help me find a barber, but she lives pretty far away, and our schedules don't always mesh. So, I opted to call in a favor, and ask my postdoc friend, Lishuang, to help. It turns out Lishuang's favorite barber is just around the corner—perfect! Late one afternoon, she led the way.

As we walk in, I'm directed to a seat with a basin. Apparently standard practice is a preliminary hair washing. That's fine by me, even though the little hair I have hardly warrants washing. But this is all about experience, right?

After washing, I'm directed to a barber's chair. The barber asks me something, which of course I don't understand. Lishuang interprets, and I say the standard fitting I use on my beard trimmer says twelve millimeters. I don't know if the fittings these guys have are measured the same way, but I'm sure not going to tell him "half inch." I might end up with half a millimeter. Very short hair means your head is always cold. And while that's not so bad in Shanghai in August, the heat's turned off now in the Institute buildings. My office is regularly 59°F (15°C).

The barber sets me up with a sheet and collar, and starts combing at my skimpy hair and snipping wildly with scissors. I can't see anything because my glasses are off, but at one point, I check length. Here's what I think is happening.

The guy has more enthusiasm than talent. With every snip, he removes perhaps 75 percent of what he's trying to cut. So, to make up for this, he takes numerous snips. And this makes statistical sense. If your first snip leaves behind 25 percent of what you want to remove, your second snip leaves behind 25 percent of 25 percent, or 6.25 percent. Do that again, and again, and again . . . eventually you have a pretty decent result. Theoretically.

After about five minutes of this wild snipping, my barber gets out a trimmer and trims down various parts of my head. I can tell some parts are bare (like the back of my neck, which is good). Other parts don't feel chilly, so I think they still have some length of hair. Eventually, after about ten minutes of buzzing, I'm directed to check out the results.

I think I look fine, and I'm ready to be done. But . . . what? What am I supposed to do? I return to the first chair with the basin, and they wash my hair again.

I think he wants to be sure he catches any stray hairs because he leads me back to the barber's chair where I'm subjected to a few more snips. Then, the barber whips everything away and dries my hair with a blow drier. Which takes about three seconds. There's not that much hair to dry on my head.

Lishuang's hair takes quite a while longer, partly because her hair is thick, plus her barber is trying to style it. That reminds me of how much I envy Chinese hair. I wouldn't say my hair gets cowlicks, but that's only because I know the size of cow tongues. My head could support only two or three licks, and usually there are more. No, whenever I get licks, they're goat licks. Or maybe puppy licks. Multiple tufts stick out in random directions. It's especially bad in a humid environment, such as here in China, if my hair gets too long.

I think I would prefer thick straight hair, like everyone I see here. And not just for aesthetics. It would certainly be warmer, now that the heat is off at the Institute.

**FINAL FORM. MY HAIR ALWAYS STICKS STRAIGHT UP ON TOP WHEN IT'S THIS SHORT, BUT IT BEATS LICKS.**

# SANDS OF TIME

The US embassy here in Beijing recently asked me to give a public talk on the science of climate change. I offered to talk about how we know what past climates were like and how we quantify temperature and atmospheric carbon dioxide concentrations, as context for evaluating modern global warming.

Although I have a talk from about ten years ago, atmospheric carbon dioxide and methane concentrations have increased so much since then, none of my slides are accurate any more. There's a useful lesson there . . .

But in addition, I wanted to rerun some calculations I made ten years ago. That means updating data sets for new measurements, running some numbers, making sure my statistics are robust, etc., etc. Basically, doing the stuff that scientists are supposed to do.

What's the question I'm trying to answer? Simply this: could modern carbon dioxide and methane concentrations be considered "normal"?

Here's one way to answer this question, using paleoclimate records:

1. Bubbles of air in ice cores are preserved continuously back to eight hundred thousand years ago (incredible, isn't it?). The concentrations of carbon dioxide and methane in those bubbles have been measured (similarly incredible). So, we have a continuous record of atmospheric carbon dioxide and methane concentrations for the last eight hundred thousand years. These show regular variations in concentration—low concentrations during glacial periods, and high

concentrations during interglacials. Today we're in an interglacial period (it started approximately ten thousand years ago), so it's not surprising carbon dioxide and methane concentrations are higher now than, say, twenty thousand years ago during the last glacial maximum. But—here's the key question—are they *unusually* high?

2. The chemistry of ocean micro-critters (called foraminifera) has also been measured continuously back to eight hundred thousand years ago (actually, all the way past sixty-five million years ago, beyond the start of the Cenozoic Era). That chemical record is one way we identify the timing of past interglacial periods, independently of the ice core record.

3. Using ocean micro-critter chemistry to identify interglacial periods, and correlating with the ice core air bubble record, I can calculate the average carbon dioxide and methane concentrations during interglacials. This gives me an average "normal" concentration during interglacials—what I would expect to see today.

4. But of course, there's variation, and the ice core data also allow me to calculate the range of values that might occur naturally. Variability is reported in terms of a quantity called "standard deviation" or "sigma," after the Greek letter "σ" used to represent it.

5. With both the average and standard deviation, I can evaluate how different today's concentrations are compared to past interglacials in the context of that "normal" variability—how many sigmas modern concentrations deviate from normal interglacials of the past.

6. Then I can convert those sigmas into a probability—how likely is it that modern carbon dioxide and methane are "normal" (that is, the result of random variation)? The more sigmas today's concentrations are from the average, the less probable it's random. For example, one, or two, or maybe even three sigmas removed from the average? Yeah, I could see how that might be natural. These correspond to probabilities of approximately one in six, one in fifty, and one in 650. But four or five or six sigmas? much less likely.

So just how different are modern carbon dioxide concentrations from past interglacials? Well, the current value is 419 parts per million by volume (ppmv). Actually, units aren't important here. Just think of it as the number 419. The average concentration of carbon dioxide during past interglacials was around 265 ppmv. OK, they're different by a little over 150 ppmv, but how variable were past interglacials? If there was a lot of variation, say one hundred ppmv, maybe it's not surprising the Earth could have a concentration in excess of four hundred ppmv. That would mean it's only approximately 1.5 sigmas removed from the average. that's not *so* unlikely, right?

Well, sigma for past interglacials isn't one hundred ppmv, it's only thirteen ppmv. So, today's value of carbon dioxide isn't 1.5 sigmas removed from the average, it's approximately twelve sigmas (I tested different definitions of interglacial periods, and values range between eleven and thirteen sigmas).

That seems like a lot of sigmas, but exactly how (un)likely is that? How unlikely is it that a twelve-sigma deviation could reflect "normal" random variation?

I had to search a while to find out how to calculate such low probabilities. Most tabulations cut off at four or five sigmas. I understand why—what's the point of calculating probabilities that are so tiny? Still, one calculator I found (keisan.cassio.com) estimates that a twelve-sigma observation has a probability of about one in 1,000,000,000,000,000,000,000,000,000,000,000 (one with thirty-three zeros after it), or one in a million-billion-billion-billion. Even for someone like me who regularly reckons time in millions and billions of years, that's a hard number to grasp.

That's like a billionth of a second out of the entire age of the universe. It's like winning the same state lottery five times in a row. It's like—well, imagine this. You take a single sand grain and place it anywhere you like. Top of a mountain, middle of a sand dune, bottom of an ocean, between someone's toes (but not in solid rock or in a pool of magma—it has to be retrievable as a single grain). Now, some other person randomly picks a single sand grain from anywhere they like on Earth. Same deal—it could be the middle of a construction site, a farmer's field in outer Mongolia, a bucket of muck from Lake Titicaca, stuck in the gill of a coelacanth in the ocean.

It is thousands of times more likely that this other person happens to pick your grain of sand—randomly placed anywhere on Earth—than the likelihood that modern carbon dioxide concentrations are normal.

Think about it. Say you choose to burrow into the middle of a sand dune in the Sahara Desert and place your sand grain thirty feet (ten meters) below the surface. This other person, without communicating with you, or in any way narrowing down the possibilities, randomly chooses exactly the same sand dune, burrows down in exactly the same place to exactly the same depth, and somehow, even then, manages to pull out exactly the same sand grain.

Or maybe you do put it in some coelacanth's gill and release it back into the ocean. This other person randomly finds the same coelacanth (which are very rare), chooses the same gill, and picks the same sand grain.

And that probability is more likely? It's more likely than the likelihood that modern carbon dioxide concentrations are the result of normal random variation? Holy cow! How much more unlikely could it be?

How about the (un)likelihood that methane concentrations are normal? Yes, methane concentrations are much less likely than carbon dioxide to reflect normal variation. Concentrations today aren't a measly twelve sigmas removed from the interglacial average, they're thirty sigmas removed. That's like winning the same lottery thirty times in a row.

That's like placing an atom anywhere in the observable universe and having that random person pick the same one. And not just once—twice in a row.

Remember, too, that there are more atoms in a bottle of water than there are stars in the observable universe. We're talking teensy-weensy-teeny-tiny! probabilities.

Now, to be fair, different approaches will yield different answers. I don't think Poisson statistics are applicable, but they would yield higher probabilities. A different scientist might choose different definitions of interglacial periods. Each bubble in an ice core averages some time period, and I compared it to an instantaneous measurement. But at the end of the day, we would all conclude that atmospheric compositions cannot be normal. In fact, I would say they're about as not-normal as it's possible for something to be.

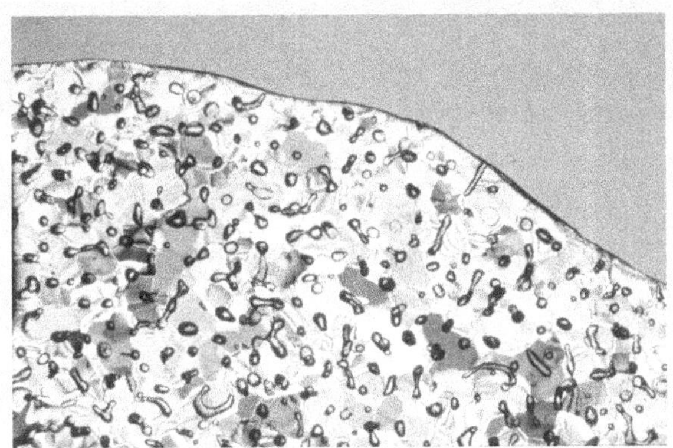

**MICROSCOPE SLIDE OF A SECTION OF ICE CORE. THE SMALL BLOBS WITH BLACK EDGES ARE GAS BUBBLES. FROM THE COMMONWEALTH SCIENTIFIC AND INDUSTRIAL RESEARCH ORGANISATION (CSIRO).**

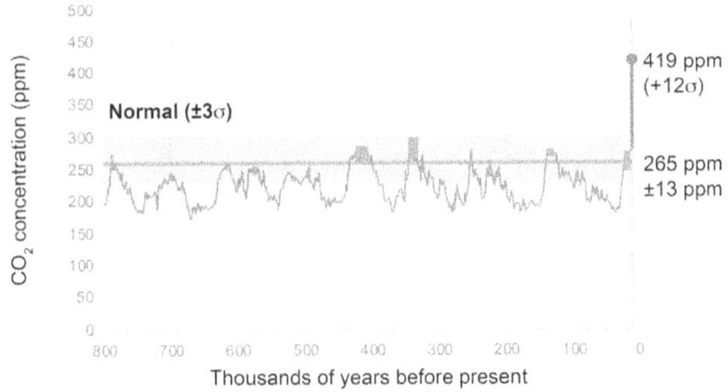


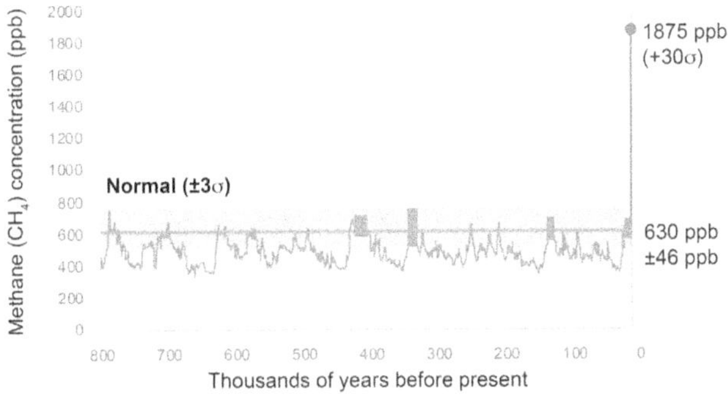


**GREENHOUSE GAS RECORD FOR THE LAST EIGHT HUNDRED THOUSAND YEARS. THE NEARLY VERTICAL LINES FOR TODAY (THOUSANDS OF YEARS BEFORE PRESENT = 0) ARE RECENT MEASUREMENTS. THE DOTS AT 419 PPM AND 1875 PPB ARE TODAY'S VALUES. SHADED BANDS ARE PLUS OR MINUS THREE SIGMAS (FAIRLY GENEROUS ON LABELING SOMETHING "NORMAL").**

# RICE IS NICE, ESPECIALLY WITH TEA

As we drive out to look at rocks in the Dabie Mountains, we pass field after field after field of some yellow crop.

| Matt: | What's that crop? |
| Lishuang: | Rice. |

Nowadays I don't eat much rice, even though I love it. When I lived by myself as a graduate student and postdoc, my standard meal, at least four times per week, was white rice cooked in bouillon with broccoli or some other vegetable, and some cubed cheese added at the end. I thought it was generally nutritionally balanced. Protein and green vegetables plus some starch to round it out.

Nowadays, starch makes me sleepy within an hour of eating—that's why I stopped eating cookies before geoscience seminar, remember? I have enough trouble staying awake without adding a sugar crash. I've also realized there's virtually nothing nutritious about white rice and flour. Eating a bowl of white rice is essentially like eating a bowl of sugar. If I'm going to eat sugar, I want it to taste sweet.

Hardly anyone here in China understands how I might possibly refuse rice or noodles. I'm constantly offered them. Would you like some rice? No? Are you sure you don't want rice? You can have as much rice as you want. No? How about noodles? Are you sure? I do eat noodles occasionally, mainly because I really do like them, but also so my colleagues and friends know I'm not morally opposed. Still, I try to stay away.

I realize now I haven't seen too many rice fields in the US, if any. But I remember the rice fields of Bhutan distinctly. Those fields are amazing terraced structures, each little terrace carefully supported by a small wall made out of stacked stones. Terrace after terrace after terrace . . . all the way up a mountainside. I realize rocks are pretty easy to come by, but the amount of work building so many stone walls is simply staggering. The lip of each wall sticks up just high enough that farmers can flood each terrace. Most walls are pretty narrow, but you can walk on top of the bigger ones. That's a standard way to cross a slope. The beauty of these fields in the morning and evening light always stops me short. I have to catch my breath for a minute. And it's not the altitude.

I wouldn't describe the fields in China with quite the same awe. I do like looking out over the fields, and their soft golden-yellow color does contrast appealingly with the bright green and dark green of other crops, especially in the morning sun. But the scale is much larger because the big rice fields are in the bottom of large river valleys. Most things in China are bigger, of course. When you have to feed 1.5 billion people in China rather than a mere 770,000 in Bhutan (or even 29 million in Nepal), bigger is better.

We've caught the farmers down in the flats just as they're starting their harvest. The edges of fields still sprout muddy rice straw stubble, but most of the fields are yellow and uncut. In the remote towns up in the mountains, the farmers have already reaped their rice and piled the straw into conical piles. Smaller, terraced fields have other crops (for example, bok choy, gourds, mung beans, etc.). We even saw one field with black sesame.

Despite a similar community structure, China obviously enjoys greater wealth and investment in infrastructure compared to Bhutan or Nepal. I see tractors occasionally in the mountains (lots in the valleys), and the walls have mortar to hold the rocks together. The roads are paved. And there actually are roads. I also didn't see any little wooden huts on stilts. These are to keep watch at night to make sure the pigs don't eat all the crops.

In the forest, loggers are cutting bamboo. We don't see them at work, but we do see trucks loaded with giant bamboo crawling along the mountain roads. This also reminds me of Bhutan, where we saw loggers hauling bamboo. But they weren't using trucks, they were hauling them on their backs. Clackity, clackity, clackity, clackity, clack! What a ruckus! And hard work too. Those guys were straining. Bamboo is a grass. How can grass weigh so much?

Bamboo has lots of uses. You can eat it (bamboo shoots), use it for water pipes, and make the bigger sections into jars. Finally, after it's used up and dried out, you can burn it. Some of the best food I've eaten in China was cooked over a bamboo fire.

But all these crops are incidental in the communities of the Dabie Mountains. No, the big deal here is tea. Tea is everywhere. And it's not just that the farmers have allocated a large fraction of their terraced fields to tea. Every little bit of flat ground also seems to have tea trees on it—in someone's backyard, by the side of a road, wherever. We passed some road construction that appeared to have taken out half a small plantation (maybe ten trees) because someone had planted it on the road's shoulder.

Stopping for rocks, I casually inspected some tea trees. These are all scrubby little things, but they bear pretty, pendulous, waxy, white flowers with yellow-orange centers. The color of the flowers reminds me slightly of white daffodils. A postdoc here tells me tea tree oil is made from the flower buds. Bees were buzzing around, sluggishly, because it was chilly.

Apparently in the springtime, when the tea is harvested, tea trees emit a strong odor. I didn't smell anything, perhaps reflecting either the wrong season or the fact that my nose was cold all the time.

Towering over the stunted tea trees, the upper branches of the stately Osmanthus tree just managed to brush low-hanging telephone wires. Yes, this tree was only about eight to ten feet (approximately three meters) high. So, it's much smaller than even the average bamboo tree. But it looked big compared to tea trees. It was blooming, and I recalled the fragrance of its flowers in Chinese wine during my first meal out with Xiaochi.

Xiaochi:        Matt, do you want to stop at a tea shop?

Matt:        Uh . . . sure! [Why not?]

Naively, I thought he meant a place where you drink tea. Not so. This was a place where you buy tea. By the handful, out of a burlap sack (or the modern plastic equivalent of burlap). In this shop, a fistful of dollars buys you a fistful of tea leaves. I'm just kidding. In this shop, a scanned QR code on WeChat plus a payment code buys you a fistful of tea leaves.

The owner pulled out three sacks of tea, each about two-thirds full, and a fourth large cardboard box, approximately one-third full. Each held dried green tea. Enough tea to last a couple lifetimes, even for the most avid tea drinker. And their family. The back storeroom held sacks and sacks more. Enough for a couple generations of descendants. Or possibly one gigantic Chinese wedding.

I bought 250 grams (ten ounces) for 120 yuan. Converting, that's roughly $18.50, or a little over two dollars per ounce. Is that cheap? Everyone here seemed to think so. I think they were right too. Looking online, I found I could buy green tea from the Dabie Mountains for a mere sixty cents—per gram! I'm not positive it was the same tea, and variety matters a lot to a tea connoisseur. But if it's the same tea, that 250 grams that I purchased for $18.50 might sell online for $150. Plus shipping. Direct from the manufacturer—88 percent discount!

Normally I think of tea as something of a luxury. It's not exactly cheap. But whereas I still plan to avoid rice here, now I feel a little differently about drinking multiple cups of tea every day. Somehow knowing the people whose lives depend on it makes it more meaningful.

RICE FIELDS STRETCHING INTO THE DISTANCE FROM MY HOTEL WINDOW

CLOSE UP OF RICE FIELDS IN BHUTAN. I DON'T THINK THE SCARECROW IN THE BACK LEFT IS VERY SCARY.

**TERRACED RICE FIELDS IN BHUTAN**

**TERRACED TEA TREE PLANTATION IN CHINA**

**HAULING BAMBOO IN BHUTAN**

**HAULING BAMBOO IN CHINA**

**ROWS OF TEA TREES**

**FOUR DIFFERENT TYPES OF TEA. THE TWO ON THE LEFT ARE SIMPLY DRIED. THE TWO ON THE RIGHT HAVE SOME OTHER PROCESS APPLIED (MAYBE DRYING IN AN OVEN?) AND ARE MUCH MORE BITTER.**

# GEE, A GEOPARK

Did you know there's a global network of geoparks? It's sponsored by UNESCO (United Nations Educational, Scientific, and Cultural Organization), and there are over 160 of them in forty-four countries. China alone holds more than forty.

But geoparks aren't quite like parks in the US, at least not the one I visited here in the Dabie Mountains, Tianzhushan Park. And it's not just the forests of giant bamboo.

First, the "visitors center" is actually a sophisticated museum. And it's huge. The exhibits are extensive and contain a lot of information at a fairly high level. The undergrads at Boise State would understand the discussion of geology, but would the average person? Not the average American, that's for sure.

A geopark isn't necessarily just geology either. Tianzhushan Park also includes rare ecosystems and cultures. For example, a monk in this area created the Chinese tea ceremony. There are special tea varieties and ceramics styles. Diverse ecosystems equate to diverse species of plants and animals, too, which the museum shows in detail.

We received a personal tour during an off day. I think museums are more fun with kids around, but all the explanatory signs were written in Chinese and English. So, while our tour guide knowledgeably and thoroughly informed everyone else about the details of geology, ecosystems, and culture (I guess that's what she was talking about), I wandered around, reading and looking at stuff at my leisure.

The two most important differences between a geopark in China and a national or state park in the US became evident the next day. First, the park boundaries encompass several towns. That's not surprising, because people have populated this area densely for at least one thousand years. I expect it would be hard to create a park in China that didn't include at least one community. But most parks in the US don't have people ploughing up land to grow their dinner.

The second important difference relates to the philosophy that a park is held in public trust for the benefit of all. Both China and the US adhere to this. But, whereas in the US that means you leave everything alone in a national park, including rocks, plants, animals, clots of dirt, bits of slime mold, etc., here it means anyone can hammer on an outcrop, as long as it's considered justifiable and sustainable. A geopark won't allow you to deface a singularly distinctive outcrop, sell rocks from the park, or use dynamite. But even signed road cuts can be fair game, if there's a good reason to collect. Mostly we sampled unsigned roadcuts. In the US, that's absolutely forbidden. You need a collecting permit everywhere, and those aren't always so easy to get. And those permits are enforced, too. Trust me, if you don't have a permit on you personally, don't walk around a national park with a rock hammer in your hand unless you enjoy having a menacing park ranger publicly rip you.

The world may have over 160 geoparks, but the number of geoparks in the US is . . . zero. Nada. Zip. Zilch.

Partly I think it's a matter of timing. The first national park in the US (Yellowstone) was created in 1872. It's not considered the first national park globally (Bogd Khan Uul in Mongolia took that prize in the late 1700s), but it was the one that got the national parks movement really rolling in the US and ultimately in other countries. The traditional story is that explorers during the 1870 Washburn-Doane expedition were sitting around a campfire talking about the incredible things they had seen. Legend goes, a guy named Cornelius Hedges proposed that the geysers, mud pots, waterfalls, etc., shouldn't be developed commercially, but should be preserved for future generations as our first national park. Even if the story isn't true, Hedges promoted the idea heavily. Together with a major report on Yellowstone the next year from the Hayden Geologic Expedition, including key paintings from Thomas Moran that were displayed prominently in Washington, DC, legislation was introduced and our first national park was created in practically record time. With bipartisan support. From both houses of Congress. Those were the days . . .

Like many of our national parks and monuments, legislators justified its creation on the basis of its geologic and natural uniqueness. I briefly scanned the approximately two hundred largest national parks and monuments, and, for most of them, geology and landscape were a principal reason for setting them aside. If we consider other preserves within the National Park System, and parks outside the National Park System (Toadstool Park in Nebraska, Anza-Borrego in California, etc.), the US could easily justify a couple hundred geoparks to UNESCO.

But UNESCO's geoparks program wasn't created until 2001, long after the vast majority of our parks and monuments had been created. At that point, why would the US sign on to UNESCO Global Geoparks? They already had hundreds of them. Wasn't the rest of the world simply playing catch-up?

I suspect there's more to it, though. UNESCO certification requires certain standards of information and accessibility. While US parks are much more physically accessible and safer (and more protected) than anything I've seen in China, I doubt the US federal government is interested in having an international organization impose standards of intellectual content and activity that the US doesn't control. After all, Grant County in Oregon is so opposed to international oversight, it actually banned the United Nations.

What does that mean, anyway, to ban the UN (or, more correctly, declare the county a UN-free zone)? If António Guterres (current UN secretary-general) decides to take a soak at Blue Mountains Hot Springs or tour the Kam Wah Chung State Heritage Site, does the sheriff throw him jail? Clap him in irons? Put him in the pokey? It seems about as effective as banning South Carolina. Or the Mounties. Or Mount Everest.

Grant County:    Mount Everest, you may no longer visit Grant County, Oregon. We are now a Mount Everest-free county.

Mount Everest:    OK . . .?

Perhaps, as a paleontologist (Matt Smith, I think) once commented, it means residents should now call it Grant Coty. That's what you get if you remove "UN" from "Grant County."

But perhaps more cynically, I'm not sure our federal government is all that interested in geology. Sure, we have a US Geological Survey, but that's a legacy of the 1800s when the government cared about mineral resources. The USGS and the core Geoscience programs at National Science Foundation aren't exactly awash in dough. If the level of information provided on signs here in Tianzhushan Geopark is any indication (admittedly it may not be) the average Chinese person knows much more geology than the average American. I suppose we don't have world-famous ultrahigh-pressure rocks in our national parks, or even all that many that feature metamorphism for that matter. The geologic significance of most parks rests on volcanoes, fossils, and time. But, I can't recall reading anything significant about metamorphism in Great Smoky Mountains National Park or Death Valley National Park, which hold two of the most spectacular metamorphic sequences in the world. And the information on volcanoes, etc., is pretty basic.

There's an ironic twist to all this.

As I've mentioned previously, the American Geosciences Institute estimates that the US will have a shortage of roughly one hundred thousand trained geologists in the next five to ten years (out of three hundred fifty thousand). Where will they come from?

If not from the US, they will have to come from other countries. And China (apparently) takes a far stronger interest in promoting geologic learning than the US. Logically, it seems like scientists from China could fill a critical gap. In fact, I read somewhere that 85 percent of students from China who receive science PhDs in the US stay in the US. So, by the numbers, they already do fill an important gap. But the US is making it harder and harder for foreigners to get visas and work permits. An extraordinarily-talented student who worked with me was unable to get a job in geosciences simply because she's Brazilian, not American. Potential employers told her she had the skills, but it was too difficult and expensive for anyone to justify hiring her. And the US actually likes Brazil (or so the State Department says). It's vastly harder for someone from China to receive a visa, let alone land a job.

Is this really in our best interest? Ironic that, for a country that's so concerned about intellectual dominance, we're deliberately shooting ourselves in the foot by pushing away good scientists.

**A SIGN NOTIFYING VISITORS OF AN IMPORTANT OUTCROP (ACROSS THE ROAD FROM ME)**

**DETAILED DESCRIPTION OF THE SIGNIFICANT GEOLOGY OF THE OUTCROP. IT EVEN HAS THIN SECTION (MICROSCOPE) PHOTOS ON THE RIGHT!**

**A DIFFERENT OUTCROP, ILLUSTRATING THE KEY MINERALS: GARNET AND A HIGH-PRESSURE SODIUM-BEARING MINERAL (CLINOPYROXENE/OMPHACITE). THIS TYPE OF ROCK (ECLOGITE) MAKES THE DABIE MOUNTAINS RENOWNED AMONG GEOLOGISTS.**

# POISONING PIGEONS IN THE PARK

Do you know the songs of Tom Lehrer? He's a mathematics professor who became famous in the 1950s and 1960s for his scathingly satirical songs about life in the US. When I was in high school, I discovered a small book of Tom Lehrer songs on our bookshelf, and learned to play many of them on the piano. My PhD advisor, Frank Spear, is a fan also.

One day in the Chinese countryside, I was reminded of Tom Lehrer and his song *Poisoning Pigeons in the Park.*[7]

| | |
|---|---|
| Professor Guo: | Matt, please try this. [He's holding out a spray of berries on a small branch of some plant that looks familiar . . . but . . .?] |
| Matt: | What is this? |
| Prof. Guo: | Try it. But eat only the black berries. They are ripe. Don't eat the green ones. |

---

7. The song hypothesizes there's a guy who feeds poison-laced peanuts to pigeons. Don't worry, it's not serious in any way.

Matt:  OK.

I eat two. They taste a little fruity, very slightly sweet, a little tart, and a little like a cross between a blackberry and a tomato. Not bad, all round. The flowers look just like tomato flowers, only white or slightly purplish, not yellow.

Matt:  But what is this?

Dr. Tang:  In China, we call it "beautiful woman," but I don't know what it is in English. It's the same name in Italy.

Matt:  And you eat this, you say?

Prof. Guo:  Yes. When I was a kid, we didn't have money for fruit, so we would eat the black berries.

Matt:  Oh. Wait. You said it means 'beautiful woman'?

Dr. Tang:  Yes, when a woman eats it, her pupils dilate, and she becomes more beautiful. That is why we call it beautiful woman.

Matt:  And it's the same word in Italian? Like bella donna!?

Dr. Tang:  Yes, it is the same fruit.

Matt:  But that's poisonous!

Prof. Guo:  Oh, well we eat them all the time. They seem safe for us.

Well, if he didn't die already from eating them as a child, I'm not likely to die now as an adult. I don't have the apparatus necessary to purge my stomach, anyway. And, unlike Lisbeth Salander (from *Girl with the Dragon Tattoo*), I never learned to barf on cue.

A few hours later, none of us have fallen asleep permanently, so I eat another one. I would eat it again. Cautiously.

I looked all this up later, and learned that, yes, the Chinese and Europeans do eat the berries of the black nightshade (*Solanum nigrum*). The fruit is a little like tomatoes (same genus), only much tinier, and black. It's poisonous, but only mildly so, at least for the ripe berries.

I wouldn't eat a black nightshade berry pie, though, and the green ones can be dangerous. But it's not belladonna in the sense of *Atropa belladonna*, which is in the same plant family (Solanaceae). Now that plant, if you eat a couple berries, you really can die. It's called belladonna because Italian women used to dilate their pupils using the juice (the concept that Dr. Tang was alluding to). Dilation has the unpleasant side effect of blurring your vision, though. My multiple trips to optometrists and ophthalmologists attest to that.

This little event, of course, illustrates why it's dangerous to use common names for plants. The same name can mean vastly different things—a tasty source of vitamin C for a poor family versus death at the hands of the Borgias. Or, in my case, a quaint but pleasant experience for a visiting scientist versus scaring him shitless.

Actually, the Borgias used arsenic (just like the guy in Tom Lehrer's song!). Arsenic has no flavor.

As none of us died that morning from eating "belladonna" (or from any other hazard), we moved on to Huating Lake National Park (Hualiangting Reservoir), and Xifeng Temple, part of the Taihu Zen Tourism Scenic Area. This area describes itself as the birthplace of Chinese Zen Buddhism.

Hiking from the lakeshore up to the temple complex isn't even close to the three thousand feet to the top of Mount Crumpit in *How the Grinch Stole Christmas* (or ten thousand feet in the movie), but it's still a bit of a hump—about eight hundred feet (250 m), and very steep. Fortunately, the stairs are well spaced, and each step is the same height. No tripping or heaving, like at the Great Wall.

The view at the top is spectacular, although China's very hazy, so you won't see the surrounding mountains clearly.

What to do at the top? Besides admiring beautiful buildings, statues, and friezes, you can visit the original cave where Zen masters hung out and light some incense sticks. I wouldn't horse around any, though, because the complex is an active training/learning center for Buddhism. At least, it looks like you can rent rooms and study there. There are some cultural displays where you can read about the history in the area. And lots of pleasant alcoves in the woods where you can sit and enjoy nature. There are cute little Buddha statues scattered about, too, all in different poses. It's not all serious.

Last, you can always feed the pigeons. There are peanuts for them. But while the pigeons will approach closely, they won't take peanuts out of your hand. Perhaps, like me, these pigeons had also listened to Tom Lehrer's song and were generally wary of Americans.

Now I realize we should have tried feeding them black nightshade berries. Would they eat them? Maybe next time . . .

**BLACK NIGHTSHADE**

**INTERIOR OF A TEMPLE BUILDING**

**TEMPLE COMPLEX OVERLOOKING LAKE**

**BAMBOO FOREST WITH ALCOVE TO SIT AND ENJOY NATURE**

**FEEDING PEANUTS TO PIGEONS IN THE PARK**

# HAPPY BIRTHDAY!

Halloween here in China happens to correspond with the birthday of Huixia's son, Xunxun. When I attended the family lunch and birthday celebration, I didn't see so many tricks, although there were certainly many treats.

Logistics fared easily—the guards at the subway didn't seem to care that I was carrying a fold-up kitchen knife, a laptop computer, and a fifth of single malt scotch whiskey as a present. They did look at me kind of funny, but then they always do that. I'm the only American dude in a billion people.

Now, why is it that it's the children who get the presents on their birthdays? It's not like the kid did all the hard work getting born. And think what their parents have had to put up with for the preceding 365 days (unless it's a leap year, in which case it's 366). No, I figure the people who deserve presents most on a little kid's birthday are the adults. And single malt seemed singularly appropriate.

Although maybe not in China. Like many a formal meal, this one was accompanied by pitchers of baijiu (rice- or sorghum-based alcohol) and lots of toasts. There was no shortage of baijiu. The guests welcomed me to China four or five times. Or maybe six. I kind of lost count. Actually, I've kind of forgotten what all those other toasts were about, too. All I remember is that there were a lot of them.

I rounded out my savory culinary experience with some new items: chicken feet (no bones, just kind of thick chewy chunks), jellyfish (also kind of thick, chewy chunks), and pickled green garlic cloves.

But the highlight of the event wasn't food, it was the traditional game: Let's-see-what-a-one-year-old-child-will-do-with-his-life.

The idea is that, at the one-year birthday, parents spread out an assortment of characteristic objects on the floor. In this case, they were spread out in an arc. The kid is placed on the floor, and encouraged to crawl (or otherwise navigate) toward these objects. Whichever object the kid picks up signifies his or her life's work. What will it be?

Will it be the string of money (miser?), the cutlass (pirate?), the bun (glutton?), the key (jailer?), the ball of string (string collector?), the gavel (next Speaker of the House in America?).

Xunxun was first intrigued by the scale (a scale for weighing things, not like a smelly bit of a dead fish). I was intrigued, too. What did it mean if he chose that? Would he become a lawyer? A drug dealer? A prospector? Actually, which is worse, lawyer or drug dealer?

Considering the circumstances, I was a little disappointed he didn't choose the passport. It was clearly fake, and we all know every family could use a good counterfeiter.

Ultimately, he chose a tiny knobby wooden thing that looked like a cross between a chess piece and Frosty the Snowman. Was it some kind of top? Was his life work going to be a break dancer? Spin doctor? Disk jockey? No, it turns out it's supposed to represent a gourd, and that he will grow up to be a doctor.

What's the link between gourds and doctors? Well, there's a phrase in Chinese about doctors, where the second character is pronounced the same as the word for gourd. I checked it out in one of my Chinese-English translator apps, and sure enough, out popped: "This guy who ran with the bulls needs a doctor. He got gored."

Doctors are good to have in families too. Although it depends on what kind of doctor. My dad told two stories from when he received his PhD.

The first was a piece of advice from his advisor, who told him that when he was introduced as "Dr. Kohn," people would likely start describing aches and pains, hoping to get some free medical advice. He was advised to wait for an opportune moment, then tell the person "OK, first take off all your clothes." That was supposed to stop the conversation.

I don't know how often Dad got to practice that little joke. I've never had an opportunity. No one ever mistook me as a person to trust with their health.

Dad also claims he was introduced to someone who then proceeded to exclaim over how great medical doctors were, how much they helped people, how kind they were, yada, yada, yada. He interrupted saying, "Oh no, I'm not the kind of doctor who does anybody any good."

I think I might have used that line once myself. It might have come from a *New Yorker* cartoon, also.

Then there was the time when my brother Andy and I both came home for some holiday. Andy has a PhD too. The phone rang, my sister answered, then called out, "It's for Dr. Kohn." We all looked at each other, started laughing, and called back "Which one?" Brief conversation. "Dr. Harold Kohn" (my Dad). "Ooooooohhhhh . . ."

Now you know what it's like to live in a family of geeky smartasses. Yeah, like anyone would call me or my brother at my parents' home and ask for "Dr. Kohn."

Actually, I often tell my students not to call me Dr. Kohn, because then I think they're asking for my dad. Usually, I tell them they can call me anything they want, as long as they don't call me late for supper. As I said, a family of smartasses.

Or, they can call me Matt. That's quite different from my Aunt Rose, who demanded that students call her either Doctor Goldsen or Professor Goldsen. Maybe now it seems stuffy, but I respect her for it.

Rosie was one of the first women to earn a PhD at Yale University (I think she might have been the third in sociology). Even before her graduation in 1953, she took up a position at Cornell University as a research associate. This is a "soft-money" position, meaning it required her to raise her salary through research funds. I supported myself for five years on soft money, and let me tell you, it's tough. After working at Cornell for nine years, a new tenure-track line opened up. Seeing that she was going to be passed over again, Rosie demanded that she be considered for the position, which she got, because she was super talented. After that, damned if she was going to let anyone mistakenly think she was inferior to anyone else on the faculty. So, it was either Dr. Goldsen or Professor Goldsen to the students, staff, faculty, and administrators (and "Rosie" to her close friends and family).

She had an impact, that's for sure. There's an Archive of New Media Art named for her at Cornell. Her book, *What College Students Think* (Goldsen, Rosenberg, Williams, and Suchman, 1960) was an eye-opener. No one had ever thought to ask.

Still, times change, and when I took a course at Massachusetts Institute of Technology (MIT) from a former student of hers, Dr. Ruth Perry, I was allowed to address her as Ruth.

In China, I'm usually addressed quite formally, as "Professor." Not "Professor Kohn." Or "Professor Matt" (which I sometimes hear from people from the Caribbean). Just plain old "Professor."

Now that I know Xunxun will be a doctor (the kind of doctor who does people good), I think I'll start calling him "Doctor." Maybe I can even the score on formal titles a little.

**THE APPROACH—WHAT WILL IT BE?**

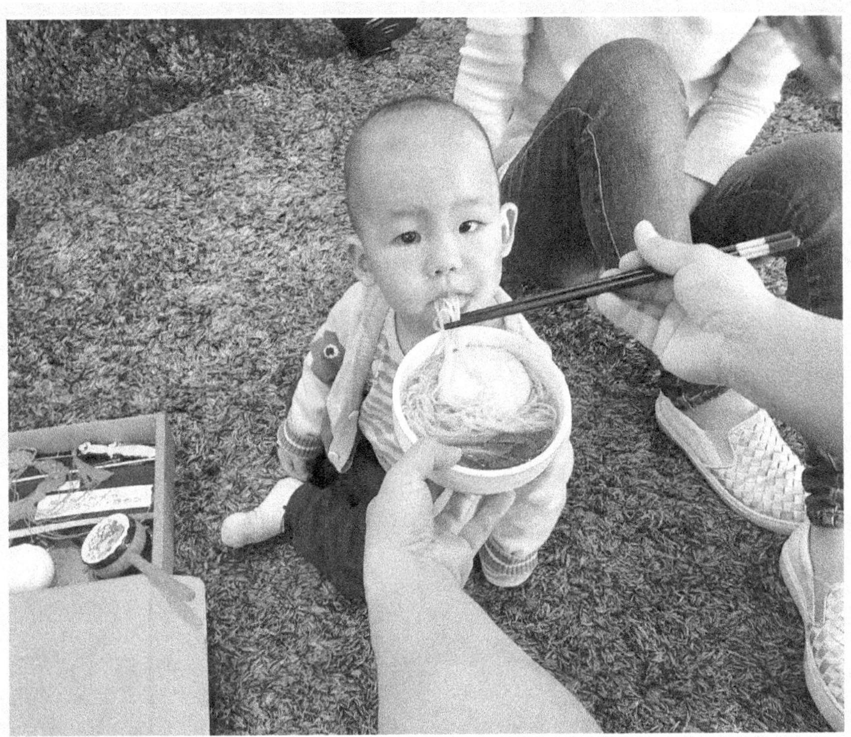

**ALWAYS EAT NOODLES ON YOUR BIRTHDAY TOO. LONG NOODLES EQUAL LONG LIFE.**

# NOVEMBER

# LET IT SNOW

Even though it hosted the winter Olympics in 2022, Beijing isn't exactly a snowy city. So, I was a little surprised (and I think everyone else was too) when we had a major snowfall in early November.

It started as rain, then shifted to sleet, then to snow. A friend and I had planned to see a movie (*Dune*) down the street that evening, and naturally, being an intrepid explorer, I decided to walk the half hour to the theater. Wow, was that impressive!

Huge north winds blew snow every whichaway. The streets were clear, so no traffic problems. But by the time I got to the theater, snow was starting to stick, and my left ear was feeling numb. By the time the movie was over, slushy snow had already accumulated a half inch (approximately one centimeter).

So, naturally, I walked home again. After all, I thought it only fair to numb my right ear. Why should my left ear have all the fun?

The next day, much of the snow on the streets had compacted into ice, and the groundskeepers at the Institute were out with shovels, trying to scrape it up. No salt here.

In some ways the storm reminded me of Boise. The winter storms in Boise mostly follow a consistent pattern. We experience what is called an atmospheric river, or "pineapple express" (not the movie). Warm moist air originating in the tropical Pacific, commonly in the vicinity of pineapple-laden Hawaii, streams northeastward and floods the west coast of the US. It's a little like a fire hose, and typically the rivers sweep south after they hit the coast.

There happens to be a low-elevation corridor between northern California and Boise, so the fire hose sends a stream of warm, wet snow our way. The kind that's good for making snow sculptures and for compacting instantly into ice on the roads.

As the atmospheric river sweeps south, cold air from Canada backs in behind it, so our temperatures drop dramatically. This ensures that our icy roads and sidewalks and bike paths are preserved for the next week or two. Like Beijing, Boise doesn't use salt, it just waits.

As someone who rides his bike to school every day, winter or summer, rain or shine (or snow), slick ice makes for an interesting commute. I think I'm now approximately 50 percent for accidents, meaning I go down once every couple years. Usually it's nothing serious, although once I broke a rib (and a lot of eggs) and another time my chin needed stitching. That's how I learned how difficult it is to use sewing scissors, tweezers, and a mirror to remove tiny black threads from the underside of my face amidst a sea of identically-thick brown hairs.

Back in Beijing, it looked like there was sufficient snow to warrant building a snow sculpture at the Institute. Apparently, others felt similarly. And that's how I found myself on the top of the building, tromping around in several inches of snow the next afternoon, where two snow people were being constructed. Actually, only one could legitimately be called a "person," the other was more of a snow pig. At least, the snout was very pig-like. Standing upright, I suppose it most closely resembled one of the characters from George Orwell's *Animal Farm*, except that it smiled disarmingly. I doubt the pigs on *Animal Farm* smiled like that. The snow pig also didn't carry a whip.

One benefit of the snowstorm is that it cleared out the air. Like Boise, Beijing has a terrible problem with thermal inversions and air pollution. With fifty times the population, it's also about fifty times worse. But the process is exactly the same: cold, stagnant air builds up against the mountains to the north, trapping pollution. With so many millions of people, Beijing's smog is legendary. My eyes sting, and I want to sleep all day. High carbon dioxide levels don't help. And it's much colder.

So, it was a relief to get a break from smog. In fact, it was the first time I was able to see many stars at night.

I've heard that in the Australian outback, where the skies are clear and the nights get cold, you cuddle up with your dog to stay warm. Or dogs. A cold night is called a one-dog night. A colder night is called a two-dog night. And a really cold night is called a three-dog night. Supposedly that's how the band Three Dog Night got their name.

Here in Beijing, a smoggy night is a one-star night (actually, all you can see is a bright planet—Venus or Jupiter; forget trying to see Mars). A moderately clear night is a two-star night. And a really clear night is a three-star night. I was surprised one evening to see a planet and four stars. That's pretty good by Beijing standards.

Of course, it's not just smog, it's also light pollution. I'm sad to say that when I first moved to Boise, I could easily make out constellations at night. Now I can still see them, but they're not nearly so clear. The price of progress, I suppose. Maybe one day Boise will be the size of Beijing.

I hope we've solved the problems of pollution and inversions by then. Otherwise, I can't imagine what Beijing will be like. Every night would be a no-star night. How sad would that be?

**SMOGGY SUNSET IN BEIJING**

**RENOWNED CHINESE PROFESSOR OF GEOLOGY FLANKED BY A SNOW PIG (HOW DID IT GET MY HAT?) AND A SPINDLY-ARMED SNOWPERSON**

# TALK TALK TALK TALK TACO

I wrote less in November because I'd been giving talks. First was the US embassy, then a talk at the Chinese Academy of Geological Sciences, then the China University of Geosciences in Beijing, then the Chinese Academy of Sciences. Only one of these talks was the same (CAGS and CAS), and talks take time to prepare. I've been busy.

I don't think I could have predicted my experience at the embassy, though, starting with the Vietnamese tacos. I was invited to dinner before my talk, and I selected Vietnamese from the list of options. When we arrived, they had a dinner special—Vietnamese tacos. The local Mexican restaurant had limited their hours because of the pandemic, so the Vietnamese place had capitalized by "honoring" them with an offering of fish tacos. I was intrigued, so I ordered them. I don't recommend Vietnamese fish tacos.

It's a little like one of my favorite sayings: The difference between theory and practice is that in theory there's no difference, and in practice there is.

In theory, cultural fusion should lead to pleasurable new combinations of flavors. In practice, Vietnamese tacos are not sufficiently flavorful to compete with Mexican, or sufficiently fresh and springy to compete with Vietnamese. It did inspire me to go out to a real Mexican restaurant the following week, though.

And that was thoroughly delightful. Pebbles is a little hole-in-the-wall restaurant. We made reservations for 5:15, but when we showed up the place was empty. The Wednesday special was pork tacos, which we ordered, along with shrimp tacos, nachos, and a margarita. The pork was super flavorful. You definitely want to visit this place on a Wednesday for their special. And after dinner we had cheesecake and carrot cake. Both were delightfully authentic, although the carrot cake had more cream-cheese frosting than cake.

The only truly bizarre bit to the Mexican restaurant experience wasn't the reggae/Caribbean music or the strangely embroidered throw pillows. It started about 5:30 when three Caucasian women came in for dinner. They sat across the room, and chattered incessantly in English. It was bizarre because I could barely understand anything of what they said. Do white people always speak so fast and inarticulately when we're together? What I could make out seemed thoroughly inane too. In some defense of Americans (who always seem to be criticized when traveling), at least one of them was British. I wanted to tell them to slow down and speak clearly. Preferably with a Chinese accent.

Back to my embassy talk. Perhaps forty people attended, nearly all Chinese. Normally, there's autotranslation for these public talks, but, unfortunately, that option fell through, so I spoke slowly. And, naturally, ran overtime. But no one fell asleep (always a good sign), and I got to document the improbability that carbon dioxide levels are normal (see "Sands of Time"). Stars in the observable universe, grains of sand on Earth, atoms in a bottle of water, etc. All that.

Afterward, a local artist presented me with a couple painted fans. Receiving personal art from a professional was a first for me. She was very kind and soft-spoken, and later I figured out that she's a nationally-recognized classical artist who exhibits at the Beijing Art Museum. Unfortunately, I have no way to contact her now to thank her again for her thoughtful gift. She also spoke to say that we should recognize that the Earth is ill, and that it is our responsibility to help heal the sickness we've inflicted. This reminded of a talk I gave about ten years ago, and the difficult question afterward: "Is it 'too late' to save the Earth?"

These sentiments always bring up a couple sticky points for me: Is the Earth sick? Does it need saving? I'm not sure it is or it does.

Please don't get me wrong. I'm extremely distressed at what humans have done to Earth's climate and ecosystems. We've created an existential threat to ourselves and many other organisms, and we have not only a vested interest in reversing our past actions (insofar as possible) but also a moral responsibility. So, in terms of actions, the artist and I are in complete agreement.

But does the Earth care? Besides philosophical questions about anthropomorphizing Earth, the scientist in me knows that Earth has experienced much bigger changes in climate and ecology than anything we're talking about now. If we do nothing, models predict the Earth will become 5°C (9°F) warmer than one-hundred-fifty years ago. That's a *big* increase with *drastic* consequences for humans. We humans have never experienced anything like that and should try to avoid it at all costs. But from Earth's perspective, she's been many times warmer in the past. Fifty-three million years ago, crocodiles and palm trees lived at 80° north latitude, well above the Arctic circle. Both groups are highly sensitive to temperature and can't survive below freezing for more than about a week. That's one reason the cousins of crocodiles (alligators) in South Carolina can live in Charleston but not in Columbia. Columbia's just a little too cold. Alligators are that sensitive. Yet, today, 80° north routinely hits minus 40°C every winter! In other words, a mere fifty-odd million years ago (only a little more than 1 percent of Earth's "lifetime" ago), some wintertime temperatures were 40°C (72°F) warmer than they are today. How crazy is that?

No, conditions on Earth have been far less livable from a human perspective (or not livable at all) compared to what we're talking about over the next century. True, I wouldn't prefer to live on a world that's any warmer than today, and I'll do my best to keep it from becoming that way. But much worse hellholes have existed before the first human appeared, and Earth has "survived" them. And it's only a "hellhole" from my human perspective. Maybe Earth likes being super warm with acidic oceans that dissolve sea creatures. Who knows? Maybe all that ice on the poles is itchy. Maybe shellfish are the fleas on Mama Earth's skin, and she's glad to be rid of them.

Also, besides the fact that I'm not sure the Earth has an innate desire to be saved, the optimist in me feels like nothing is ever too late. I think we can still fix many of the mistakes we've made (and I do agree they're mistakes), although I agree it does get harder every year.

Unfortunately, COVID-19 scuttled my plans to give the same talk at other consulates around China. Not many people have contracted COVID-19 here. As I write this, the case rate dropped from approximately eighty per day to approximately twenty per day, or about five thousand to ten thousand times lower on a per capita basis than in the US. But there have been a few tens of cases in Beijing in the last week. That's a lot by Chinese standards. The embassy didn't want me to travel to, say, Shanghai and then get stuck there for two weeks (or more) if China suddenly cut off all travel back to Beijing. It wasn't just that the embassy didn't want me to be inconvenienced. They also didn't want to have to pay for a hotel for me for two (or more) weeks. That kind of reasoning always makes me laugh.

My other science talks at CAGS, CUGB, and CAS reinforced my perspective that there's simply much more enthusiasm in China for the Earth sciences than in the US. For context, these were hard-core science talks, very specific to my discipline. On a good day at a US institution, I might get twenty-five people. Undergraduates listen to this stuff only because I'm selfish, and I put it in my lectures for classes that they have to take to graduate.

The setting for our CAGS talk was a little unusual. We met in a swanky meeting room with mood lighting, soft chairs and couches, and tea served all around. The only thing missing was a jazz band in the background with a classy singer and martinis. I gave my one-hour talk, then was subjected to a delightful one-and-a-half hours of highly intense grilling about science.

Maybe you think I'm being sarcastic when I say "delightful," but scientists always appreciate sharp questioning. Or most do, anyway. It shows people are interested. And it helps me think and develop new ideas.

Still, it seemed the tiniest bit of a letdown. There were probably only thirty people there, mostly from the group of a professor I work with (they have big groups). I wondered, how many arms had been twisted? Cynically, I thought it was probably fifty (two times twenty-five).

Then I heard that my talk had been live-streamed, and nearly fifty people tuned in. So, attendance was really at least seventy-five people, and most of them were under no pressure to listen in. That's pretty big for a hard-core science talk. CAGS is not a big institution.

My CAS talk was similar (in fact I gave the same talk). Maybe thirty people attended, but intense questioning and interest followed.

But CUGB was beyond believable. Huixia and I arrived at the room (which held fifty) almost two hours early. We arrived early because we wanted to discuss a project, and it was convenient.

> Matt: Why are there students here in the classroom?
>
> Huixia: They came to hear your talk.
>
> Matt: But it's not for two hours.

A half hour before my talk, the room was overflowing. After calling around, we moved to a new room. One that held two hundred. That filled, too. Not quite overflowing (there were a few empty chairs), but many people chose to stand.

Of course, I hope students came because they were interested in the topic, but I suppose I'm also a novelty. How many American scientists are they likely to see in the next year?

The funniest part, though, was the follow-up. Feeling inspired, I offered to give my climate talk at CUGB (the same talk I gave at the embassy). I thought a more general talk might be a little more accessible, and I don't mind being a novelty. Huixia said that would be great. But when she called the university administrators the next day, they asked me not to give a talk, at least not right away. Why not? They didn't want to risk a super-spreader event. How crazy is that?

If only we could harness that scientific excitement worldwide, we could solve the climate crisis in no time! Sorry, Mama Earth . . .

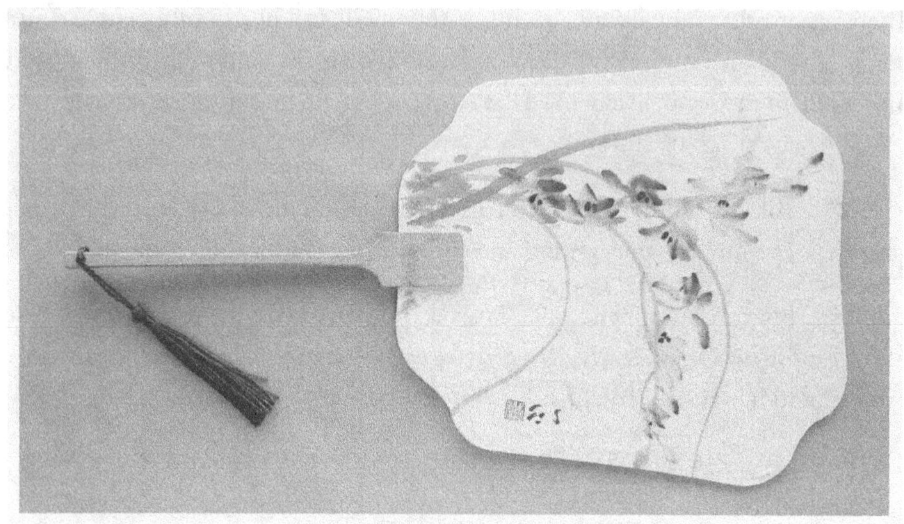

ONE OF THE FANS I RECEIVED

THE BIG ROOM AT CHINA UNIVERSITY OF GEOSCIENCES, BEIJING

SPEAKING AT CUGB. I WORE MY SUPER-SPECIAL, WESTERN-STYLE BOLO TIE.

# VISA-
# TATION DENIED

I was wrong. I thought that if I was persistent, I could reach the right people and convince them that a Chinese student who studies the collision between India and Asia over time spans of millions of years ago does not pose an existential threat to the United States military or business interests, and that we should extend him a visa. No dice.

To recap the situation (see "Visa in, Visa Out"), a student here in China has a fellowship to come work with me in the US. In parallel, another student here at the Chinese Academy of Sciences has a fellowship to work with a colleague at the University of California at Santa Barbara. Both students asked my advice for help in obtaining a visa. Both were ultimately unsuccessful. Presidential Proclamation 10043 prohibits visas for Chinese students in science, unless their work poses no threat to the US military or American businesses.

But how do students show that? I tried to obtain direct answers from visa offices both at the US embassy here in Beijing and at the US consulate in Guangzhou. Ultimately, I failed. First, there's no phone number. My attempts at navigating their phone tree concluded with an automated invitation to send them an email. Which I did, several times. This resulted in a couple relatively formulaic emails saying that visa officers won't talk to anyone except visa applicants or their lawyers. Attempts to engage in any meaningful conversation about procedures went nowhere. They simply stopped responding to my questions about how visa applicants should make the case that they're exempt from the proclamation.

I talked to contacts at the US embassy, asking for a meeting with anyone in the visa office. They tried to help, but the visa office brushed us off. Too busy. Not important.

One of my senators tried hard to help. After three messages from his office, the visa office in Guangzhou said yes, visa applicants are allowed to present documentation at the time of the interview that they are exempt from the proclamation. True, I was prohibited from attending the interview to help explain. And true, there's no information on any website that says this. And true, it seems a little suspicious that visa officers don't routinely ask an applicant "Do you have anything else you would like to add to your application?" After all, the presidential proclamation specifically calls out opportunities for exemptions. But at least we knew it was possible. Theoretically.

Except the US still wouldn't issue visas to these students, regardless of what they did. Both students provided documentation that their work was benign. The student with a fellowship to visit UC Santa Barbara had a letter from his prospective supervisor—a member of the US National Academy of Sciences, no less—saying that he was exempt from the proclamation. Boise State refused to allow me to submit a similar letter for the student who wanted to work with me, but his advisor here in China explained all this thoroughly. Both students were denied.

The State Department claims there's no significant impact on Chinese students or US academic institutions. They comment that they've issued tens of thousands of visas to Chinese students. Maybe, but in what fields? To do what? Anecdotally, I've heard of more visa rejections in the Earth sciences than approvals. At this point I have only small numbers, but 5:3 in favor of rejections seems pretty bad.

Why does this matter? Two reasons.

First, I don't like sending intellectual talent to my competitors in other countries. Why should Canada or Switzerland or England get all the good students? Why can't the US bring in the smartest kids? Many of them stay here. America has always welcomed talent in the past. Why change now?

Second, it makes the US look petty and racist. At least, that's how the Chinese are describing us now.

I talked to a contact in the public relations wing of the US embassy here, and he understands my concern. We're simultaneously shooting ourselves in the foot (sending brilliant students away) and giving ourselves a black eye (making ourselves look bad). Brilliant policy.

I wish I knew how to change it. But when your employees in the government refuse to talk to you, and you can't directly fire them, there's not much you can do.

# ORANGE YOU THANKFUL?

It's kind of sad to spend a holiday by yourself when you'd normally be with your family. I was a little surprised at how lonely I felt, because I don't make a big deal out of holidays. My dad didn't either, possibly because he was a recovering Orthodox Jew in a family that drifted gradually to a rather devout form of Protestant Christianity.

> Dad:   I just realized I now have seven children.
>
> Matt:  How do you figure that?
>
> Dad:   Four who were born once. And three who were born again.

I was the child who wasn't born again. Does that make me a middle child now? Number four in a line of seven?

Anyway, I inherited many of his perspectives on holidays, either through direct genetics or through social conditioning. I received a healthy dose from my mom too. Holidays were times to give people stuff they needed, like pencil erasers or a scraper for your car. Or maybe do something nice, like replace their splintery toilet seat. If I don't need anything (and most tenured faculty with grown children don't), I don't really expect to receive anything. It drives my family crazy.

My friends here in Beijing wanted to help me celebrate Thanksgiving, and they knew that the holiday focuses on food. So, I started receiving presents.

| | |
|---|---|
| Shaoxiong: | I didn't want you to feel lonely on Thanksgiving, so I brought you this. |
| Matt: | Wow, that's a big bag. What's in it? |
| Shaoxiong: | Some Chinese special foods. I don't know what you call this one, but it's very traditional. |
| Matt: | I don't know what you call it either. It looks a little like a cream puff. But is that seaweed? [Answer: Yes, it's two soft sponge cake-like rounds bonded with custardy filling, the whole thing covered in sugary shredded dried fish/shrimp(?) and seaweed flakes. Sort of a sardine-flavored cream puff. It tastes about like you would expect.] |
| Shaoxiong: | And these are traditional cookies. |
| Matt: | Wow, that's a lot of cookies. I don't know how I'm going to eat them all. |
| Shaoxiong: | And there are two types of oranges. |
| Matt: | Thanks, oranges are one of my favorite fruits. |

Actually, for a long time, oranges were my most favorite fruit. I ate them every day. Perhaps I was compensating for my childhood in Tennessee, when oranges were very expensive. We could eat them when they were in season in Florida. And we were allowed one while we watched the Orange Bowl on New Year's Day. Otherwise, that was it. Now, persimmons slightly edge them out, partly because I like the texture but also they're still a seasonal fruit, so they seem special. But a good orange is hard to beat.

| | |
|---|---|
| Huixia: | My husband is in Hangzhou. I will ask him to buy some oranges for you. He said last week they didn't taste good, but if they taste sweet this week, he will buy some. |
| Matt: | Oh, thanks! Of course, you know I love oranges. |

Wangchao:     Dear Dr. Kohn, I have sent you a box of navel oranges, a specialty of our hometown. Very delicious, very sweet.

Matt:     Thank you! I like oranges very much.

Wangchao:     The package should arrive in the next couple days.

Matt:     Great. I'll keep an eye out for it.

Lishuang:     Hi, I brought this for you. Happy Thanksgiving!

Matt:     Thanks! What's in here?

Lishuang:     The box is from rose-flavored moon cakes, but that's not what's in it.

Matt:     Oh, oranges! Wait, what's that written on them? "Happy Thanksgiving" and a big smiley face. Thank you!

Lishuang:     You're welcome. I hope you have a happy day.

The smiley face has definitely been the high point of oranges here for me.

The only problem with all the gifts I'm receiving, is that they make me a little teary-eyed. Partly because it reminds me of home, which is far away. But I'm also going to miss everyone here.

So, what do you do for Thanksgiving dinner if you're an American alone in China? The same thing (I'm told) that Jews do for Christmas in America—you go out for Chinese food. Of course, in Beijing, it's not very hard to find a Chinese restaurant that's open. After all, it's not a holiday here.

Perhaps knowing of the Jewish dilemma in America (or, more likely, because they're thoughtful and kind), Xiaochi and Summer treated me to Chinese Hotpot at a famous restaurant, named "Hi." I've had hotpot in America, although not at a restaurant. The meal consists of several tubs of boiling water, each flavored differently (hot pepper, mushroom, mutton plus chicken, and mushroom plus . . . tofu water?). The server delivers plate after plate after plate of thinly sliced foods. You drop these into the boiling water, and after a few seconds, fish out the cooked food, dunk it in some sauce (that you prepare from a sauce bar), and eat. It's a little like fondue except with much greater variety.

We ate many old favorites—mutton, beef, six or seven kinds of mushrooms (seriously), tofu, bamboo, and kelp. Plus a couple new twists on old themes: duck intestines (a favorite of Xiaochi), shrimp balls, and pork stomach. No, I don't know why the shrimp doesn't disintegrate in the water, but it's hard to pick up round slippery balls, even when they don't disintegrate.

I expect Jews in America probably don't eat shrimp balls and pork stomach very often, even for Christmas.

The dinner concludes with a guy stretching out noodle dough, which he cuts up and dunks in your hotpot. His performance is just like throwing a pizza, if a pizza were five meters (sixteen feet) long and two centimeters (one inch) wide.

Because I'll be leaving next month, I've been seeking out new food experiences. On the corner near the Institute, a guy sets up a cart every evening, selling roasted chestnuts. The method of cooking them is ingenious. There's a big tub, heated from below, that's filled with oiled pebbles (or maybe they're beans). The chestnuts are placed in the tub, and a stirrer moves them around. The pebbles help transfer heat, the oil keeps the chestnuts from getting too dry, and the stirring heats everything evenly. Xiaochi bought me some chestnuts the other day. I'm glad I tried them, although I don't need to eat them again anytime soon. Even cooked professionally, they're kind of dry, and they don't have much flavor. Something warm on a cold night is comforting, though.

On the other hand, I really don't recommend silkworm chrysalis. A couple days ago, I was taken out to dinner at a local dumpling restaurant and saw barbeque silkworm on the menu. Ever the intrepid adventurer, I ordered a skewer. I think what I expected was something crunchy and oily. Instead, the chrysalis shell reminds me of paper (actually, maybe it is a type of paper)—dry, flavorless, and tough. Reasoning that I rarely eat paper napkins, and regret it when I do, I chose not to swallow it. The inside was soft and gooey, also without much flavor.

Recalling what Euell Gibbons said about the bobcat, I can report that the silk part didn't bother me (even though I spit it out), but the worm was hard to swallow. I still get a little shuddery thinking about it.

Some of my friends here say they've never eaten silkworm. Cicadas, yes. Silkworms, no. But every one of them has commented that silkworm has a lot of protein. I'm thankful I tried it, but never again. Not even on Thanksgiving.

**SUGAR COOKIE AND SEAFOOD CREAM PUFF. THE DARK BITS ARE SEAWEED FLAKES. TOOTHPICK FOR SCALE.**

**ORANGE YOU GLAD IT'S THANKSGIVING?**

**HERE'S THE RANGE OF FOODS AT THE HOTPOT:**
Counterclockwise from the upper left: five kinds of mushroom, mutton, Vienna sausage sliced into a flower shape, my little bowl of sauce, my little plate with chopsticks, pork tripe, Xiaochi's little bowl of sauce, tofu, duck intestines (pink), ground shrimp (gray), bamboo slices, mutton. The two dishes on the rightmost side are kelp and hot spicy bamboo. There are also some small bowls of soup (with spoons). The hot water in the middle is (from upper left) mutton plus chicken, mushroom, hot pepper, and mushroom plus (maybe?) tofu water.

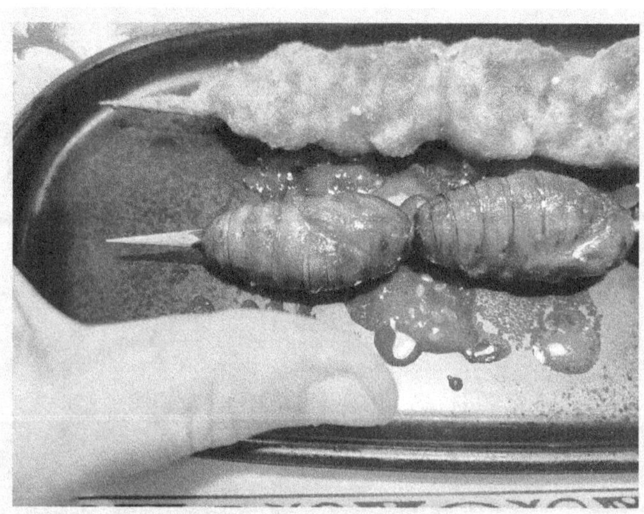

**BARBECUE SILKWORM CHRYSALIS. THUMB FOR SCALE.
THE SKEWER ABOVE IS CHICKEN.**

# THE GREAT STAIRCASE

Many people out west know of Grand Staircase–Escalante National Monument, although probably not for what the park offers. Rather, it became a famous political football after Bill Clinton established it by Presidential Proclamation No. 6920 in 1996.

A big problem was that the monument was so big. Some legislators questioned whether the president has authority to set aside so much land. The courts ruled on this multiple times—yes, the president can.

A coal mine had been proposed, and some were angered when that plan was scuttled. But, besides the fact that the government bought out the handful of leases, the quality of the coal and viability of the mine were always marginal at best. And, even then we knew the US shouldn't be burning coal. Global warming, remember? In fact, since then, we've made substantial progress in cutting back. In 2000, coal accounted for 50 percent of all power production. Now it's dropped to less than 20 percent. Coal is not coming back. This is a dead issue.

There is some uranium potential too. But nuclear power isn't exactly booming in the US. More to the point, some of the richest sources of uranium are in . . . dinosaur fossils. Yep. Bone can take up substantial uranium when it fossilizes. I know because that's one of the things I study. But, I think most would agree the value of dinosaur fossils probably lies more in science and less in energy production. And dinosaur fossils are a major scientific resource in the monument, especially in the Kaiparowits Formation on the Kaiparowits Plateau. That's where critters like *Kosmoceratops* were discovered.

And, of course, there were cultural and economic pluses to setting aside the monument, not least the preservation of Native American sites, and an increase in tourism dollars to the region.

No, most of the original controversy centered on the old states' rights versus federal rights argument that's been going on since the country was founded. The same argument that helped spark the Civil War. The same argument that caused local officials in Utah to put up signs on dirt two-tracks, claiming they're official county roads, so they have to remain open under a provision of the 1866 Mining Act. Among other things, public roads make it impossible to set aside land as wilderness.

Mostly the problem was that setting aside so much land without discussing it more with state and county officials pissed off a lot of people. Mostly on principle, less on fact.

What really set people off, though, was twenty years later, when President Trump tried to reverse Clinton's Proclamation No. 6920 with Proclamation No. 9682, reducing the size of Grand Staircase-Escalante by nearly half (also the nearby and much more politically sensitive Bears' Ears National Monument). He claimed he wanted to support fossil fuel and uranium development, but those were never major considerations. I'm sure a few people and companies would have benefited, but it was clearly a political hack job.

So, no one was surprised when President Biden reversed Trump's Proclamation No. 9682 with Proclamation No. 10286, restoring Grand Staircase–Escalante to its original boundaries. All this political badminton brought fame to an otherwise obscure park.

Why is it called "Grand Staircase"? Geology! There are a series of resistant sedimentary rocks, layered one on top of the other. Each forms a cliff of a different color: chocolate, vermilion, white, grey, and pink[8]. Zion is cut into the strata that form the white and vermilion cliffs. The cliffs are stepped across the landscape. Each step is something like one thousand feet (three hundred meters) high and ten miles wide (sixteen kilometers). A little too large even for dinosaurs. But on a *grand* scale, it's a little reminiscent of a staircase. Hence, "Grand Staircase."

I encountered some fairly grand staircases myself this last weekend. But they weren't geological. Rather, Xiaochi, Summer, and I took a day trip to another section of the Great Wall, at Mutianyu. And that's when I realized it shouldn't be called just "The Great Wall." No, it should also be called "The Great Staircase." Because, excepting a few inclines here and there, the whole thing is stairs. Steep pitch, shallow pitch, variable pitch. But step after step after step, for miles and miles and miles. The Great Wall of China is over twenty thousand kilometers long. That's long enough to go around Grand Staircase-Escalante National Monument about fifty times. But until now I had never thought directly about the vertical elevation gain/loss.

The elevation gain at Badaling (which I visited before) is approximately one thousand feet (three hundred meters), expressed over three to four kilometers. At Mutianyu, a couple sites say the elevation gains are similarly about one hundred meters per kilometer. I believe it. That's not super steep, only a 6° slope on average. But it's nearly all stairs. And some of those stairs are steep, too, apparently up to an 80° pitch. Best practices for setting a ladder recommend a shallower pitch (75°). Remember that stairs don't have rungs, though, so if you slip, there's not much to grab hold of.

Of course, it's risky to extrapolate from a couple small sections to an entire wall, but if I do anyway, all the elevation gains for the Great Wall of China would add up to approximately two thousand kilometers. That's about one third the radius of the Earth. Or one thousand Grand Staircases! Once again, the scale of the construction is staggering.

---

8. Hey, don't blame me for the choice of colors or spelling. Instead, talk to the ghost of Clarence Dutton. He's credited with the names from his work in the 1870s.

After climbing stairs all day, I was kind of staggering, too. But riding back to the Institute on the subway in Beijing was flat. I even took the stairs up to my fifth floor apartment.

**GOTTA LOVE THAT GREAT WALL GRANITE!**

**OOH, THAT'S STEEP!**

# DECEMBER

# THE SUMMER, IN WINTER

Almost exactly eighty years ago (as I write this), the Japanese attacked Pearl Harbor. The next day, the US declared war on Japan. And nine days later, Congress authorized the Tennessee Valley Authority to begin constructing Fontana Dam, in western North Carolina. Construction began only two weeks later, and the dam began generating hydroelectric power three years later, in January 1945. Record time for building a dam—the fourth highest dam in the world at the time, and still the highest east of the Rockies.

Why the rush? After all, the plans had been on the books for years. Answer: power. Power for the Aluminum Company of America (Alcoa), so they could make aluminum faster. Aluminum was needed for airplanes. One reason the allies were able to defeat Germany is because, as airplanes were shot down, we were able to replace them faster.

Power for the new Oak Ridge research facility. Oak Ridge was created to develop nuclear weapons, which helped us defeat Japan.

Fontana Dam didn't just generate a ton of power, though, it flooded out over 1,300 families. To compensate, the government agreed to build a thirty-mile-long (about fifty-kilometer-long) road on the north side of Fontana Lake (reservoir), along the southern edge of Great Smoky Mountains National Park, so folks could go visit their old family cemeteries. But after completing just six or seven miles (about ten kilometers) of road, construction stopped. Why? Geology is one reason.

Unfortunately, the road cuts through the Anakeesta Formation, which is a sulfide-rich, carbonaceous schist. Sulfides react with oxygen and water to make sulfuric acid, and the new road threatened ecological disaster. Great Smoky Mountains is an ecological hotspot, with the highest biodiversity of all the National Parks. The government didn't want to risk killing off a bunch of diverse faunas and floras, so people could access graveyards.

Eventually, the government compensated the county for the unfinished road to the tune of fifty-two million dollars. North Carolina manages the funds, the county gets the interest, and the government ferries families across the lake every year to visit the graves.

One attraction of the road is a quarter-mile (four hundred meter) long tunnel at its very end. Walking through it can be something of a surreal experience. When you first start in, there's still light from the opening behind you. You're just taking a walk through a tunnel, right? But after you get about half-way through, it's too dark to see much around you. All you can see is the light in the opening ahead of you. Except that the light is so far distant, every step you take doesn't seem to bring you any closer. You're walking and walking and walking, and getting nowhere. Like walking the wrong way on a moving sidewalk. Eventually, the light levels increase, the opening appears bigger, and the feeling goes away. But for a few minutes, it's like you're walking on a never-ending road to nowhere.

In fact, although "Lakeview Drive" is the official name of the road, everyone calls it the "Road to Nowhere." The name is generally thought to refer to the abrupt end of the road in the middle of a southern Appalachian rainforest. After walking that tunnel a couple times, I'm not so sure that's the only reason.

The Long Corridor at the Summer Palace reminded me of the tunnel at the end of the Road to Nowhere. I visited the Summer Palace again with Huixia on a cold and sunny Wednesday. It was a great time to visit. Hardly anyone was there. We could actually see down long stretches of the Long Corridor. Walking along wasn't quite the surreal experience of the tunnel at the end of the Road to Nowhere. But sometimes it was hard to tell we were actually going anywhere.

Huixia commented that she's visited the Summer Palace many times, but this was the first she had ever walked the corridor end-to-end. There were too many people during her other visits.

Without the crowds, it was easier to appreciate the paintings too. Many images are scenes of animals, plants, famous old guys (for example, Confucius), or buildings. We found one scene from the Summer Palace itself. Other paintings are based on four classic Chinese works, including *Journey to the West* (aka *The Monkey King*), which I've read in translation. Fortuitously, I looked up just as we came to one of the Monkey King paintings. I recognized him not only from his face (surprise!—the Monkey King has the face of a monkey), but also from his long iron staff. Just like the story says.

The disadvantage of visiting an outdoor park in December is that there's an overwhelming sense that everything is closing down. Hardly any shops are open, but, more significantly, many trees have lost their leaves, the bushes are dusty and drab, the lotus plants that cover large sections of the waterways are withered and brown, there's ice on surfaces . . . For those who notice these things, the sun is lower on the horizon than in the summertime too.

Sadly, this is also how I feel about my travels in China. With only a little more than one week left (out of twenty-one), every day feels like closing doors. This is the last time I'll see the Summer Palace. The last time (probably) I'll go on an adventure with Huixia. One of the last times I'll be outside for any length of time. And the truly sad part is that, unlike winter, my endings may be more than seasonal. Will I be able to return next year? Probably not.

To obtain an academic exchange visa, I would need to accept travel support from my collaborators here. And, if I do that, new legislation means I could lose all access to federal research funding for my students. No one knows for sure, but the consequences could be disastrous. The State Department's behavior toward Chinese researchers makes me wary.

In principle, Heather and I could pay our way on tourist visas. But Idaho salaries are . . . conservative. And Tibet probably won't allow tourists, especially from the US.

There's little chance my friends here can get visas to travel to the US anytime soon.

It's like I'm back on the Road to Nowhere. I'm walking through the tunnel, marking time as I approach the exit. And, just like the first time I walked it, I don't know what I'll find. Maybe there's a path through on the other side. Several trails do take off from the Road to Nowhere. Maybe there's a way for me to return to China next year or the year after. But it could be just a dead end. Time will tell.

**LEAFLESS WILLOW, GARDEN OF HARMONIOUS INTERESTS, SUMMER PALACE**

**THE LONG CORRIDOR, ALMOST PEOPLELESS**

**370-YEAR-OLD TREE**

**SMALL TEMPLE, NORTH SIDE OF PALACE**

**BRIDGE, NORTHEAST SIDE OF PALACE. THIS REMINDS ME A LITTLE OF OHIO IN THE WINTERTIME.**

**SCENE FROM JOURNEY TO THE WEST**

**CONFUCIUS**

# GOING . . .
# GOING . . .

. . . not going.

Agent: Why didn't the American know he can't fly to the US today?

Xiaochi: How was he supposed to know you canceled his flight when you didn't tell him?

Agent: We tried calling him.

Xiaochi: Matt, did you receive a call from China Southern about a cancellation?

Matt: All I got was an email two days ago saying I was on an earlier flight.

Xiaochi: He never received a call.

Agent: Yes, we tried calling him, but the phone never connected.

Xiaochi: Matt what phone number did you list when you made your reservation? Was it your US phone?

Matt: I have no idea. That was two months ago.

Agent: And we sent him an email.

Xiaochi:   Matt, did you receive an email?

Matt:     Yes, two days ago saying I was on an earlier flight.

Xiaochi:   Did you receive any others?

Matt:     No. I think I'd remember if I received an email.

This may rank as one of the bigger screwups an airline has ever dropped on me. Two days ago, China Southern Airlines sent me an email saying my flight was delayed. Uh-oh, that could be serious. I was scheduled to leave Beijing at 3:30 p.m., arrive in Guangzhou at 6:45 p.m., and leave Guangzhou for the US at 9:30 p.m. (just under three hours later). If the flight from Beijing was delayed, I might not make my connection.

However, the subject line of the email completely misrepresented its contents.

I wasn't delayed at all. Rather, it said my 3:30 p.m. flight had been canceled, and did I mind transferring to the 1:30 p.m. flight, arriving at 4:45 p.m.? I responded, yes, that's fine.

Whew! Disaster averted. Again. Sure, that means less time in the morning with my friends, but that's better than missing my flight home.

Now, I've traveled extensively, and I know that things can change unexpectedly. Still, I was a little surprised when we arrived at the Beijing airport at 11:30 a.m. this morning, and was told that there was a problem, and I couldn't travel to the US. OK, sure, the thought had crossed my mind that there might be a complication. No, I was surprised because the airline seemed a little offended that I didn't know about this. Apparently, I was supposed to be monitoring my email an hour before leaving for the airport in case they suddenly canceled my flight. Because that's how they told me my flight to Guangzhou had been canceled, and I'm now scheduled on a later flight that leaves at 5:30 p.m. A flight that arrives at 8:45 p.m. Forty-five minutes before my flight to the US. Leaving (at most) forty-five minutes to make it through immigration, security, check in, etc. Nope, not going to happen.

What to do? Xiaochi starts talking vigorously with the gate agent:

> Huixia:   China Southern can reschedule you, but the earliest you can return to the US is on the sixteenth.
>
> Matt:   The sixteenth? That's crazy! That's almost a week from now.
>
> Huixia:   Right. I'll tell them we won't do that.

[more conferencing]

> Huixia:   Another airline, Xiamen Airlines, has a flight that leaves Beijing tomorrow and connects through Xiamen to LA. You would get in twenty-four hours later than you planned. What do you think? Should we do that?
>
> Matt:   Well . . .

Of course, yes, I can do that, but there are many downstream dependencies (like rescheduling flights, making new hotel reservations, etc.), all at unknown expense.

Then Xiaochi uncovers another wrinkle.

> Xiaochi:   Do you remember exactly what you paid for your flight on China Southern?
>
> Matt:   Let me think, do I remember the exact cost of a flight, in Chinese yuan, for a reservation I made two months ago? Uh . . . no.
>
> Xiaochi:   Can you look it up? China Southern says they need to know.
>
> Matt:   Why do they need to know this? Surely they can look it up themselves.
>
> Xiaochi:   I don't know why, but they want to know from you.
>
> Matt:   OK, let's see . . .

So, now I start a frustratingly useless search of websites, credit card statements, and bank statements, trying to track down the value of the original reservation. I know already the cost of the flight was not listed in any of my email confirmations.

So, everything depends on reliable Wi-Fi. And the Wi-Fi at Beijing airport is not reliable.

On several levels, this is hard for me to understand. First, why does China Southern need to know this? (Can I just make up a number?) What possible purpose does it serve? Second, why can't an airline monitor its own transactions? Third, what kind of airline doesn't confirm the cost of a ticket with its passengers, then turns around and asks its passenger to confirm the cost of a ticket?

Anyway, after twenty minutes (I'm still searching . . .) China Southern says they don't need that information anymore. I never really find out why, but I think some computer genius figured out how to look up my reservation in their own computers.

So, we make a new plan: I will cancel my flight with China Southern. I will make a new reservation through Xiamen Airlines. I will move my flight home to Boise to the next day. I will cancel my Airbnb reservation (and notify the owner I'm not showing up). I will make a new hotel reservation. And I will not allow my head to explode.

Except that, other than the last task, "I" can't really do any of this. I need help from others. Why? Because half of this is in Chinese, and the other half is dependent on reliable Wi-Fi. Which I don't have.

First, the flight with China Southern is canceled. Or . . .? Now that I think about it, no one actually said this, they just stopped asking me questions. I resolve to check my bank account when I get home.

Second, the flight to Xiamen is reserved, except . . .:

> **Agent:** You shouldn't take the flight at 2:50 p.m. That arrives only three-and-a-half hours early for your flight to the US. You should leave earlier.
>
> **Matt:** Are you kidding me? That should be plenty of time. Why would I want to leave earlier?
>
> **Agent:** No, you're asking for trouble if you fly that late.

Matt:    What are you talking about? What could take that long in the airport that I have to arrive earlier? Customs? Immigration?

Agent:    If the flight is delayed or canceled, you have no option. If you take the earlier flight, you can still get to the US.

Matt:    OK, whatever, just do it.

So we do it.

Actually, Xiaochi does it because the app that we're required to use is entirely in Chinese, and my phone (even though it's Chinese) can't process the QR code. This means that Xiaochi pays more than one thousand bucks to help me out, on the promise that I'll pay him back. He's a good friend.

And that's how I'm now scheduled to get up at 5:30 a.m. on a Sunday morning to catch an 11:00 a.m. flight to Xiamen, so I can arrive nine and a half hours early for a flight to the US.

Heather helps me deal with the hotel and flight to Boise. That's relatively easy because it's all in English, I can give her my login information, and Wi-Fi in the US is reliable. Plus, she's really good at this kind of thing.

By some miracle, I manage to connect to the Airbnb website while Wi-Fi is working and send a message to the Airbnb guy.

Thank goodness that's over, right?

Nope, not so fast . . .

China and the US both require a COVID-19 test the day before boarding a flight. My COVID-19 test from Friday isn't valid on Sunday. So, I need to find a testing center. We've been at the airport for three hours solid, and poor Xiaochi has been arguing almost nonstop with airline personnel. Now it's 2:30 p.m., and we have to find a testing center in time for me to receive results before 11 a.m. tomorrow. And, because the Beijing airport is far outside Beijing, and Beijing traffic is notoriously bad, it will take at least an hour, maybe two, to get to a clinic . . .

Oh, and not just any testing center either. Actually, there's one in the airport. But, apparently, the US now requires COVID test results in English. Many Chinese testing centers report results in Chinese only. Of course, there are numerous translation apps that would allow officials to verify that results are valid. But that would require an extra step, right?

So, Xiaochi keeps searching until he finally finds the closest testing center that will accept my credentials and provide results in English. Off we go on another crosstown adventure!

**IN THE LONG PARK WITH LISHUANG BEFORE LEAVING FOR THE AIRPORT. APPARENTLY, I WAS RECEIVING AN IMPORTANT EMAIL ABOUT NOW . . .**

# EVERY CLOUD

. . . has a silver lining, right?

It sure doesn't seem that way after the airport. I still have to get COVID-19 tested again!

Xiaochi calls a taxi, and he, Huixia, and I zoom off to God knows where so I can get my test. Actually, I know we're traveling to a branch of Anzhen Hospital because Xiaochi asked me if I had my insurance card from them. But it's probably not the branch downtown. I doubt we'd arrive in time.

I'm exhausted, so I fall asleep.

An hour later, I awake as we arrive at a hospital. Xiaochi is very agitated. I feel agitated too. Huixia's the only one who seems calm.

Is it her training as a mom? The stress of dealing with children can knock down the stress you feel toward other things. Kids do such crazy things, maybe everything else seems tame in comparison. Or, maybe she's just a calm person. Period.

We rush up to the guard (there's always a guard), and explain. Xiaochi fills out some form and we go in. He scans a QR code, enters a bunch of information, and takes it to a window. The woman there checks it, and tells us to go pay our fee at a kiosk. We pay, using my card from the hospital, and it issues us a receipt—thirty-five yuan for that special desiccating scrub down my throat. So far, so good.

We go to the next window, and the woman there says, no, she doesn't deal with Americans, we have to go down to the next window. We go down to that window, and the woman there says, no, she can't help us, we have to go back and talk to the first woman. We go back and talk to the first woman, who refuses to help us.

I start thinking again of the first letter of the last 3 days of the workweek, in sequence . . .

We go back to the guard guy, and he says no, we should be able to get the test. Xiaochi tells him we're being rejected. The guard guy takes us into a back office where there's another official from the hospital. The official assures us, yes, I can get the test. The guard guy accompanies us back to the first obstinate woman, and she reluctantly relinquishes two labels with bar codes.

That was it? All this obstructive folderol over two tiny labels? Third time's a charm, I guess. Except I'm feeling less than charming. At this point, only Huixia could be mistaken for charming.

We return to the second window, where the woman takes the two labels, puts one on a centrifuge tube, takes out a swab, assiduously dries my uvula, then shoos us away.

Test completed! Whew! Everything's good now, right?

We take Huixia back home, then return to the Institute. I arrange to have dinner with Lishuang (Liu), Xiaochi (Liu), and a guy named Peng Liu at a barbecue restaurant nearby. Three Lius and a Kohn. There must be a joke in there somewhere . . .

On our way to the restaurant we see the luminous trail of a rocket in the west. Lishuang and Xiaochi tell me this is a special event. And the trail is certainly spectacular. It's a little disturbing, though, because it's not vertical. Of course, I know the wind rearranges and flattens it, but it still reminds me of failed rocket launches in the US.

We also see Jupiter and Venus clearly. The wind has cleared out much of the smog. What a relief!

At the restaurant, I insist we should drink some beer. Everyone is agreeable, but they balk at the price on the menu. Instead, Peng runs out to a local store and buys five big cans of beer. Two Budweiser, and one each of three other Chinese brands. They're all light, essentially like Bud.

Everyone is laughing, for the first time today. What a relief after the airport and hospital. This is truly a silver lining—I get to spend a last evening with at least a couple of my best friends here.

At the restaurant, I discover I missed out on a couple varieties of barbecue: chitlins (euphemistically called "sausage"), chicken feet, and squid.

There's not much to chicken feet, mostly skin and tendon with some fat. Hardly any muscle to sink your teeth into. I eat one, but leave the other for Lishuang.

I look over at the table next to us. The two guys there have a plate piled with chicken feet! Dozens and dozens of them. I guess some people like them.

After dinner, I get my towel and shampoo back from the student office (I donated all my useful stuff to the students and postdocs), take a shower, and go to bed. It's been a long and eventful day. Tomorrow starts at 5:30 a.m. But everything will go smoothly, right? I mean, what could go wrong now?

**THE STRING OF LIGHTS ON THE HORIZON
IS THE TRAIL FROM THE ROCKET.**

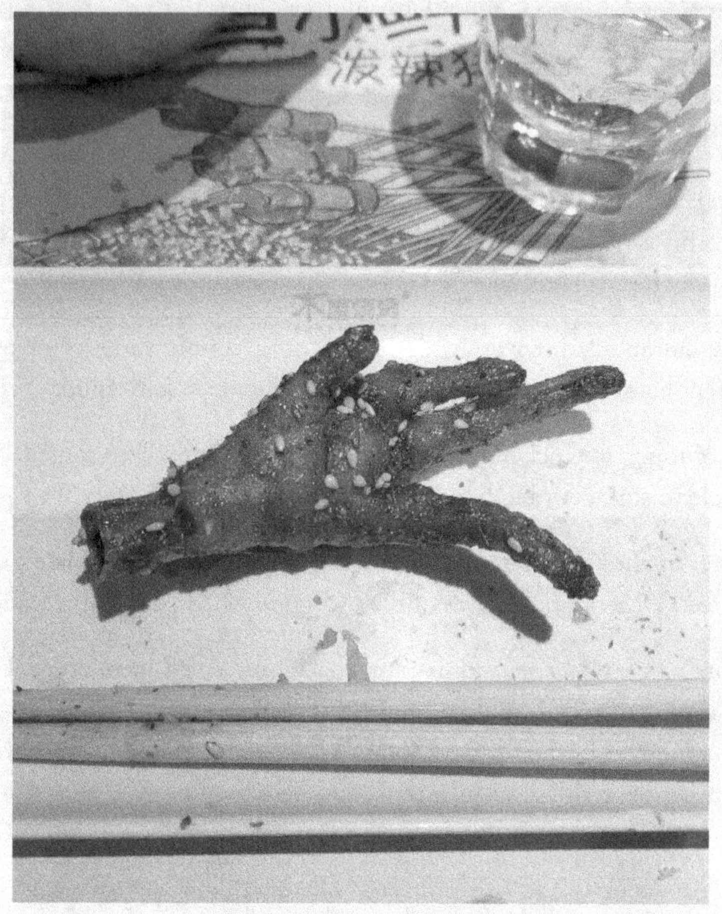

**BARBECUED CHICKEN FOOT**

# . . . GONE?

Me:        What do you mean I can't leave?

Xiaochi:  The COVID-19 report we received from the hospital yesterday doesn't have all the information that the airline wants. You tested negative, so you can travel to Xiamen, but not to the US. Also, the report is in Chinese only. We don't know if the US will accept it.

It's Sunday morning. Attempt number two to send Matt home. An attempt that's not looking too likely to succeed at the moment. But Xiaochi never gives up.

Keep in mind that the number of COVID-19 cases in Beijing is *zero*.

As in *no cases*.

Xiamen had one yesterday, none the day before. The average daily case load in the US now is one hundred thousand. Los Angeles alone has fifteen hundred per day. There are more cases every day in LA than Beijing has had since the pandemic began two years ago.

A traveler from China is the least of LA's worries. And translation apps can tell you my test is negative. But the gate agent is adamant.

Xiaochi:  OK, let's try to export your test to Alipay. Alipay has all your information. I know it works for me. Maybe it will work for you.

Me:        OK.

Xiaochi messes with my phone for a while until . . .

Xiaochi:  Not working.

Me:        What's not working?

Xiaochi:  It won't accept a US passport. It only works with a Chinese
          ID number.

This must be the thirty-second time we've experienced this problem in the last
four-and-a-half months.

Xiaochi talks vigorously with a senior gate agent again. For a long time. Then:

Xiaochi:  OK, come with me.

Me:        Where are we going?

Xiaochi:  Now we go downstairs.

Me:        Why? Where are we going?

Xiaochi:  Now you get tested again.

Me:        Here at the airport?

Xiaochi:  Yes, here at the airport.

Me:        But I thought the report from the airport would be only
          in Chinese.

Xiaochi:  Yes, but we think Xiamen Air will let you fly to
          America with it.

So, we leave Lishuang on guard duty with my bags and drop down to the first
floor makeshift testing center. For a mere thirteen times the cost of yesterday's
test, I can get tested, again, for COVID-19. And receive results in two to
four hours.

Again, we struggle with the requisite app. Again, it doesn't like my name. Again, it doesn't like my passport number. It's designed for Chinese citizens, not Americans.

Xiaochi confers closely with the clinic gatekeeper. I notice the gatekeeper has an unusually long fingernail on his pinkie—a coke nail. Just my luck to need help from a cocaine addict.

Eventually, the cokehead lets us through. Xiaochi fills out some paperwork that I sign (I don't know what I just signed away . . .), and I get my uvula scrubbed again with a cotton swab. At least I don't gag, like the woman ahead of me.

Back to the gate. Surely everything is OK now, right? Wrong.

What's the problem now? Xiaochi is arguing with the gate agent. Ooh, it's getting hot! He's practically shouting.

Now the senior gate agent who sent us downstairs is approaching. More shouting.

Yes, it's all in Chinese, but I can still tell Xiaochi is saying something along the lines of "You told us we could go get a COVID-19 test downstairs and everything would be all right. Now, we come back, and you say there's a problem? We did exactly what you said. This is unfair! You have to process Dr. Kohn."

And the senior gate agent is saying something along the lines of "Yes, we told you to go downstairs to get the test. You should get results within two to four hours. Probably you will hear before he has to board his plane."

To which Xiaochi replies "Are you kidding me? Listen to what you're saying! Four hours from now is after his flight leaves. He can't wait that long. You have to process his flight paperwork now."

To which the senior gate replies [blah, blah, blah].

| | |
|---|---|
| Xiaochi: | Blah, blah, blah!! |
| Senior gate agent: | Blah! blah blah. |
| Xiaochi: | Blah blah blah!! |
| Senior gate agent: | Blah blah, blah blah . . . |

Eventually everything gets worked out. I sign some kind of form (maybe it's a special form, maybe not?). They check my bags through to LA (at least, that's what they say). Now, it's 8:30, and we've been arguing and testing and arguing and messing with apps and arguing since 7:00 a.m. I'm kind of glad we got here so early. Super-stressful for Xiaochi, though. Lishuang seems a little shell-shocked.

Xiaochi, Lishuang, and I go get some breakfast noodles, then I head to security.

With my boarding card and passport, the guards let me through, and they even speak a little English, so it's easy to unload my computer and phones, and send everything through their X-ray machine. This looks promising!

On the other side? A little more intense scrutiny than I'm used to.

First, I set off the metal detector (my boots), so am wanded, very carefully. They don't have the same combination shower stall spin drier scanners like we have in the US, so maybe they have to be more careful. Regardless, they check every square inch on my body. Every square centimeter, too.

The security agent is surprised by all the microscope slides I have in my pack. I decided to carry them with me because they're fragile. There are close to two hundred. She checks to be sure I can't somehow slit throats with them, but seems to think that anyone who uses a microscope is probably not a threat.

Hey, all you petrologists and microbiologists out there, remember to tell security you use microscopes next time you travel.

The security agent checks my portable Wi-Fi (wondering if it's an explosive battery). She also seems worried about one of Xiaochi's presents. Of course, I didn't pack his presents, but I doubt it's anything explosive. None of our friends are into explosives. At least, I don't think they are. But she realizes it's a present, so instead of unwrapping it, she rescans it. All clear.

After five or ten minutes of intense scrutiny, I'm allowed to go to the gate!

Which turns out to be at the bitter end of the terminal. But that's OK because I'm not going to get much exercise for a while, plus I get to see some interesting features along the way. Like the fake (but beautiful) lotus flowers with fake (but beautiful) mist bubbling up around them.

I wait around a while, then an announcement is made, and everybody gets into a line. I assume it's for boarding, so I join.

To board, I have to submit a health code. Everyone else is submitting their green code (a separate mini app I have on WeChat). I could find it, but I already have my COVID-19 test from this morning out on my phone. Hey, will it work? I decide to try. The gate agent seems impressed with my report and takes a picture. Is it for airport security, or does he want to show his kids at home? "Hey, guess what I saw at the airport today!" Another guy scans my boarding card and sends me down the jetway.

On the plane, the seat is cramped, but the flight is only about half full, and there's no one next to me. We take off for Xiamen, and I fall asleep almost immediately.

Xiamen is described as a beautiful city, a real tourist destination. It's on the coast, and has some nice hills. Xiamen may be beautiful sometimes, but not today. The air pollution is so indescribably bad, I can barely make out the city or the hills. I'm certainly glad to be on my way. But I can't recommend Xiamen in December. Not if you go outside, anyway. Which I won't. There's so much more adventure awaiting me in the airport!

**BEIJING (DAXING) AIRPORT AT 7:00 A.M.**

**LISHUANG ON GUARD DUTY. DON'T MESS WITH HER!**

**LOTUS DISPLAY INSIDE BEIJING AIRPORT**

**INVERSION OVER XIAMEN. THE DARK GRAY IS TRAPPED POLLUTION FROM DENSE COLD AIR. YOU CAN BARELY MAKE OUT THE UNDEVELOPED HILLS.**

# . . . GONE!

Arriving in the Xiamen airport is a bit confusing. Do I have to pass through security again to get to my international flight? Fortunately, one woman at an information desk willingly uses the translation app on my phone (about the third or fourth person in China who seems to understand intuitively what it's about).

She tells me I have to go downstairs, then straight ahead, then upstairs again.

I walk that way, realize I'm headed out of the terminal, turn back, ask them again if they are sure I need to exit security. They reassure me, and I go downstairs to baggage claim.

I have to pass through health screening again (essentially I'm entering Xiamen city), and the people there give me more explicit directions to international departures. I make the first turn too early and end up at the missing baggage desk. I decide—why not?—to ask whether they can verify whether my bags are checked through. It doesn't hurt to be sure. They assure me that, yes, bags from Beijing are automatically checked through to LA. No worries.

I exit baggage claim, wend my way upstairs, find international departures, and am stopped cold at the entrance to international departures. Why?

Because it's only 2:00 p.m. International departures won't open until "8:00 or 9:00 p.m." (so says the customs agent there). Customs agents manage entry to international departures.

I have six or seven hours to wait.

In the meantime, one customs agent helps me fill out the customs form. She's very kind, helpful, and understands the translation app. Person number five? And the second, today. All goes smoothly.

Well, the benches outside the entry to international departures are thoroughly uncomfortable. I manage to find an electrical outlet near the floor (one of two on the entire floor, I think), and sit on the stone floor, WeChatting with friends, writing, and occasionally snacking.

Four hours later, at 6:00 p.m., I get up to stretch my legs, and I ask the customs agent when they'll open. She says 9:30 p.m. Nine thirty p.m.!? Wow, that's a long time to wait. So, I ask whether she might let me in a little early since I'm a clueless American. I'm joking, but she says she might. I go back and sit down.

At 8:00 p.m., I get up to check what's going on, and find 150 people already standing in line. I find the customs agent, ask her if I should go to the end of the line, and she says (essentially) "Sorry, dude. If you had been here first, maybe, but now all these people are ahead of you."

Yes, I screwed up our agreement, so I sheepishly go to the end of the line. And wait . . . and wait . . . and wait.

A Chinese woman in front of me, named Jenny, asks in beautiful English whether I will watch her stuff while she uses the bathroom. I'm a little shocked because it's the best English I've heard in two months. I'm momentarily thankful for my mask because it covers my surprise. I agree. When she comes back, we start talking. Now it's 8:30.

Everyone has anxieties about travel to the US. The kid in front of us is in a master's program at Duke University. He's worried that if he gets turned back for any reason, he won't be allowed to reschedule a flight until after classes start.

Jenny has a paper copy of her test, but it's in Chinese only. I've been told it must be in English.

I, of course, don't even have a written report. Mine is electronic. That won't be a problem, right?

Then, at 8:50, I get a frantic call from Xiaochi:

Xiaochi:   Matt, you have to go to gate seven to pick up your bags.

Matt:   What?! They didn't check them through?

Xiaochi:   No, they have them at gate seven.

Matt:   Gate seven? That doesn't make any sense. Don't you mean baggage claim?

Xiaochi:   No, gate seven. Please go get them and recheck them.

Matt:   Ok, on my way.

This, of course, could be disastrous. If I lose my place in line, I'll no longer be number 150, I'll be number 300. This flight could easily be overbooked and I could lose my seat. Even if I don't, who knows where I'll end up on the flight. The broom closet?

I already know they don't cram passengers into overhead bins. Anyone who travels regularly knows that space is too valuable.

I frantically ask Jenny to please watch my stuff while I run get my bags. We exchange WeChat info and agree that if the line starts moving, she'll move my stuff along with it. I don't know when international will open. Security said "8:00 or 9:00 p.m." and it's already 8:55. Off I run.

I run downstairs, plead with the guards to let me back into baggage claim (surely that's what Xiaochi meant, right?). I'm directed to a different entrance, and am searched thoroughly, but allowed in. To find—there's no baggage claim number seven.

Just as I'm about to run for the missing baggage desk (again), I hear a guy shouting. Some airline worker has a cart with my two bags on it. Glory be! I don't have to figure out what they hell they meant by gate seven (probably actually gate seven, but why would they take the bags there?).

I grab the cart, thank the guard lady at baggage claim, and head for the elevator. It's after 9:00, now, and international departures might be open!

I don't know who designed this stupid cart, but it develops static electricity as it rolls that discharges through my hands. My hands tingle constantly as I push the cart rapidly along the line of people to where I was before. Except, where's Jenny and my stuff?! They're not there anymore. Why? Because international departures opened. Where are they now?

I move up the line, receiving baleful glares from people, until I find my little carry-on in safe hands with Jenny and the guy from Duke. I rejoin the line.

Disaster averted. Once again. By Xiaochi. Once again. And Jenny.

I enter customs. They direct me to the non-Chinese line, which moves much more slowly. An agent scans my code, checks my passport, subjects me to facial recognition software (creepy), then directs me onward.

All my bags are scanned. I'm carrying a rock hammer shaped like a pickaxe, several pounds of glass, several X-ray impenetrable rocks, and dense electronics. The guards just wave me through. I don't think they even looked at the X-ray images. They must have heard I use microscopes.

Now I enter a series of short lines, each in front of a counter. Will I be able to check in without a paper COVID test result?

My line moves *very slowly*. I'm seven people deep, and it takes thirty minutes to get to the desk. Now it's pushing 10:00 p.m. But, all goes smoothly. The gate agent looks at my passport, looks at my vaccination card, checks my COVID-19 test (I give him the Chinese language version). And issues me a boarding card.

I guess it didn't have to be in English.

The only snag is that my bags manage to jam in the scanner, shutting down all operations for a few minutes. But someone reboots the scanning system, the gate agent returns my passport, and I'm on my way.

I go downstairs to wait for a shuttle bus. Eventually, the gate agents check my boarding card, passport, subject me to more facial recognition (creepy), and I'm on the bus.

Ten minutes later (it takes a while to fill the bus), I'm on the plane. Headed home at last.

Oh, but wait, there's more! Shortly before the flight leaves, a flight attendant leans across a seat and asks "Is this yours?" She's holding something in her hand. "Why, yes, it is!" Where did they find my passport and boarding card? Maybe I set it down on a seat while I was lifting bags into the overhead. Maybe it fell out of my pocket as I bent over for something. At any rate, disaster averted. Again. Except, this time, for once, without Xiaochi's help.

**LINE TO CHECK IN TO INTERNATIONAL DEPARTURES, LOOKING TOWARD THE ENTRANCE**

**LINE TO CHECK IN TO INTERNATIONAL DEPARTURES, LOOKING AWAY FROM THE ENTRANCE**

# FINAL THOUGHTS

"So, Matt, what do you think of China. How was it?"

It's 11:00 p.m. back at the gate in Xiamen, and Jenny asks me the question I've been asking myself for the last four-and-a-half months.

"I love it!"

She looks at me both skeptically and pityingly.

I quickly (and sheepishly) amend: "I love the people. I have great friends here now. The surveillance really creeps me out."

And that sums up most of my feelings. There were things in China that were hard for me, like surveillance, but its people more than made up for that. Huixia and Xiaochi from the start and throughout, but also my new friends and collaborators, especially Lishuang, Shujuan, Yang (close friend of Xiaochi's at the Institute), and Fuyuan (Xiaochi's boss). Huixia's family all welcomed me enthusiastically. Their kindness and generosity helped me through the daily frustrations and loneliness. There were many other people, also, too numerous to list by name.

So, what were the things in China that bugged me? The top ones are:

1. Surveillance. I like my freedoms. Being monitored all the time, especially with facial-recognition software, makes me uncomfortable. Yes, I know, the US uses it too. In fact, that's how I passed through immigration in LA. I simply walked up to a monitor, it automatically

activated (I didn't do anything), took my picture, compared it to my record, gave me the green light, and I walked over to baggage claim. Literally thirty seconds. The difference is that I requested special security privileges when I travel, and have willingly given up my surveillance liberty at that one point in exchange for convenience—I made that single choice. I don't have a choice in China, and surveillance isn't limited to immigration. Privacy is important to me, but cameras are everywhere.

And, why does every building need a guard?

2. Air pollution and water quality. Please remember that China can't help its geography. Boise and Salt Lake City are very clean cities in the US, and we get inversions and air pollution, too, at least in the wintertime. Fire-season air can be dangerous to breathe if the wind blows the wrong way. But the smog in Beijing (and Xiamen, apparently) is vastly worse. After walking outside in Beijing (but not vigorously) for an hour or two each day during my last week, I ended up with significant lung irritation. Even as I write this, days after my return, my lungs still hurt. Beijing should never host the Olympics again. No offense, China, it's a question of health. If you host the Olympic Games again, please hold them somewhere else. And not Xiamen.

"Don't drink the tap water." That's what everyone told me, anyway. It isn't just that this means I'm drinking bottled water all the time, which creates mountains of waste. It means water quality is generally worse. The implications for health make me uneasy.

3. Technological failures. These drove me crazy. Yes, technology is cool when it works, but it's aggravating when it doesn't. Because China's software often has no English language option and is designed for Chinese citizens with (a) local phone numbers, (b) local bank accounts, and (c) Chinese ID cards, it routinely failed for me. You know how aggravating it is when the software on your computer screws up? Well imagine that happens every day for four-and-a-half months.

4.  Role of women. Gender discrimination is everywhere. Some of it is cultural. For example, if your teacup needs filling, the men in the group often look to the women to do it. A critic might say, no, the task generally goes to the lower-status members of a group, who can be men. And that's true. A male postdoc will usually jump to the task of filling teacups before a female associate professor.

    But, besides the fact that status rarely impresses me when it comes to basic needs, there aren't very many professionally senior/powerful women. Clearly, it's harder for women to succeed, especially if they have children, so they are often in less powerful positions—filling teacups rather than having their teacups filled. The number of female professors and associate professors at the Institute is very low, roughly 10 percent and 15 percent, respectively. In fairness, the pot of America's geosciences has been every bit as charred as China's kettle. Only ten years ago, the number of female faculty in our department was also around 10 percent. What's different is that American scientists have been working hard the last couple decades to institute policies to support women. The process is slow, but it's showing results (although race, regrettably, is a different story). Now our department is nearly 40 percent for female tenure-track faculty (seven female, eleven male), and just over 45 percent for all faculty (eleven female, thirteen male). Gender representation at most geoscience departments across the country has also improved. And, unlike at the Chinese Academy of Sciences, where I learned that a husband and wife cannot both hold positions (say what?!), American universities have policies that facilitate professional double hires.

    The pressure on women to have children is enormous. And although, unlike in America, Chinese grandparents often support young mothers (for example, Huixia's father moved from western China to Beijing for four months while I was visiting, to help with Xunxun), many professionals now live in different cities from their parents. So, in principle, support is possible, but in practice it's failing. To sustain their careers, some professionals send their children to their parents in other provinces. My experience is extremely limited, but it seems like Chinese men generally help less with children than American men. Women's responsibility for children takes a big toll on professional advance.

More generally, there's a fear of women's sexuality. In movies, China censors women's breasts by blurring them. I still remember the intro to a James Bond film, where naked women dance in silhouette. You can't really see anything in the original, but China still blurs out circular areas that bounce and wobble around—an effect that is simultaneously comical, annoying, and disturbing.

5.  Cell phone obsession. Yes, nearly all of us love our cell phones, but on the sidewalks or walking around the subway the love affair between the Chinese and their phones is singularly exasperating. People are constantly getting in my way because they aren't paying attention. Yes, I do occasionally text as I walk, but only when there's no one close by. I also stay out of the way and don't drift erratically.

6.  Western models. Why do ads have to show people who are barely Chinese-looking or even western? It's one thing to promote a barely attainable body shape (which is also a problem). Quite another to promote a standard of beauty that's absolutely unattainable. Black hair, dark skin, and brown eyes are every bit as beautiful as other colors of hair, skin, and eyes. Trust me on this one—I've been to every populated continent on Earth.

7.  Scientific recipe for success. To succeed in science means following very strict conventions. You have to get grants funded (similar to the US), but also publish a certain number of papers per year, in highly-specific journals. If you don't publish in the top journals—and every journal is ranked into specific tiers—you're hosed.

In the US, what counts is impact. Publishing a paper in a top-ranked journal is good, but it won't count for much if it has no impact (maybe it seems like every paper in a top-ranked journal should have impact, but they don't always; the major hype of "high-impact" journals isn't always justified). Publishing an impactful paper even in a medium-ranked journal counts for a lot.

At the time I came up for tenure and promotion to associate professor, all the journals I had published in would have ranked as third tier or lower in China. I was also already five years beyond the maximum age for consideration at some Chinese institutions. So, my American career record would have failed in China's system. Yet, the papers I had published were highly impactful, and since then I've received a scientific medal and am a fellow of three major geosciences societies—recognitions that I've been told would qualify me for membership in the Chinese Academy of Sciences, the highest professional recognition in China. In other words, the Chinese system could easily have cut me off, despite other measures of quality. How many outstanding Chinese scientists never got the chance, simply because their successes didn't fit the recipe?

8. Fish bones and shrimp shells. Sure, this is a trivial aggravation, and eventually I learned to chew them like everyone else. But I so appreciated the lox I had for breakfast and the boneless salmon we had for dinner when I arrived home.

Some people would add censorship and idea theft to my list. I didn't experience any of that, so it never affected my day-to-day living. Perhaps that's because exchange of ideas is foundational to the advance of science, so bouncing ideas around with scientists of any nationality seems like part of my job description. As a scientist and professional educator, I don't care if the email address of the person who contacts me with a science question originates from Iran, Italy, or Indiana—I'll answer all three emails. Regardless, Chinese scientists wanted only to work with me, not take my ideas, and Chinese institutions agreed in advance to make no claims to intellectual property for my activities. That's a big deal, because the US claims the Chinese try to sucker US scientists into signing away their ideas. Clearly, that wasn't true in my case. Exactly the opposite, in fact.

There are many things I do dearly appreciate about China. Some of these are:

1. Kindness and generosity. My friends' kindness and generosity in China vastly exceeded anything I ever extended to visitors to the US. Frankly, I'm a little ashamed of the sink-or-swim attitude of Americans. We could be kinder. More generally, I was impressed at how often strangers would step forward to try to help me, for example offering translating skills when there were snags with officials and apps. Would Americans help a foreigner in the US, especially someone from China? After seeing China's example, I'm much more likely to step forward myself.

2. Passion for science. I'm not sure I've encountered such enthusiasm for science, especially my specialty (metamorphic petrology), anywhere else. Clearly, China respects science and scientists much more than the US does. In that sense, maybe I would have succeeded in China's system. I wouldn't have had so many barriers to professional success, like crappy funding and lack of professional opportunities (also huge student debt). I might actually have had a secure job when I was thirty, not five years later. And I might have been promoted to professor at thirty-six, not ten years later. That kind of job security, of course, lowers stress and improves science.

3. Fit people. Many people rode bicycles or went for walks. I never felt squashed when I sat on the subway. I felt like China adopts a more holistic view of personal health.

4. Vegetables. Goes with fitness. When I ate the buffet breakfast at the hotel in LA, I realized everything was meat/eggs/dairy, fruit (sugar), and bread (sugar). If there were any vegetables, they were well-hidden. Every meal at the Institute's dining hall has multiple options for vegetables. I ate more eggplant in the last four months than in the previous four years.

5. Public transportation. My kids must have taught me to love trains because I do like to ride the subway. The buses are pretty convenient too. None of my friends owns a car, which I think is generally a good thing. There are still plenty of cars in Beijing, but the average Chinese person pollutes much less than the average American. The bike rental systems in Beijing and Shanghai are awesome!

6. Respect. People respected me for my knowledge and for making the effort to come to China. Partly that's cultural, but I think they also realized what a pain in the ass it was for an American to buck US policies and collaborate in person with Chinese scientists (although Xiaochi is the true hero of this story). They genuinely seemed to like helping me do things, even the simplest of tasks. Becoming old in China doesn't seem so scary as in America because age is respected, not feared.

7. Technological successes. When the technology works, it's really nice. Other than the fact that I don't read Chinese, paying for stuff was easy. Having my health status checked at every door seemed a little overkill at times (I have to get checked at the mall entrance *and* the store entrance?), but the apps worked nearly all the time.

8. Safety. China is very, very safe. I never felt threatened on the streets, or worried about walking around after dark. In contrast, as soon as I exited the terminal in LA, I encountered a disturbingly aggressive woman. Much of safety must depend on culture. The safest place I've ever felt is in Bhutan, where people simply don't do bad things. The Bhutanese view theft as an abhorrent sin, and it's almost nonexistent.

   Safety in China, however, also reflects widespread surveillance. Think about domestic terrorism in the US. We celebrate how the FBI solves these cases (most of them, anyway) using really cool technologies. But the reason we need these technologies is because we don't have a universal surveillance system. If we did, the FBI wouldn't need special techniques. In fact, if we had universal surveillance, many of these crimes probably wouldn't happen, and we would all be safer. I definitely don't view this as justification for surveillance, however. I'd rather be a little less safe to hold onto that particular freedom. But I can't deny that surveillance improves personal safety.

9. Geology. The rocks in China are truly spectacular. No, I didn't get to the northern edge of the Himalayas (southern edge of Tibet), like I had hoped. But there's much more to Chinese geology than the Himalayas. My geologic horizons broadened considerably.

> 10. Naps. It's normal to take a nap in the afternoon, sometime after
> lunch. How nice is that?

Would I go back?

Yes! Well, probably. Maybe? China would welcome me back (I think I could get a visa), and I would like to continue collaborating. My only hesitation is US policy. If I accept, say, airfare from Huixia's grant from the Chinese equivalent to the National Science Foundation, or housing from the Chinese Academy of Sciences, will the federal government cut off all future research funding, try to throw me in jail, pillory me? Even now, I'm at risk for federal prosecution under Trump's China Initiative. Not that I've done anything wrong. I've tried to follow all the rules. But I think some of the scientists who are being prosecuted at the time I'm writing this probably didn't do anything wrong either. The rules are vague (what is "foreign talent recruitment"?) and can be applied capriciously. Judges have thrown out some prosecutions, but it's still a huge pain and expense for those who are wrongly accused.

After talking with Fuyuan, Xiaochi, and Huixia, I've decided to start planning a return, tentatively. After all, I do still want to see those rocks in southern Tibet. But it's all with the knowledge that I might have to cancel everything at the last minute. It all depends not only on permissions from China, but also on how US policies develop over the next six to eight months.

In the US, we question China's motives and policies. I, too, share concerns. Serious concerns. But, from an immediate personal perspective, I worry less about China, and more about the US government. This, from a guy who worked directly with the US State Department to promote scientific diplomacy in China.

Maybe this is a price we pay for democracy—the chaos of inconsistent policies driven by political debate.

Well, I don't want to end my stories on a down note. Yes, I'm anxious about the future, but many factors still encourage me. I keep coming back to Jenny's question in the Xiamen airport, and my immediate enthusiastic response.

Yes, governments have their agendas, and these can seriously mess with people's lives. In the past I had many reservations about China's policies and practices, and after four-and-a-half months in China I still do—that hasn't changed much. I also see more clearly the effects of different policies on our lives, which now leads me to question the US government more than I ever have previously.

But individuals are basically the same everywhere, and their goodness gives me hope. In my world of science and education, I see the same passions and generosity for learning in China that I do in the US. If anything, even stronger. The popular myth in America that the Chinese only want to steal ideas is just that, a myth. Yes, scientific and technological espionage does happen, and by most accounts China is more aggressive than other countries. But the US' over-the-top response damages our own interests and aspirations, and betrays fear and political agenda, rather than fact. It's the proverbial use of a (rock)hammer to swat a fly—you miss the fly and break the window instead. Oops.

Just like scientists everywhere, including me, curiosity about the natural world drives China's scientists to advance science and share knowledge. Thinking back, I realize now that I learned far more about their science than they learned about mine. I also realize now that my colleagues were the ones taking the most intellectual risk: whereas everything I talked about has been published, most of theirs was unpublished. Still, despite now-deeply-engrained mistrust between our governments, these scientists trusted me, and, likewise, I trust them.

I have to think that trust among individuals, regardless of nationality, can transcend politics and ultimately benefit the human condition. This is perhaps why the first medal established by the American Geophysical Union—the world's largest geoscience society—honors unselfish cooperation in research (the Bowie Medal). Maybe things look bleak in the short run, at least from this American scientist's perspective. But, as long as scientists worldwide keep talking and sharing, the long run seems brighter.

# ACKNOWLEDGEMENTS



So many people contributed to this book, how can I possibly thank them all? Xiaochi, Huixia, and Heather, of course, invested countless hours in making all this possible and introducing me to China's culture. Lishuang, Shujuan, Summer, Shun, Fuyuan, and Dingding led me on many adventures, from movie theaters and parks in Beijing to the geology and countryside of northern and central China. Huixia's family members—Mingchao, Xunxun, and Zeying— taught me what home life is like in Beijing. Yang was an entertaining lunch companion, and Zeming, Bo, Feng, Hu, Jiamin, Shaoxiong, Wangchao, Yang, and many others helped exercise my mental hamsters. To all the strangers who stepped forward to help me out of awkward situations—I never learned your names, but I'm ever so thankful for your generosity. I'm grateful to my many friends and family members back home who laughed at my stories (or so they said…) and reminded me I had a home to return to. Janica Smith managed all the tasks of publishing, which was a huge load off my shoulders, and my other editors and designers fixed many mistakes and handled all the tedious work. Any remaining errors are my own, however.

# INDEX

Notes are indicated by the page number followed by an italicized *n* and the note number. Photos are indicated by a bold page number.

## B

Badaling section of Great Wall
 batholith, 242
 general discussion, 241–246,
  **246–249**
baijiu, 202, 207–208, **209**, 287
*Ballad of Cordillera Darwin* (Kohn),
 219
bamboo, 269, **273**, 314, **316**
banking
 account setup in China, 132–134,
  **135**
 via WeChat app, 47, **48**
baozi (steamed bun), 97
barbecue, 237–240, **240**, **316**, **340**
"Barbeque" (Mumbo Gumbo), 237
bat guano, 170
batholith, 242
bathrooms, 137–138, **142**
Beagle Channel, 143
Bears Ears National Monument,
 318
beef, 314, **316**
Beijing. *See also* China University of
 Geosciences, Beijing
 author's fifth COVID-19 test at,
  125–127
 author trip to, 119–123
 bank account setup in, 132–134,
  **135**
 COVID-19 case rate, 302, 341
 hospitals, 251–256
 license plate restrictions, 154
 liver of mutton soup, 144–146,
  **147**
 monitoring/surveillance in, 134
 pollution, 175, 296–297, **298**
 setting up cell phone service in,
  129–132

snowstorm, 295–297, **298**
Beijing Art Museum, 300
Beijing Daxing International
 Airport, 341–345, **345–346**
belladonna plant, 282–283
beryl (aquamarine) crystals, 229
Bhutan, 62, 137, 268–269, **271–
 273**, 361
bicycles, 114–115
Biden, Joe, 318
Bilibili, 52, 67, **69**, 167
birthday party, Xunxun's, 287–289,
 **290–291**
Black Death, 224
Black Lives Matter movement, 2–4
black nightshade, 281–284, **284**
black sesame, 268
blood pudding, 146, **147**
blood sausage, 144
Blue Iris Stone, 182, 183
bobcats, 189–190
body temperature
 checks, 47, 75, 77, 130, 155
 general discussion, 96–97
Bogd Khan Uul national park, 276
Boise State University, 1, 3, 10, 14,
 26, 217, 308
bok choy, 49, 268
Bone Wars, 180–181
bottled water, 94–95, 97
Bowie Medal, 363
*Brighty of the Grand Canyon*
 (Henry), 188
Buddhism. *See* Chinese Zen
 Buddhism
business visas, 13, 14

## C

CAGS (Chinese Academy of Geological Sciences), 299, 302–303

California, 9, 115, 237, 277, 296, 341

CAM (Crassulacean acid metabolism) plants, 107–108, **110**

Cambrian *Fuxianhuia*, 232, **233**

Cambrian Maotianshan Shale, 230

cannibalism, 190

carbon dioxide concentrations, 261–264, **265**

carbon isotope geochemistry, 107–108

car culture, 114–116

care package story, 59–64

carnivores, 190

carved tourmaline seals, 229, **232**

CAS. *See* Chinese Academy of Sciences

castor oil plant, 218–219

cats, 189–190

causation/correlation fallacy, 225–226

cell phone service, 129–132, 358

Cenozoic Era, 261–262

censorship, 359

chestnuts, 314

chicken feet, 287, 339, **340**

chicken meat, 101–102

Chile, 143–144

China. *See also* Geological Museum of China

American myths regarding, 359, 361

author arrival to, 41–48

bamboo logging, 269, **273**

bathrooms, 137–138, **142**

car culture, 114–116

care of trees, 179–183, **183**

cell phone service setup, 129–132, 358

climate, 223–227

COVID-19 pandemic, 2–4, 302, 341

COVID-19 testing entry requirements, 33, 34

COVID-19 testing for travel within, 251–256

dogs as food source question, 187–190

enthusiasm for Earth sciences, 302–303, **304**

fruits in, 107–110, **110**, **111**, **216**

geology in, 232, 361

Google in, 47, 79–80, 84

napkins in, 140–141

naps in, 362

passport laws, 37, 43, 87, 89, 99, 195–196

Proclamation 10043 and, 197–199

public transportation system, 119–123, 153, 360

quarantine rules, 44–48, 75–78

reverence for rocks, 179–180, 182–183, **184**

rice cultivation, 267–269, **271**

US foreign talent recruitment law, 25–29

US mistrust toward, 359, 361

visa application, 9–20

Wi-Fi in, 42, 57, 79–80, 120, 122, 333-335

China Southern Airlines, 331–335

China University of Geosciences, Beijing (CUGB)

# ABOUT THE AUTHOR

Matt Kohn is an internationally-recognized Distinguished Professor in Geosciences at Boise State University. His research uses geochemistry to investigate how mountain belts form and how climates and ecosystems have changed over millions of years. He and his wife, Heather Steele, live in Boise, Idaho, and have two sons, Tavi and Asa. When he's not teaching or hammering rocks out of outcrops, Matt enjoys contra dancing and backpacking.